D0236133

AN ILLUSTRATED GUIDE TO
FLOWERING TREES AND SHRUBS

AN ILLUSTRATED GUIDE TO
FLOWERING TREES AND SHRUBS

Edited by
Cyril C. Harris

TIGER BOOKS INTERNATIONAL

This edition published in 1998 by
Tiger Books International PLC, Twickenham, UK

First published by Orbis Publishing Limited 1979
© 1998 Little, Brown and Company (UK)

ACKNOWLEDGEMENTS
A-Z Collection 12–13, 14, 23, 24, 30, 40, 42, 47, 49, 69, 71, 75,
    76, 79, 88, 94, 95, 118, 119, 127, 138, 139
Bernard Alfieri 20, 76, 81, 108
Alphabet & Image 125
Heather Angel 138
Pat Brindley 9, 22, 23, 24, 26, 289, 29, 32, 34, 36–7, 45, 51, 52,
    53, 67, 72, 73, 82, 88–9, 103, 115, 119, 121, 129
R.J. Corbin 15, 17, 18, 18, 21, 30
John K.B. Cowley 59, 75, 101
Derek Fell 120
Brian Furner 16
Iris Hardwick Library 64–5
G.E. Hyde 23, 41, 94, 139
IGDA 60, 78
Elsa M. Megson 12, 48
Tania Midgley 13, 45, 93, 140–1
J. Parkhurst 75
Ray Procter 14, 124
Kenneth Scowen 44–5, 60
Harry Smith Collection 2–3, 6–7, 10, 11, 12–13, 22, 25, 26, 27,
    28, 32, 33, 34, 38, 39, 42, 50, 51, 52, 53, 55, 56, 58, 59, 61, 62,
    63, 65, 66, 74, 75, 77, 78, 79, 82, 83, 84, 85, 86, 87, 90, 91, 92,
    96, 97, 98, 100, 101, 102, 103, 104, 105, 106, 107, 110, 111,
    112, 113, 114, 115, 116, 122, 123, 126, 127, 129, 131, 132,
    134, 135, 136, 137, 142
Michael Warren 17, 46, 54, 55, 57, 63, 64, 64–5, 68, 69, 70, 71,
    72, 73, 82–3, 90, 91, 97, 98, 106, 107, 109, 114–5, 118, 128,
    130, 132, 133, 138, 140–1, 142
D. Wildridge 41

The right of Cyril C. Harris to be identified as the author
of this work has been asserted in accordance with the
Copyright, Designs and Patents Act 1988

All rights reserved. No part of this publication may be
reproduced, stored in a retrieval system, or transmitted in
any form or by any means, without prior permission in
writing of the publisher, nor be otherwise circulated in any
form of binding or cover other than than in which it is
published and without a similar condition including this
condition being imposed on the subsequent purchaser.

ISBN 1-84056-051-7

Little, Brown and Company (UK)
Brettenham House
Lancaster Place
London WC2E 7EN

Printed and bound in Czech Republic

CONTENTS

INTRODUCTION

A well-laid-out garden presents an exquisitely beautiful tableau in which flowering trees and shrubs, ably accompanied by a supporting caste of herbaceous plants, hardy annuals and bulbs, are the principal performers. Perhaps everybody is now so used to seeing them in public parks and private gardens that there is a tendency to take them for granted. This can be offset by thinking of what a landscape would look like if it was devoid of such plants, and after all a garden is the gardener's landscape.

Apart from the natives, trees and shrubs were introduced into western gardens from the wild in early times. There is little doubt that the Romans brought over quite a number when they settled in Britain. From a gardening aspect they have endured many vicissitudes over the years. Before the 14th century people were too preoccupied with war to cultivate trees and shrubs. In the more settled times that followed and after the Black Death, noblemen and cottagers planted them in their gardens. Because of the popularity of the knot garden and other topical features during Tudor times they were generally banished to the deer park, outside the confines of the castle.

Trees and shrubs became of real interest from the mid-17th century onwards, undoubtedly inspired by the publication of John Evelyn's *Sylva, or a Discourse of Forest-Trees*, in 1664. Great impetus was given to the introduction of trees and shrubs. This continued through the 18th and 19th centuries into the early years of the 20th century when, sponsored by wealthy patrons, the Royal Horticultural Society, other learned bodies and prominent nurserymen, numerous intrepid plant hunters sallied forth to distant lands and brought to Britain and other western countries the many flowering trees and shrubs that grace our gardens today.

Not unnaturally, in the course of time, competing types of plants and forms of gardening – herbaceous borders, wild gardens, Victorian ferneries, formal beds and so on – have caused the fortunes of tree and shrubs to fluctuate. Now, after two World Wars and rapid changes in economic conditions over the past sixty years, bringing higher costs, lower availability of labour, and exorbitant prices of building land, gardeners have been forced to find more labour-saving means of gardening. This meant that the incidence of features, such as herbaceous borders and formal bedding out, while not completely abandoned, have been reduced to a minimum. Their place has been taken by trees and shrubs, with other types of plants playing a lesser, though still important role.

There is also an ecological reason why trees and shrubs, perhaps not by design, have assumed a greater significance. Essential changes in agricultural policy and development in some countries have destroyed many miles of trees and hedgerow, leaving many birds homeless. In many cases these have taken refuge in the thousands of trees and shrubs, hedges and climbers that

7

adorn the many gardens. From an aesthetic viewpoint this has brought great advantages to gardeners because the birds have tended to move from the country more into the residential areas, where they give immense pleasure to townsfolk and where, in gardens, they introduce movement – a most valuable factor in making a garden attractive.

The bulk of this book consists of a dictionary of trees and shrubs. Under each item their countries of origin are included. Quite a number are native to Britain or they have been growing here so long that they have become naturalized. It will be found, however, that the greater proportion has been brought from foreign climes, largely China, Japan and nearby Far East countries, while others have been introduced from the continent of Europe and many more from Canada, the United States and South America. Although this particular information appears to be of academic interest only, there is a more practical relevance which can be useful when selecting trees and shrubs, particularly from a catalogue. For example, numerous shrubs such as the hebes come from New Zealand, which has a long coastline, usually ensuring that its plants flourish in coastal districts; on the other hand there are some, like *Rosa pimpinellifolia altaica*, that are natives of Siberia and it is reasonable to suppose that they are very hardy and withstand severe cold. Some of the most beautiful climbing shrubs are indigenous to tropical or sub-tropical areas, such as the glorious *Eccremocarpus scaber*, which hails from Chile and needs to be planted against a warm sheltered wall in a southern garden if it is to flourish.

As already mentioned, the end result when planting out a garden is to obtain the effect of an attractive tableau which is three-dimensional. It is the intention of this book to equip the reader for this purpose, irrespective of whether he is planting out a whole garden or a shrub bed or border, or whether his garden is relatively large, or small, or just a patio. In the following sections he is given detailed characteristics of thirty-five groups of plants containing a total of nearly 600 species, hybrids and varieties, which can be combined in many different ways to produce a variety of planting schemes. In addition details about origin, history, specific uses, cultivation, pruning, methods of propagation and other relevant information are supplied, together with attractive illustrations of many trees and shrubs, invaluable in making a selection. These individual plant profiles are prefaced by a number of sections dealing with more specialized aspects of handling trees and shrubs.

Many plants can contrive to produce a beautiful garden. According to one nurseryman's catalogue, there are up to 8000 trees, shrubs, conifers and bamboos available in Britain, of which the majority are flowering trees, shrubs and climbers. These form the backbone of all gardens, large and small and give enormous scope for garden-making on any scale.

It should be superfluous to state that trees and shrubs are decorative but this is the obvious quality that attracts people. One particular factor that all take notice of is floral colour, followed by the range of fruit colours after flowering and, often, brilliant autumn tints. Study of the plant profiles below shows that it is possible to sustain floral colour in a garden by selection during the greater part of the year. To do so must be the object of any gardener when he is planting out. The heyday of flowering trees and shrubs comes in the spring when Japanese cherries, prunus, crab apples, magnolias, rhododendrons, laburnums and philadelphus follow one after the other.

Summer and autumn bring their quota of colour too, slightly more sober in colour, with such lovely plants as the hydrangeas, buddleia, hypericum, hebes, *Magnolia grandiflora*, potentilla, fuchsias and many others.

Even in winter there can be a cavalcade of colour bravely produced by stalwarts like *Prunus subhirtella* 'Autumnalis', witch hazel, *Viburnum farreri*, the winter flowering rhododendron Lee's Scarlet, and *Daphne mezereum*.

As a bonus to this spectacle of colour many trees and shrubs produce berries that are mostly red, but also blue, white, black, brown, yellow, orange, pink and mauve.

Trees and shrubs have other valuable functions. Trees can give privacy, shade and screening, form wind-breaks and filter out sea salt at the seaside. A tree can be usefully planted as a focal point around which the garden is planned; it can be used to direct the line of vision over the greater distance and create a sense of spaciousness. Equally as valuable, shrubs can screen an ugly fence or shed, shroud a manhole, give excellent ground cover and provide blackdrops for more forward planting. Most important they make excellent boundary or division hedges. Trees and shrubs, with their varying shapes and sizes, create great 'architectural' interest in the garden. This is something which is supplemented by their variation in texture and the size of their leaves. Lastly, climbers or climbing shrubs and wall plants, while exceedingly decorative, can cover walls and sheds; left unsupported they sprawl over the ground, hang down over walls or clothe a dead tree trunk.

The pruning of flowering trees and shrubs is a concern of many gardeners. Actually most do not need regular pruning, but some should be cut back occasionally. Thinning is often a problem but this is really quite simple, if two rules are followed: trees and shrubs that bloom on the previous year's growth of wood (which generally flower early) should be pruned immediately after flowering; those blooming on the current year's wood, (and generally flowering during summer) should be pruned in late winter or early spring. Winter-flowering trees and shrubs should be pruned in the spring.

Most of the trees and shrubs described later can easily be propagated. This, of course, affords an inexpensive way of increasing stock. Some, like hebes and holly, seed freely. Self-sown seedlings are a bonanza and they should be transplanted to a nursery bed.

January, 1979   Cyril C. Harris

SELECTION, CULTIVATION AND USES

CHOOSING A SPECIMEN TREE

One of the best ways of showing a tree to advantage is to plant it as a specimen in a carefully-chosen site. Appearance, however, is by no means the only factor that must be considered; by following the guidelines given below you should be able to choose a tree that will both look attractive and serve a useful purpose.

Choosing a tree for a garden of any size needs careful consideration. Trees can have a functional role quite apart from their decorative appearance, and there are practical considerations to be taken into account, such as the local soil conditions. Bear in mind that large trees give a great deal of often unwanted shade and that their roots deprive other plants of nutrients. Trees with spreading canopies keep the rain off anything planted underneath: this area will therefore be of limited use for flowers or shrubs after the tree becomes established.

In siting a tree you must take care that neither its top growth nor its root system encroach in any way on to your neighbour's property. If the tree is likely to cast shade over the next-door garden, for example, you must get permission from the neighbours before planting it. It is important not to plant large trees too close to the house as their roots could undermine the foundations, and interfere with drains, electricity cables or gas pipes. Members of the salix and populus genera, in particular, have very thirsty roots that spread a great distance in search of moisture, penetrating and blocking drainage systems even.

What is required?
Choose the right tree for the specific purpose you have in mind. Perhaps the most frequent requirement of a tree is to form a screen; in this case it is better to choose one, or a group, that will break up the line of vision rather than form a solid block – a comparatively low-growing tree with a spreading head is often sufficient as it will not block out too much sun.

A very important function of a tree, particularly a columnar one, is to give a focal point around which the garden design can turn. A tree that has branches growing low down from the trunk can be planted between the house and the entrance or driveway, to give the effect of length by obscuring the actual distance involved. Similarly, a tree can be an accent or high point in an area where the

Above: slow-growing Acer palmatum *has glorious autumn foliage*
Right: Gleditschia triacanthos Sunburst *can reach a height of 9m (30 ft)*

garden is fairly flat. A tree such as *Salix babylonica* (weeping willow), planted on the brow above a dip in the ground can give an illusion of a pool underneath it.

You can also use trees to create the illusion of movement, which is important to a good design. Introduce actual movement by selecting trees with flexible leaf-stalks and leaves that tremble in the breeze. Habit and form also play an important part; trees with arching or pendulous branches give a great sense of serenity, while those with very large leaves impart an exotic, sometimes subtropical touch.

Selecting a specimen tree
Trees have five main qualities – colour, habit, shape, size and texture – that must be considered when you are selecting a specimen. One of the first decisions to

make is whether you want an evergreen or a deciduous tree. After that, the factor which most often predominates is colour. With this, the colour of the flowers is often the least important because it is short-lived in comparison to the leaves. Remember that fruits and bark can also provide colour throughout the summer and autumn and even into winter.

Geometric shape, coupled with habit, is the next important element to be considered. There are round-headed, pyramidal and columnar trees, and also those with fastigiate growth and arching or weeping branches and those with a wide-spreading habit. There are trees for almost any purpose or position in the garden, but you must study catalogues and books to find them, and visit gardens and parks to see them *in situ*. Columnar trees, for example, are often more suitable in a small garden as they do not throw too much shadow. And bear in mind when choosing a deciduous tree what sort of shape its bare branches will give in winter.

Trees with a bold texture have the same sort of visual effect as strong, bright colours – they appear to push themselves forward. Fine-textured trees (with small leaves) are like blue or greyish colours that visually recede into the background, and create an illusion of distance. These characteristics, if used with care, can give a feeling of movement that always adds interest.

The size that a tree is going to be after, say, 20 years' growth must be considered. Be sure that the eventual height and spread will not overwhelm your garden in years to come; even in a large garden it can be a mistake to plant forest trees such as elm and beech. There are many ornamental acers, birches, cherries and other prunus, ornamental crabs, and sorbus that graduate in size, making them suitable for the largest down to the smallest gardens. You will find more details about many of these later in the book, and also, of course, in catalogues from specialist growers.

Although there are few trees that are really suitable for very tiny gardens, their design functions can often be fulfilled by a weeping standard rose, such as Dorothy Perkins. In addition, it is possible to obtain a low-growing shrub, such as *Cotoneaster* Hybridus Pendulus, grafted on to a standard stem, that is very suitable for this purpose.

A choice of specimen trees

Unless otherwise stated, assume that the trees listed will grow satisfactorily under normal garden conditions, and in ordinary, good soil. The first dimension given is the average height and the second is the spread, both after 20 years' growth.

COLOUR

Red foliage

Acer palmatum Linearilobum Atropurpureum
Has bronze-red leaves that are divided to the base into long, narrow, serrated lobes. 4·5 × 2·5m (15 × 8 ft).

Acer platanoides Crimson King
A big, vigorous, deciduous cultivar with large leaves. 10 × 6m (33 × 20 ft).

Malus Jay Darling
Has large, wine-red flowers produced before or with its similarly-coloured leaves. Bears purplish red fruits. 6 × 5m (20 × 16 ft).

Gold/yellow foliage

Catalpa bignonioides Aurea
Has a rounded habit and is a vigorous grower, with large, velvety leaves. Excellent for town gardens, particularly in a mild climate. 9 × 8m (30 × 26 ft).

Gleditschia triacanthos Sunburst
Unlike the type species, this form has thornless stems. 9 × 8m (30 × 26 ft).

Laburnum anagyroides Aureum
A much-branched tree that prefers light soils and dislikes wet or heavy ones. Spreads with age. 4·5 × 3m (15 × 10 ft).

Purple foliage

Malus Profusion
An upright tree, producing wine-red flowers in late spring and early summer (April and May), succeeded by red fruits. 6 × 5m (20 × 16 ft).

Prunus × blireana Moseri
Has pale pink blooms in late spring (April). 4·5 × 3m (15 × 10 ft).

Quercus robur Atropurpurea
A slow-growing cultivar of the common oak, with stems that are purple when young and become greyish on maturity. 9 × 9m (30 × 30 ft).

Grey/silver foliage

Eucalyptus coccifera
A fast-growing, hardy, gale-resistant tree, with bluish green, elliptical juvenile leaves that become lanceolate and greyish on maturity. Grows in acid soil. 10 × 6m (33 × 20 ft).

Pyrus nivalis
An attractive tree with ascending branches, producing white flowers in late spring (April), followed by yellow-green fruits. 4·5 × 2·5m (15 × 8 ft).

Pyrus salicifolia Pendula
A slow-growing, weeping tree. 8 × 9m (26 × 30 ft).

Variegated foliage

Acer pseudoplatanus Nizetii
Has variegated yellow and white leaves, suffused pink, purplish beneath. 4·5 × 2·5m (15 × 8 ft).

Ilex × altaclarensis Golden King
Has almost spineless green leaves with a golden margin and bears large red berries. 8 × 4·5m (26 × 15 ft).

Liriodendron tulipifera Aureomarginatum
A variegated variety of the tulip tree, with leaves bordered with yellow. 10 × 6m (33 × 20 ft).

Autumn-tinted foliage

Amelanchier canadensis (snowy mespilus)
Has white flowers in late spring (April), followed by black berries. The twigs are purple in winter. It likes a moist position. 3·5 × 3m (12 × 10 ft).

Liriodendron tulipifera (tulip tree)
A large tree with leaves that are cut off square at the top, and become bright yellow in autumn. Its tulip-shaped, yellow-green flowers, borne in late summer (July), first appear after about 15 years' growth. 15 × 10m (50 × 30 ft).

Malus tschonoskii
A strong-growing, deciduous tree with pink-tinted and white flowers appearing in early summer (May), followed by yellowish fruits that are tinged reddish purple. 9 × 3m (30 × 10 ft).

Coloured fruits

Ailanthus altissima (tree of heaven)
A large, round-headed tree with compound leaves and conspicuous bunches of reddish, key-shaped fruits. Tolerates polluted atmosphere. 18 × 12m (60 × 40 ft).

Malus Golden Hornet
Has white flowers appearing in late spring (April), followed by persistent, bright yellow fruits. 8 × 6m (26 × 20 ft).

Prunus cornuta (Himalayan bird cherry)
Has white flowers in early summer (May), followed by grape-like bunches of brownish crimson glossy berries. Prefers soil with a little lime. 8 × 8m (26 × 26 ft).

Sorbus Joseph Rock
An erect, deciduous tree that produces leaves with autumn tints and clusters of yellowish amber fruits. Dislikes chalk. 12 × 8m (40 × 26 ft).

Coloured stems and bark

Fraxinus excelsior Aurea (or Jaspidea)
Has yellow leaves and yellowish bark. It can tolerate chalk, and exposed and coastal conditions. 4·5 × 3·5m (15 × 12 ft).

Parrotia persica
The bark of the older trees flakes off, giving a patchwork effect. Its large leaves have brilliant autumn colours, and it likes chalk. 6 × 4·5m (20 × 15 ft).

Tilia platyphyllos Rubra (red-twigged lime)
A large deciduous tree with reddish young stems. It does not suffer from aphid attack, so its leaves do not drip honeydew – which can be a problem with common lime. 12 × 9m (40 × 30 ft).

SHAPE AND HABIT
Round-headed

Acer pseudoplatanus (sycamore)
A large deciduous tree, with leaves that turn yellow in autumn. Forms a good windbreak, and tolerates seaside conditions. 13·5 × 6m (45 × 20 ft).

Crataegus monogyna (hawthorn, may, quick)
This thorny, deciduous tree produces clusters of scented white flowers in early summer (May), and crimson berries later on. 8 × 5m (26 × 16 ft).

Malus coronaria Charlottae
Has pink, violet-scented flowers in mid summer (June), and orange and yellow autumn tints. 4·5 × 4·5m (15 × 15 ft).

Ornamental flowering trees are suitable for almost any size of garden. Prunus
Hokusai *(above) grows 6m (20 ft) high;* Crataegus monogyna *(left) reaches 8m
(26 ft) and* Amelanchier canadensis *(far left) only 3·5m (12 ft)*
Below left: Pyrus salicifolia Pendula *has unusual variegated leaves*

Prunus cerasifera (cherry plum or myrobalan)	Has white flowers in early to mid spring (February to March), followed by yellow fruits. It likes some lime in the soil. 8 × 8m (26 × 26 ft).
Sorbus Mitchellii	Has mature leaves about 15cm (6 in) across, green above and white-felted beneath. 11 × 12m (36 × 40 ft).

Pyramidal

Acer rubrum Girling	Has dark green foliage that becomes vivid orange-red in autumn. 6 × 2·5m (20 × 8 ft).
Magnolia kobus	Produces white flowers in late spring (April) after about 12 years' growth. Can tolerate chalk. 3 × 3m (10 × 10 ft).
Malus tschonoskii	See under Autumn-tinted foliage.
Populus candicans Aurora	Has young leaves that are white, often pink-tinged, becoming green later. Grows well in chalky soil. 11 × 6m (36 × 20 ft).

Spreading

Acer negundo Elegans	Has leaves with a bright yellow margin, and young shoots with a white bloom. 6 × 6m (20 × 20 ft).
Malus Chilko	Has purplish leaves, and produces blooms 5cm (2 in) across in early summer (May), followed by crimson crab apples. 6 × 3·5m (20 × 12 ft).
Mespilus germanica (medlar)	A much-branched, deciduous tree with dull green leaves that become russet and yellow in autumn. It bears medlars in autumn, and likes a sunny position. 8 × 6m (26 × 20 ft).
Prunus Hokusai	A vigorous, wide-spreading Japanese cherry that produces large, semi-double, pale pink flowers in late spring (April). Likes chalk. 6 × 9m (20 × 30 ft).

Erect-growing (columnar)

Carpinus betulus Fastigiata	Has a narrow shape when young, but tends to broaden with age. 6 × 1·8m (20 × 6 ft).
Eucryphia × nymansensis Nymansay	A quick-growing evergreen with cream flowers borne during early and mid autumn (August and September). It is

Above: bold-foliaged Aralia chinensis *accents the line of the house nearby, as well as the columnar conifer in the background*
Above left: Carpinus betulus *Fastigiata is erect-growing when young, but broadens with age.*
The fine foliage of Betula pendula *Youngii (far left) and* Robinia pseudoacacia *Frisia (left) gives the impression of distance to a garden*

hardy in milder areas and tolerates chalk. 4.5×1.8m (15×6 ft).

Morus alba Pyramidalis — An erect-branched, slow-growing tree similar to the Lombardy poplar. 9×1.8m (30×6 ft).

Populus nigra Italica (Lombardy poplar) — A large, deciduous tree with close, upright branches. It is covered almost to its base with leaves. 24×5m (80×16 ft).

Prunus Amanogawa — Has fragrant, pink flowers during early summer (May). Can tolerate some lime in the soil. 6×1.8m (20×6 ft).

Prunus Umineko — Has white flowers that appear in late spring (April), and foliage that turns to brilliant autumn colours. 6×1.8m (20×6 ft).

Pendulous (weeping)

Acer saccharinum Pendulum — A form of the silver maple, with weeping branches, and leaves that are silver-white below. 11×4.5m (36×15 ft).

Betula pendula Youngii — A mushroom-headed, weeping tree that will grow on thin, acid or sandy soil. 8×9m (26×30 ft).

Caragana arborescens Pendula — Produces yellow, pea-like flowers in early summer (May), and succeeds in exposed positions and in poor, dry areas. 4.5×4.5m (15×15 ft).

Laburnum × *watereri* Alford's Weeping — Produces long racemes of yellow blooms in mid summer (June), and has a wide-spreading head. 5×3.3m (16×11 ft).

Salix × *chrysocoma* — A weeping tree with arching branches terminating in slender, very long, golden branchlets. Produces yellow catkins in spring. 8×4.5m (26×15 ft).

Tilia petiolaris (weeping silver lime) — Has mid green leaves that are downy above and silvery below. It produces highly-scented white flowers in late summer (July). 8×4.5m (26×15 ft).

TEXTURE
Bold foliage

Ailanthus altissima — Has leaves about 90cm (3 ft) long. See Coloured fruits.

Aralia chinensis (angelica tree) — Has leaves up to 1·2m (4 ft) long and 60cm (2 ft) wide, and white flowers borne in huge panicles during early and mid autumn (August and September). 3.5×3.5m (12×12 ft).

Catalpa bignonioides (Indian bean tree) — A tree of rounded habit with large, heart-shaped, bright green leaves. Its white, foxglove-like flowers have yellow and purple markings and appear in late summer to early autumn (July to August). These give way later to long, slender seed pods. 11×13.5m (36×45 ft).

Magnolia macrophylla — A slow-growing tree with large, thin-textured leaves. It yields large flowers that are fragrant and parchment-coloured with purple centres, and appear in early and mid summer (May and June). It will not tolerate alkaline soils, and ideally should be given a sunny position sheltered from wind. 8×4.5m (26×15 ft).

Parrotia persica — See under Coloured stems.

Paulownia tomentosa — Bears heliotrope-coloured flowers during early summer (May), and leaves that are often 60cm (2 ft) across. It needs protection from frost. 6×3.5m (20×12 ft).

Fine foliage

Azara microphylla — Has tiny, vanilla-scented, yellow flowers that appear in mid and late spring (March and April). 3×1.5m (10×5 ft).

Betula pendula (silver birch) — A white-stemmed, deciduous tree that thrives on thin, acid and sandy soils in sun or shade. 8×3m (26×10 ft).

Laburnum anagyroides (common laburnum) — Bears racemes of yellow flowers in early summer (May), and has trifoliate, dull green leaves. 4.5×3m (15×10 ft).

Nothofagus antarctica (Antarctic beech) — A fast-growing, deciduous tree, often having a distorted trunk and main branches. Its small, rounded, heart-shaped, dark green leaves turn yellow in autumn. It cannot tolerate chalk. 9×6m (30×20 ft).

Robinia pseudoacacia Frisia — A deciduous tree with small leaflets that are golden in summer, becoming a yellow-tinted apricot in autumn. 12×12m (40×40 ft).

CHOOSING CONTAINER-GROWN SHRUBS

As all keen gardeners know, the modern way to buy shrubs is in containers – generally polythene bags, but sometimes rigid polythene or plastic pots. These are all available from the many garden centres that have sprung up all over the country in recent years.

Reputable garden centres sell only good-quality plants, but nevertheless it pays the customer to know how to recognize top-quality as well as inferior-quality plants.

In Great Britain many garden centres have been approved by the Horticultural Trades Association. These centres sell plants of the highest quality only and are easily recognized as they fly a blue flag bearing the emblem of the International Garden Centre Association.

Too young or too old?
Shrubs should be well rooted and established in their containers, otherwise they may not 'take' successfully. A good test is to lift up a plant by the stems; it should

remain firm and secure in the pot. If a shrub is not well established, the container and soil are liable to fall away from the roots: the soil ball should remain intact when planting so that the roots are not disturbed.

Beware of shrubs that have rooted through the base of the containers and established themselves in the underlying medium; this is an indication that they have been in the pots for too long. In order to move such plants from the containers, you would have to cut the

roots away and this, of course, would check growth and mean that the shrub would take longer to establish itself in your garden. If, however, just a few roots show through the base of the container when you lift it up, the plant is well-established in its container and this can be taken as a sign that it is ready for transplanting.

Shrubs that have been containerized for a long time may also be showing signs of nutrient deficiencies – looking generally sickly and rather stunted. Leaves may be unusually small and yellowish, perhaps with marginal scorch or browning, or show abnormal red coloration.

Plants to avoid
Never buy shrubs that are not clearly labelled. Each shrub should have an

individual label, in which case you can be reasonably sure you are buying the right plant. Do not buy any shrubs that are in very dry soil and are obviously suffering from water shortage. This will result in a severe check to growth and even premature leaf fall.

Try to pick shrubs that have a generally healthy appearance, and that seem to be growing well. Avoid any plants with wind or frost damage; again this shows up in the leaves, which may have brown scorch marks, and also in the buds which, if dry and brown, will never spring into life. Reliable nurserymen will keep the more tender shrubs – some of the camellias, magnolias, rhododendrons and azaleas – in a suitably protected area like a lath structure, a polythene or netting tunnel, or a cold glasshouse.

Many people think they are getting better value for money if they buy really tall shrubs from a garden centre or nursery. But these are suspect, especially those with only a few 'leggy' stems, that are devoid of foliage at the base. Instead buy shorter plants that are well branched from the base – really bushy specimens with plenty of strong stems. These plants will already have been stopped; a 'leggy' plant will generally remain so unless you cut it back hard.

Avoid any plants with pests on the foliage as it is foolish to introduce any more trouble into your garden. Likewise beware of containers full of weeds: there is always a risk here of introducing a particularly pernicious weed to your garden, which may prove difficult to eradicate. And perennial weeds cannot be extracted from the soil ball without a great deal of root disturbance to the shrub. You may sometimes find liverwort

Far left: buy your shrubs from a good garden centre. Above left: shrub being removed from its container prior to planting
Left: conifer suffering from erratic watering
Below: azalea with lime-induced chlorosis

(flat, green, plate-like growth) on the surface of the soil, but this is harmless and can easily be scraped off before planting.

Flowering shrubs
One of the ideas behind containerized shrubs is that the customer can buy them when they are in flower. You can thus be sure that the plants have reached flowering age and that you will not have to wait several years for a display. It probably goes without saying that you should choose well-budded plants, or those with plenty of flowers. For instance, rhododendrons and camellias are generally offered when in bud, so ensure that they have plenty of fat flower-buds.

If you decide to buy some shrubs that show no signs of flowering, ask the sales assistant or nurseryman to give you an idea when you can expect the particular specimen to come into flower. Some subjects, for example chimonanthus (winter-sweet), take a number of years to reach flowering size.

Climbing plants
Climbing plants are generally supplied with some kind of support such as a stout bamboo cane, and are regularly trained in by the nursery staff to prevent plants becoming entangled with each other. But if this has not been done, do not attempt to untwine them; your plant's stem may well be damaged in the process. You will find that clematis are often grown in a netting sleeve to contain them; remove this immediately after planting.

Diseased shrubs
Reliable nurserymen would never offer diseased plants. But there is one serious disease of shrubs whose symptoms you should be able to recognize. Conifers and heathers are prone to attack by a fungus called phytophthora that causes the roots to rot and the plants to die. It affects some other shrubs too, such as rhododendrons, and is highly infectious – it can spread like wildfire in a nursery. Obviously you do not want to introduce it into your garden. Conifers suffering from this disease lose their natural foliage and turn greyish. They start to die from the base upwards. Heathers have similar symptoms and also the tips of the shoots wilt in the early stages of infection. Rhododendrons generally show a somewhat stunted appearance, the leaves being smaller than normal and often of a pale colour.

Rhododendrons, camellias, heathers and other lime-hating shrubs with yellowing foliage are probably not diseased but suffering with chlorosis from being potted in a compost containing lime.

PLANTING TREES AND SHRUBS

Here we describe the steps taken in planting trees and shrubs to achieve the best results. During the dreary winter months, when many plants die down or at least lose their leaves, the evergreens come into their own. They provide a welcome touch of colour when the garden is at its barest and are effective all year round as screens or hedges.

In prepared soil, dig a hole a little wider than the rootball of new shrub

Remove plant from container, taking care not to disturb its roots or soil ball

Put plant in centre of hole, adding a supporting stake at this stage if necessary

Replace soil carefully round shrub, but no higher than soil mark

Firm each layer of soil with your heel before adding the next

18

Planting time

Nowadays trees and shrubs are either in plastic or bitumenized paper-containers or the root-ball is wrapped in hessian when they are bought. Shrubs especially must have their roots kept moist.

It is important to be sure that no plants are planted where there is a severe frost or the ground is soggy. In the former case they should be stored unopened in a frost-proof place, watering those wrapped in hessian, or in the latter, heeled under in a sheltered spot until the weather improves.

Regarding planting time, evergreen trees and shrubs never become completely dormant in the winter, unlike deciduous ones that drop their leaves and rest during a cold period. Evergreens should therefore be planted when the ground is warm and not too dry so that their roots will grow and become established. This is best achieved in mid-to-late autumn (September to October) and late spring to early summer (April to May). Deciduous plants should be planted between late autumn and mid spring.

Preparing the ground

Prior to planting, the ground should be thoroughly dug to the depth of a spade or fork, or if you have the energy, double dig it to two spits. Add a good quantity of organic matter, such as well-rotted farmyard manure, garden compost, peat, leaf mould or spent hops. A top dressing of sterilized bonemeal at 135g per sq m (4 oz per sq yd) can then be forked into the surface. Firm down the soil with your heels and the site is ready for planting. Dig a hole, a few centimetres wider than the diameter of the soil ball and deep enough for the top of the ball to be slightly below the level of the soil surface after planting – about 13mm ($\frac{1}{2}$ in) is enough.

Planting

Remove the plant from its container or hessian wrap, taking great care not to disturb the roots or the soil ball around them, otherwise there may be a check to the plant's growth. The ties securing a hessian wrap should be cut, and then the wrap can be pulled back and the plant carefully lifted out. If your plant is in a flexible plastic bag, the bag should be slit two or three times with a knife, the plastic pulled right back, and the plant lifted out. Bitumenized containers are often held together by staples and these make it easy to pull them apart and lift out the plant. If a plant is in a rigid plastic pot you will have to invert it and sharply tap the rim on the edge of a bench, at the same time holding the base of the stem and the top of the rootball with your other hand. The rootball should then slide cleanly out of the pot with no disturbance.

The plant should be placed in the centre of the hole and the soil returned, firming all round with your heel as you go. The soil must be level with the soil mark on the stem.

If a plant requires a stake, this should be inserted first, for if you drive it into the ground after planting, it may go straight through the soil ball and damage the roots.

Shrubs such as cytisus, genista, spartium and some conifers, that have weak root systems, would benefit from staking for the first few years until they become really well-established. This applies particularly if they are in a windy situation. A stake would help prevent them being buffeted by the wind and so not rooting properly.

Care after planting

Correct care of newly-planted evergreens is of vital importance if they are to become properly established. On no account must the plants be allowed to become dry at the roots, otherwise they are liable to drop their leaves and die. Water them well immediately after planting and continue to do so whenever the surface soil starts to dry out. Until they are well-rooted in the surrounding soil, the evergreens may lose a lot of water through their leaves and be unable to replace it. To counteract this you can give them a good spray all over twice a day – early morning and in the cool of the evening. A less time-consuming method is to spray the leaves with a product called S.600. This forms a film over the surface of the leaves and so prevents rapid water loss. It may have to be re-applied after heavy rain. This product (usually available from garden centres and shops) need only be used until the plants have rooted in the soil – a matter of four to six weeks.

To ensure that the soil does not dry out too rapidly, it is a good idea to mulch the plants after planting. Place an 8cm (3 in) deep layer of organic matter around the plant, over the root area, but not quite up to the stems or trunk. Suitable materials for this purpose are well-rotted farmyard manure, garden compost, peat or spent hops. Fresh lawn mowings, provided they have not been contaminated by weedkiller during the past six weeks, could be used for mulching.

Young evergreens should be well protected from the prevailing wind, especially in the winter, as cold drying winds and gales often cause the edges of the leaves – and sometimes the entire leaf – to turn brown. If the plants are protected on the windward side by larger well-established plants, they will be better off. Otherwise it is a good idea to erect some form of temporary windbreak on the windward side. This could be a sheet of hessian stretched between two posts, or a wattle hurdle or fencing panel would give good protection if securely fixed to wooden posts. A windbreak should be higher than the plant it is protecting. With most shrubs, wind protection may only be necessary until they are well-established – say for the first two or three years, and then generally only in the winter.

If shrub is in exposed position, erect a windbreak to shield it

TRANSPLANTING LARGE TREES AND SHRUBS

There is a trend nowadays to transplant large or semi-mature trees and shrubs. This is often done by local authorities to provide an immediate effect in streets, parks and open spaces, or new housing estates. There may be occasions, however, when the private gardener wishes to move a fairly large established tree or shrub from one part of the garden to another. Here we look at the preparation that is necessary, and describe how to carry out the operation.

Although many trees and shrubs can be moved when fairly large without suffering any ill effects, there is also the question of whether or not you are physically capable of moving a mature tree from one position to another. Think carefully about this problem before you begin, and be sure that sufficient people are available to help you.

Preparation

Trees should preferably be prepared for transplanting one or two growing seasons before lifting, depending on the genus. Some trees – such as acer (maple), aesculus (horse chestnut), alnus (alder), platanus (plane), populus (poplar), fibrous-rooted rhododendrons, tilia (lime) and ulmus (elm) – move easily and re-establish themselves quickly. These can therefore be got ready only one season in advance.

Difficult and coarse-rooted genera, however, should be prepared over two seasons. In this category are abies (silver fir), betula (birch), carpinus (hornbeam), castanea (chestnut), cedrus (cedar), chamaecyparis (false cypress), crataegus (thorn), cupressus (cypress), fagus (beech), fraxinus (ash), ginkgo, ilex (holly), laburnum, larix (larch), liquidambar (sweet gum), malus (flowering crab), metasequoia (dawn redwood), nothofagus (southern beech), picea (spruce), pinus (pine), prunus, pyrus (pear), quercus (oak), robinia, salix (willow), sorbus, taxodium, taxus (yew), thuya (arborvitae) and tsuga (hemlock or hemlock spruce).

A plant with a good quantity of fibrous roots has a far greater chance of survival than one with coarse roots. Some pruning is necessary, therefore, and this is done by excavating a trench around the tree, about 90cm (3 ft) from the trunk and 60cm (2 ft) deep. This will sever coarse lateral roots, thus encouraging a fibrous root system. Fill the trench with topsoil and firm the surface area.

For trees needing two seasons' preparation, *don't* cut a trench right the way round in one operation; instead, remove half of the circle in the first year and the other half the following year.

In the case of deciduous trees or shrubs, this operation can be carried out while they are leafless – that is, between early winter and mid spring (November and March); for evergreens, the best time is late spring or mid autumn (April or September).

Transplanting

First, prepare the planting hole, so that the tree can go right in when it is ready. Dig a hole wider than the rootball and break up the subsoil, incorporating well-rotted farmyard manure or other organic matter; then firm the base well. The prepared hole should be deep enough to allow the tree to be replanted to its original depth. Place a layer of good topsoil in the bottom to assist rooting.

Now you are ready to move the tree. First dig out another trench around the base, making it the same size as before, but being careful not to damage too much of the fibrous root system. Then sever any down-growing roots beneath the tree.

Carefully tease away soil from the soil ball until you think you will be able to lift the tree; the more soil you are able to leave around the roots, the higher the chances of a successful transplanting. Once you have reduced the soil ball to manageable proportions, wrap it tightly with hessian and twine to prevent soil falling away during the move. Try to take

*To encourage fibrous root system in tree to be transplanted, **1** mark out trench around trunk; **2** excavate to adequate depth; **3** sever coarse lateral roots; **4** refill trench and firm; **5** replace turfs*
Left: mulching after the tree has been transplanted will help conserve moisture

the hessian underneath the soil ball if possible, and also over the top, right up to the trunk.

Now you will need as many willing hands as possible to raise the tree out of the hole and move it on to its new site. Set it in the planting hole, remove the hessian, and then backfill with good-quality topsoil, firming really well with your heels as you go.

After-care
The tree will probably need supporting for a few years until well established. This could be done by guying. Insert three angle-iron stakes, evenly spaced, around the tree and attach a length of seven-strand, galvanized wire to each stake through an eyelet or hole. Loop the other end of each wire around the lower branches; thread a piece of rubber or plastic hosepipe onto the wire to protect the bark. Try to get the wires as tight as possible, making sure that you pull the tree into a perfectly upright position.

Alternatively, you could insert three stakes around the tree an equal distance apart, about 60cm (2 ft) from the trunk, and secure the tree to them by means of proprietary, heavy-duty tree ties. These should be available at good garden centres. Use 75mm (3 in) chestnut stakes, at least 2m (7 ft) in length, and insert them about 45cm (18 in) into the ground.

Mulch the tree with well-rotted farm-yard manure or some other organic matter. Keep it well watered during dry spells, at least for the first season after transplanting.

For evergreens, an anti-transpirant spray, such as s.600, used immediately after transplanting would help to reduce

water loss from the foliage until the plant has rooted into the soil. Otherwise, spray the plant with plain water every morning and evening for a few weeks after the move.

If you plant in a lawn or other grassy area, don't allow the grass to grow right up to the trunk until the tree is really well established. For a few years leave a circle of cultivated soil around the trunk, about 90cm (3 ft) in diameter.

To sum up, then: provided you move the tree or shrub at the correct season, with as much soil as possible around the roots, and keep it well watered after transplanting, there is every reason to expect it to survive.

SHRUBS FOR SMALL GARDENS

It is often difficult to make small gardens look really decorative, especially in built-up areas where there is a preponderance of buildings and walls. In such gardens, where too many annuals and bedding plants can look messy, the many attractively-foliaged, flowering shrubs provide the ideal answer.

In a very small garden, the first consideration is to ensure privacy. This is not always easy, since many tiny gardens exist in built-up areas and are consequently surrounded and overlooked by walls and buildings. Light, ornamental trees are often planted to screen the garden area, but even these block out a substantial amount of sunlight and rain from other plants – particularly when they are also in the shadow of neighbouring houses. In spite of these drawbacks, trees are used in purely functional ways – to form screens or focal points, or to divert attention from the ugly, permanent eyesores that exist in congested urban areas.

This is not to say, of course, that trees have only functional value – most are decorative and some are exceptionally beautiful. Nevertheless, small gardens cannot always afford the space necessary for trees. This is where shrubs come in.

Shrubs for cover and concealment

Although grown primarily for decoration, shrubs, like trees, can have a utilitarian purpose. The most common uses made of them are to hide bare boundary walls and fences, to conceal ugly objects such as sheds and to form a generally decorative background.

Unfortunately, there is a drawback to the indiscriminate use of some shrubs. Since the walls surrounding a small garden are often high, large shrubs are needed to cover them; after a fairly short time, such plants encroach on ground space and sap the nutrients and moisture from the soil, leaving it infertile for other decorative plants. Shrubs planted to cover or conceal have, therefore, to be chosen with care, and with an eye to their eventual size and spread.

Evergreen climbers

As some bushy shrubs grow too large for the small garden, it is better to cover walls and fences with evergreen climbing

Small shrubs come in a wide range of foliage colour and texture

shrubs trained along wires or trelliswork. Some climbers send out shoots that can be trained horizontally on either side of the stem for a distance of at least 2m (6½ ft). One climber can cover the same wall area as three or four shrubs, and in much the same time – consequently the demand on the soil is much smaller. Most such climbing shrubs are amenable to regular light trimming, so there is little encroachment on precious ground space. Two evergreen climbers that are particularly good for this purpose are *Pyracantha atalantioides* (firethorn) that has long-lasting scarlet berries, and the fragrant *Lonicera japonica* Halliana (honeysuckle).

Decorative infilling

Once the trees and shrubs for constructional and functional purposes have been planted, the remaining area can be infilled with decorative plants. Of course, there is a considerable amount of overlapping between the shrubs classed as functional and those classed as decorative. A single plant can be utilized for either purpose, depending on the conditions available. These infilling shrubs are the plants, that, ultimately, will form the body of the garden and impart colour and form to it.

Before placing any plants, it is worthwhile studying the layout of larger gardens. Many of the large-growing shrubs that are so valuable in big gardens have rather less vigorous dwarf counterparts that will give much the same effect in a smaller space. Careful visualization and planning is really all that is needed to make a 'pocket-handkerchief' area as relaxing and pleasant a place to be in as a much larger garden.

Colour, shape and texture

To create a garden that is pleasantly varied and yet well organized, first consider the 'three harmonies' of garden design – shape, colour and foliage texture. These are particularly valuable for a small garden where there is normally very little room for error.

The harmony of shape is perhaps the most important; shrubs can be round, conical or pyramidal, and prostrate, erect or spreading – all in a variety of dimensions. Careful mingling of these different sizes and shapes in a border can produce a pleasing, contoured effect. To avoid monotony, an occasional upright-growing, pyramidal shrub can be planted to form an accent point.

The second harmony to consider is that of colour. Here it is important to bear in mind that the foliage of many shrubs lasts much longer than the blooms. Therefore, intermix leaf colours – green, purple, gold, grey and variegations – rather than flower colours. Some very striking combinations can be achieved just through foliage alone. The subtle use of colour will, of course, add emphasis to shape and form.

The third harmony – foliage texture – is often not as easily recognized as the other two. Optically, plants with large, bold foliage seem to push themselves forward, while those that have very tiny leaves appear to recede. By judicious positioning of these two types you can create a sense of gentle movement and flow that compliments the shape and colour of the chosen shrubs. This illusion of movement can also be obtained by planting blue-foliaged and gold-foliaged shrubs in close proximity.

Some varieties to choose

The shrubs listed below are excellent for planting in combination in a small area. The first dimension given is the ultimate height and the second is the spread.

SMALL SHRUBS

Of the plants listed below, some are naturally low-growing and spreading, while others can be kept in check by regular trimming.

Andromeda polifolia Compacta (bog rosemary)
Round, evergreen shrub with small leaves that turn purple in winter, and pink flowers borne in early summer (May). 30 × 30cm (12 × 12 in).

Berberis stenophylla Corallina Compacta
Low-growing, evergreen shrub with dark olive-green, close-set leaves and orange flowers that appear in early summer (May). 45 × 60cm (18 × 24 in).

Ceratostigma plumbaginoides (plumbago)
Low-growing, round sub-shrub with mid green leaves that assume red tints in autumn. Blue flowers open from late summer to mid autumn (July to September). 30 × 38cm (12 × 15 in).

Cytisus × beanii (broom)
Semi-prostrate, deciduous broom. Bears golden flowers in early summer (May). 45 × 90cm (18 in × 3 ft).

Euonymus fortunei Emerald Cushion
Dwarf, mounded, evergreen shrub with dark green leaves. 30 × 30cm (12 × 12 in).

Euonymus fortunei Silver Queen
Variegated evergreen shrub with grey, silver and white small leaves that are tinged pink in winter. 45cm × 1·2m (18 in × 4 ft).

Helichrysum splendidum
Globular, silvery-grey, deciduous shrub. Bears yellow everlasting flowers from late summer to mid autumn (July to September). 60 × 90cm (2 × 3 ft).

Hypericum × inodorum Elstead
Erect-growing, semi-evergreen shrub with deep green leaves. Produces small, pale yellow flowers from late summer to mid autumn (July to September). Its size can be controlled by pruning back to the ground in spring. 90cm × 1·2m (3 × 4 ft).

Laurus nobilis (bay laurel)
Dense, pyramidal, evergreen, aromatic shrub with mid green leaves. It stands clipping well, so its size can be controlled; but if not, it will reach 4·5m (15 ft).

Pachysandra terminalis
Dwarf, evergreen, carpeting shrublet with deep green leaves, carrying white flowers during early and mid spring (February and March). Variegata is an attractive form with mottled white leaves. 30 × 45cm (12 × 18 in).

Below: Hypericum *Elstead can be kept under control by hard pruning*
Below left: dwarf Pachysandra terminalis
Bottom left: lovely deciduous Cytisus × beanii *takes up a minimum of space*

Below: aromatic Laurus nobilis, *the laurel crown plant, is perfect for all-year-round cover*

Right: tiny Ceratostigma plumbaginoides

Potentilla Elizabeth
Dome-shaped bush with small, silver-green leaves and single rose-like yellow blooms borne from mid summer (July) onwards. 60cm × 1·5m (2 × 5 ft).

Potentilla fruticosa mandshurica
Dwarf, semi-prostrate, grey-leaved shrub with white flowers appearing from early summer to late autumn (May to October). 30 × 75cm (12 in × 2½ ft).

Rhododendron microleucum
Tiny-leaved, dwarf species with clusters of white flowers opening in late spring (April). 23 × 60cm (9 × 24 in).

Rosmarinus Jessop's Upright (rosemary)
Strong, erect-growing evergreen shrub with green leaves that are white on the undersides. 1·2 × 1·2m (4 × 4 ft).

Syringa velutina (Korean lilac)
Dwarf, deciduous shrub with 5cm (2 in) long, rounded, velvety, dark green leaves. Produces lilac-pink flowers in early and mid summer (May and June). 90 × 90cm (3 × 3 ft).

DWARF CONIFERS
The selection given below is very limited, since there are many different dwarf conifers available today. You should be able to find a reasonably good selection at any reputable nursery, or alternatively write to one of the specialist growers.

Chamaecyparis lawsoniana Gimbornii (Lawson cypress)
Globular, compact bush of slow growth. Has foliage that is bluish-green, tipped mauve. 60 × 60cm (2 × 2 ft).

Chamaecyparis obtusa Pygmaea (Hinoki cypress)
Low, spreading dwarf conifer with fan-shaped green foliage that reddens at the tips in winter. 45cm × 1·5m (18 in × 5 ft).

Juniperus communis Compressa (juniper)
Column-shaped, compact, slow-growing dwarf conifer with dense, tiny, bluish-grey foliage. 60 × 15cm (24 × 6 in).

Picea glauca albertiana Conica (Alberta white spruce)
Attractive dwarf, conical, slow-growing bush with leaves of bright grass green. 1·2m × 75cm (4 × 2½ ft).

Taxus baccata Standishii (yew)
Very slow-growing and columnar, with golden leaves. 1·8 × 30cm (6 ft × 12 in).

Above: compact Chamaecyparis obtusa *Pygmaea is a good conifer for small areas*

SHRUBS AND CLIMBERS FOR SUNLESS WALLS

Although north- and east-facing walls are traditionally difficult to cover with plants, there is, in fact, quite a range of hardy shrubs and climbers – most with good foliage and flowers – that can be grown very successfully in such positions. A selection taken from the list given below will ensure more than adequate coverage of almost any house or boundary wall.

Generally, walls with a north- or east-facing aspect are regarded as difficult to cover, whether with wall plants or climbers. This is unfortunate, since many houses have north- or north-east facing walls at the front or back – usually the most important walls.

Of these two different aspects, there is little doubt that the north-east facing walls are the most difficult to clothe satisfactorily. In general only the very toughest of shrubs and climbers can grow in such a position. Almost any rose, however, will be quite happy either standing against or climbing up a wall with an eastern aspect – mainly because they like some shade during at least part of the day.

Although all walls facing directly towards the north will certainly be dark and dreary, particularly when the days are short, they are somehow not quite as bad for plants as east-facing ones. Generally, but particularly in the summer, the wall of a house that has a northerly outlook – provided it is a fairly flat one without any deep recesses – seems to get a little (possibly reflected) sunshine on it very early in the morning and last thing before sunset. Also, any plants positioned against such a wall are exposed to a north light that seems to be of benefit to them. Fortunately, there are a good number of interesting shrubs and climbers that will grow quite contentedly in such a position.

If the bed to be planted is overshadowed by a tall building or a group of trees farther to the north, then the problem becomes even greater. Under such circumstances it will be necessary to fall back on the 'toughies' – such as *Fatsia japonica* (fig leaf palm), skimmia, elaeagnus and *Ilex altaclarensis* (holly). There are also some hardy rhododendrons and cultivars of *Camellia japonica* and *C.* × *williamsii* that are tolerant of comparatively heavy shade.

Camellias for north walls

Camellias, almost without exception, are excellent as plants for a sunless wall. They can be chosen to flower from early

Shade-tolerant camellia Donation does well against a north-facing wall

winter to early summer (November to May). During the rest of the year they provide an attractive appearance with their shiny, mid green, moderately large leaves. For clothing walls most varieties of *C. japonica* and *C.* × *williamsii* are most suitable – as is *C.* Inspiration, with its large, deep pink blossoms. Although camellias are fairly slow-growing, it is possible to obtain good wall coverage after a number of years; their ultimate height and spread can attain 4m (13 ft). At all times these shrubs are shapely, bushy, and very decorative plants.

You must, however, bear in mind that although camellias will flourish against a north-facing wall, they must not, on any account, be placed at the foot of one with an easterly aspect. This is because camellias come into bloom when severe frosts are likely; the real danger lies in the damaging effect of the warmth of the early morning sun on the frozen tissues of the blossoms. An east-facing wall is, of course, particularly exposed to this.

Roses for walls

In a small garden the wall of a house is often the only space that can be spared to grow roses; fortunately many will grow vigorously on a north- and east-facing walls. If you decide to grow bush roses at the foot of a wall, it is best to choose those that are vigorous and tall-growing – floribundas are generally just a little bit stronger than hybrid teas and can withstand more adverse conditions. The tall, vigorous Queen Elizabeth, with clear pink blooms, or the golden yellow Arthur Bell are both worth trying. Other bush roses that have withstood the test of time are the rugosa shrub Conrad F. Meyer that produces very full, silvery pink blooms in early summer (May), repeating this colourful display in autumn, and the hybrid perpetual Hugh Dickson, that has full, globular, very fragrant, red blooms during the summer.

Climbing roses such as disease-resistant Hamburger Phönix (left and below) and the exceptionally vigorous, fragrant Maigold (below left and bottom) are excellent for clothing high walls. Kerria japonica *Pleniflora (above right) and* Desfontainea spinosa *(below right) can brighten up most shady corners*

The best choice of roses for growing on almost sunless walls will nevertheless come from among the large-flowering climbers and the *Rosa kordesii* climbers. The former are colourful and vigorous and will soon cover a good area of the wall of a house. Possibly one of the most spectacular large-flowering climbers is the flamboyant, fiery scarlet Danse du Feu. It is moderately vigorous, growing to a height of 2·5m (8 ft). Rather taller-growing is the bronze-yellow, fragrant, free-flowering Maigold, which attains a height of 3·4m (11 ft), and the very fragrant, free-flowering Guinée, with dark scarlet, shaded black, full flowers. The *R. kordesii* climbers Hamburger Phönix (crimson) and Parkdirektor Riggers (blood red, semi-double flowers) are more modest-growing.

Hints on general cultivation

Remember that very often a foundation bed at the foot of a wall is very dry; therefore dig it as deep as possible and incorporate into it a good deal of humus-making material such as well-rotted manure, garden compost or peat. Plant nothing closer than 38cm (15 in) to the wall, and train climbers to the wall along a sloping bamboo cane. Water well before and after planting, and mulch.

Bear in mind also that the soil in such a bed often contains a lot of mortar, dropped during building. It is therefore likely to be alkaline, so if you intend to grow lime-haters, first neutralize the soil by adding plenty of peat.

Some plants for north and east walls

Any selection from the plants listed below should give adequate coverage of a north- or east-facing wall. It is a good idea to choose an evergreen to go next to a deciduous flowering plant, so that coverage is maintained throughout the year.

SHRUBS

Berberis × stenophylla

This is a graceful bush with long, arching branches and small, evergreen leaves. It has orange-yellow blooms, opening during late spring and early summer (April and May). 2·5m (8 ft) high.

Chaenomeles speciosa Moerloosii
(flowering quince)

A deciduous shrub with an arching, spreading habit that enables it to cover the lower half of a house wall very effectively. It has delicate pink and white blooms, borne in thick clusters between early and late spring (February and April), followed by fruits that are flushed pink. 1·8m (6 ft) high.

Choisya ternata (Mexican orange blossom)
A beautiful evergreen with glossy foliage. It produces sweet-scented, white, star-like flowers in clusters in early summer (May). 2·5m (8 ft) high.

Desfontainea spinosa
This somewhat less well-known evergreen appreciates the shelter of a wall. It has small, holly-like leaves and tubular, scarlet flowers that bloom from late summer to mid autumn (July to September). 1·8m (6 ft) high.

Jasminum nudiflorum (winter-flowering jasmine)
Has golden-yellow blooms carried on bare stems throughout the winter. It looks most attractive if planted so as to grow through the branches of an evergreen pyracantha. East-facing aspects should be avoided, however, because early sun after frost damages the flowers. 4m (13 ft) high.

Kerria japonica Pleniflora (jew's mallow)
A graceful, deciduous shrub with dainty, arching, bright green stems, that becomes garlanded with golden-yellow ball-like flowers during mid and late spring (March and April). 3m (10 ft) high.

Pyracantha (firethorn)
There are several very attractive species of pyracantha that can be trained to cover a wall. They are all evergreen, and are covered with masses of hawthorn-like flowers during the spring and early summer months. They reach a height of 4m (13 ft). Suitable forms for virtually sunless walls are *P. atalantioides*, with crimson berries during the winter, *P. coccinea* Lalandei with orange-red berries, and *P. rogersiana* Flava with bright yellow berries.

CLIMBERS
Akebia quinata
This semi-evergreen, twining climber can reach a height of 3m (10 ft). It produces very dark purple, scented flowers in late spring (April), followed by peculiar, 8cm (3 in) long, dark purple sausage-shaped fruits that are quite decorative.

Celastrus orbiculatus (climbing spindle berry)
A strong, deciduous, twining climber, reaching 3m (10 ft) high. Its leaves turn clear yellow in autumn, forming a splendid backcloth to its brownish seed capsules that split open to show a yellow lining and red seeds.

Hydrangea
H. anomala, reaching 4m (13 ft) high, with slightly domed, up to 20cm (8 in) across, corymbs of yellowish-white flowers, has brown, peeling bark when it is mature. *H. petiolaris* is a deciduous, strong-growing, self-clinging, climbing hydrangea that reaches 4m (13 ft) in height. It bears white flower-heads 15cm (6 in) across, and serrated leaves, in mid and late summer (June and July).

Top: well-grown Choisya ternata *and* Rosa banksiae *at Kiftsgate Court*
Winter-flowering Jasminum nudiflorum *(above) prefers a northerly aspect*
Above left: Hydrangea petiolaris

Parthenocissus quinquefolia (Virginia creeper)
This tall, self-clinging deciduous vine is treasured for its rather dull green leaves that turn orange and scarlet in autumn.

FLOWERING TREES AND SHRUBS

AZALEA

Type	mostly hardy, deciduous, semi-evergreen and evergreen flowering shrubs
Family	ERICACEAE
Planting season	mid spring (March); container-grown plants at any time
Flowering dates	late spring–mid summer (April–June)
Mature size/shape	usually round, sometimes erect; height 10cm–2·5m (4 in–8 ft), spread 60cm–3m (2–10 ft)

Modern garden azaleas are a group of attractive and useful deciduous, semi-evergreen and evergreen flowering shrubs, created by extensive interbreeding. At one time botanists considered them to be a separate genus, but now they are included as a group, known as Series (S) Azaleas, of the rhododendron genus.

There are at least 40 species of azalea available commercially in Britain; of these about a dozen are cultivated for garden use. Several of the remainder have played an important part in producing the many decorative hybrids so popular today. These include the deciduous Ghent, Knap Hill and Exbury, mollis and occidentale types that have been developed in Europe since the early 19th century. The majority of the evergreens originated from a collection of kurume azaleas from Japan, and were known as 'Wilson's Fifty' because they were introduced by the plant collector and explorer, E. H. Wilson, in 1920; a further range was developed in Europe and the United States.

Azaleas are characterized by brightly-coloured flowers that appear, according to type and variety, in late spring and early summer (April and May), occasionally extending into mid summer (June). Some of the deciduous Knap Hill hybrids have bronze-tinted or coppery red young leaves, and others – such as the mollis group, the species *Rhododendron arborescens*, *R. calendulaceum*, *R. occidentale* and *R. reticulatum*, the Ghent azalea Corneille and the kurume Hinodegiri – follow their flowers with brilliant autumn tints. Quite a number are also pleasantly scented. They range in size from prostrate forms such as *R. nakaharai*, to the occidentale hybrids that grow to 2·5m (8 ft) high and 3m (10 ft) wide. Normally the evergreen hybrids are smaller, with a height and spread of about 1·2m (4 ft) after 20 years' growth. They are usually rounded or erect in shape.

Deciduous azaleas

Ghent hybrids are a popular category, originally produced in Belgium in the middle of the 19th

century. Their variously-coloured, fragrant blooms have long, tubed flowers rather like those of the honeysuckle – and so are popularly known as 'honeysuckle azaleas'.

Knap Hill hybrids were originally raised at Anthony Waterer's nursery at Knap Hill in Surrey, hence their name, but their development was continued afterwards on a much larger scale by the late Lionel de Rothschild at Exbury, Hampshire. Those raised there, although similar in character to the original cultivars, are often called 'Exbury' azaleas. This group has large, trumpet-shaped, usually unscented flowers in varying colours.

Occidentale azaleas, a most valued race of garden hybrids, are characterized by pastel-coloured flowers – a quality possibly derived from *R. occidentale* that has creamy white to pale pink flowers with a pale yellow or orange basal stain.

Rustica hybrids, created by crossing double-flowered Ghent azaleas with *R. japonicum*, have sweet-scented, double, brightly-coloured flowers that are profusely produced and daintier in flower and growth than other deciduous azaleas, as well as being shorter and more compact.

Evergreen azaleas

The kurume group of evergreens, very widely grown in present-day gardens, and usually of comparatively small dimensions, has small, brightly-coloured flowers, and is eminently suitable where space is restricted.

Kaempferi hybrids are modest-growing azaleas, created in Holland around 1920 by crossing *R. kaempferi* with the cultivar *R.* Malvaticum (a seedling of the evergreen Hinodegiri). The Oldhamii group are also hybrids of *R. kaempferi*, but their other parent is *R. oldhamii* (the Formosan azalea); most have large blooms.

Satsuki hybrids, with medium to large flowers, have been produced mainly by crossing *R. indicum* with *R. simsii*, but there have been other crossings involving some of the Belgian hybrids.

Vuyk hybrids, with large flowers, are frequently grown in gardens today; their parentage is probably *R. molle* crossed with the kurume hybrids.

Glenn Dale hybrids, raised by B. Y. Morrison of the US Department of Agriculture at Glenn Dale, Maryland, are characterized by very large flowers, and are dwarf in growth.

Indian azaleas are mainly tender hybrids with very large flowers, bred chiefly in Belgium and Britain during the 19th century. Some varieties are specially forced by florists for the Christmas trade.

Hardy azaleas are excellent for shrub and mixed borders, and are particularly valuable because of their wide range of sizes. Possibly their greatest garden asset is that many bloom from early to mid summer (May to June) and sometimes into late summer (July), thus avoiding damage from frost. Another advantage, particularly with the deciduous Knap Hill hybrids and *R. luteum*, is their ability to exist in industrial areas.

Evergreen azaleas such as Hatsugiri, Izayoi and Rosebud are particularly useful for ground cover; *R. luteum* is sometimes planted as a hedge because of its yellow, honeysuckle-like flowers and the rich red hues of its leaves in autumn. The dwarf evergreen azaleas also make excellent – but rather expensive – low-growing division hedges. There are several species that are valuable for shrubberies; these wild species are largely indigenous to Japan and North America, but a few originate from the Caucasus, China and eastern Europe. Most were introduced to Britain during the 19th century, but earlier ones were *R. viscosum* (1734), *R. canadense* (1767) and *R. luteum* (1793).

Cultivation and propagation

Deciduous azaleas do best in moist, partially-shaded positions. The evergreen types are rather more tender than the deciduous and need to be sheltered from cold winds. They will grow in full sun provided they are kept moist. The best soil is a light, acid one; you can create such conditions by adding peat or leaf mould to existing soil. On no account must the soil be chalky or limey.

Provided the weather is good, you can plant bare-root azaleas at any time during the winter, but the best time is probably mid spring (March), when the soil is warming up. Plant container-grown ones at any time in good weather. Determine planting distance by adding together the spreads of two adjacent plants and then dividing by two.

Dig a hole large enough to take the rootball comfortably; on no account must this rootball be disturbed. When planted, the azalea should not be any deeper in the soil than it was before. Fill in the soil round the roots and firm gently. After planting, mulch with leaves, well-rotted compost or peat. Position early-flowering cultivars where they will be protected from the early morning sun, to avoid damage from frost on the petals that might thaw too fast.

Mulch the plants with leaves, well-rotted compost or peat in early summer (May) every year. Feed with 135gm per sq m (4 oz per sq yd) of J.I. base fertilizer, or rhododendron or rose fertilizer every spring. Where possible, dead-head the flowers as they fade.

Propagate deciduous azaleas by layering at any time when the shoots are young. Evergreens are grown from cuttings taken in late summer and early autumn (July and August). Root them in cutting compost in a cold frame for the winter, then pot them on and transplant them to a nursery bed in spring.

Pests and diseases

White fly particularly infest azaleas; treat with nicotine used according to the manufacturer's instructions. Azalea gall causes the young leaves and flowers, particularly of the kurumes, to form small swellings that are red or pale green, then white and eventually brown. Remove the galls if there are only a few of them, before they turn white; if there are a great many, spray them with Bordeaux mixture.

Left: deciduous azalea Coccinea Speciosa grows best if planted in a partially-shaded position
Below: the evergreen foliage of Kaempferi azalea Willy provides good ground cover during the winter

The jewel-bright blooms of evergreen azaleas Vuyk's Scarlet (right) and Blue Danube (far right) make a magnificent display in early summer (May) Centre right: the foliage of R. luteum *turns to spectacular shades of crimson, purple and orange in autumn Below right: Knap Hill azalea Persil blooms from early to mid summer (May to June)*

Some varieties to choose
The following is a list of some of the most popular varieties of azalea grown today. A careful selection of plants will ensure a continuous display of flowers throughout the summer months.

DECIDUOUS HYBRIDS
Ghent hybrids
Flower in early and mid summer (May and June). Height and spread usually about 1·8m (6 ft).

Bouquet de Flore	Bright pink, deepening at the edges of the petals, with a white stripe down the centre of each.
Coccinea Speciosa	Brilliant orange-red; one of the best.
Corneille	Cream, double flowers, flushed pink outside, with pink buds and excellent autumn foliage tints.
Daviesii	Creamy white, flushed pale apricot on the reverse side, with orange-yellow blotches; buds are buff pink. Late-flowering.
Nancy Waterer	Golden yellow with orange-yellow top petals. Compact.
Pucella (Fanny)	Deep rose with top petals blotched orange.
Sang de Gentbrugge	Bright red.
Unique	Orange-yellow, in globular trusses. Tall-growing.

Mollis hybrids
Flower in early summer (May), and have good autumn tints. Height and spread of about 1·5m (5 ft).

Directeur Moerlands	Golden yellow with an orange flare. Also known as Golden Sunlight.
Dr. M. Oosthoek	Orange-red.
Floradora	Orange-red, spotted.
Goldball (Christopher Wren)	Orange-yellow, flushed flame and spotted a dark orange.
Hortulanus H. Witte	Brilliant orange-yellow.
Hugo Hardyzer	Bright rose-pink, strongly blotched orange.

Knap Hill and Exbury hybrids
Bloom from early to mid summer (May to June). Have a height and spread of 1–1·8m (3–6 ft).

Gibraltar	Orange-flame, with orange-yellow blotch.
Harvest Moon	Amber-yellow.
Persil	White, with an orange flare.
Satan	Geranium-red.
Seville	Brilliant orange.
Tunis	Deep crimson, with an orange flare.

Occidentale hybrids
Flower in early and mid summer (May and June). Have a height of up to 2·5m (8 ft), and a spread of up to 3m (10 ft).

Exquisitum	Cream, flushed pink, with an orange flare.
Graciosa	Creamy pink, with an orange-yellow basal blotch.
Irene Koster	Rose-pink; late-flowering.
Superbum	Pink, blotched apricot, with fringed petals.

Rustica hybrids
Have double flowers in early and mid summer (May and June). Height 1·8m (6 ft), spread 2·5m (8 ft).

Byron	Double white, tinged pink.
Freya	Pale pink, tinted salmon-orange.

EVERGREEN HYBRIDS
Kurume azaleas
Bloom from late spring to early summer (April to May). Height 1·2m (4 ft), spread 1·5m (5 ft).

Addy Wery	Deep vermilion-red.
Benigiri	Bright crimson.
Blaauw's Pink	Salmon-pink. Early.
Hatsugiri	Bright crimson-purple flowers. Dwarf habit.
Hinodegiri	Bright crimson.
Shin-seikai	White. Dwarf habit.

Kaempferi hybrids
Bloom during early summer (May). Height 75cm (2½ ft), spread 1·2m (4 ft).

Alice	Salmon-red.
Arendsii	Pale purple, with red spots.
Fedora	Deep pink.
Kathleen	Rose-red.
Orange Beauty	Salmon-orange.
Willy	Soft pink.

Vuyk's hybrids
Flower in early summer (May). Height about 90cm (3 ft), spread 1·5m (5 ft).

Blue Danube	Bluish violet.
Palestrina	White.
Vuyk's Rosyred	Deep rose.
Vuyk's Scarlet	Bright red.

Glenn Dale hybrids
Flower in early and mid summer (May and June). Height and spread about 1·2m (4 ft).

Buccaneer	Brilliant orange-scarlet.
Martha Hitchcock	White, edged with magenta.
Polar Sea	White.

SPECIES AZALEAS
Deciduous

R. albrechtii	Green-flecked, deep rose flowers appearing in late spring and early summer (April and May). Height 1·2m (4 ft), spread 90cm (3 ft).
R. luteum	Rich yellow, very fragrant blooms appearing during early and mid summer (May and June). Height 2·5m (8 ft), spread 1·5m (5 ft).
R. vaseyi	Pink or white flowers appearing during late spring and early summer (April and May). Has beautiful autumn tints. Height 4m (12 ft), spread 1·8m (6 ft).
R. viscosum (swamp honeysuckle)	White or pink fragrant flowers in late summer (July). Height 2·5m (8 ft), spread 1·8m (6 ft).

Semi-evergreen

R. kiusianum	Deep pink or purple flowers borne in early summer (May). Height 90cm (3 ft), spread 1·5m (5 ft).

BERBERIS

Type	evergreen and deciduous flowering and fruiting shrub
Common name	barberry
Family	BERBERIDACEAE
Flowering season	spring
Planting date	outdoors: deciduous varieties late autumn to mid spring (October–March); evergreen varieties mid to late autumn (September–October) or early to late spring (February–April); anytime from containers
Mature size/shape	prostrate to 3·6m (12 ft) high; round, dome-shaped, pyramidal or erect

Although only a fraction of them are widely available, berberis (barberries) are members of a large genus containing over 400 species. Some of these are deciduous, while others are evergreens but, irrespective of this, most of them have similar rosette-like clusters of leaves and generally spiny stems. In some instances the evergreens have holly-like leaves, and despite their smaller size, they can be equally uncomfortable to the touch.

Some of the evergreen species and their cultivars are grown for their very handsome glossy leaves. The deciduous species, on the other hand, are more particularly cultivated for the autumn colour of their foliage and their brightly-coloured berries (or fruits). These usually last well into the winter to enliven the somewhat duller garden scene. The production of berries in autumn is not, however, entirely the prerogative of the deciduous shrubs because many of the evergreens also have them. With several important exceptions, the evergreen shrubs generally yield berries of black, blue, purple and violet while those on the deciduous types are brilliant scarlet, orange-red, coral-red, crimson, pink and, in at least one instance, orange.

Apart from a few species that come from South America, all berberis are hardy and can be grown in most gardens without difficulty.

Most berberis flower in the spring and at that time their blossoms vary in colour largely from pale yellow to orange, occasionally with a touch of red. They are often borne singly, when they sometimes wreathe the arching branches of the shrubs, but can also grow in panicles, spikes or racemes or in flat or dome-shaped flower-heads. Whatever their form, they are always beautiful, but the loveliness of their spring blossoms is only a curtain raiser to the brilliance of their autumn tints and the plethora of vividly-coloured berries of varying shapes and sizes that follow later.

Most berberis are excellent for present-day gardens, being reasonably small in stature, labour-saving and largely trouble-free. They range in size from dwarf – up to 30cm (12 in) in height – to large shrubs – but most of these do not exceed 3·6m (12 ft) in height. A large number of them have ultimate heights and spreads from 60cm to 1·5m (2–5 ft), which makes them fairly reasonable for planting in somewhat restricted spaces. It is usually possible to find a berberis to suit almost any situation, be it sunny or shady, by the sea, in country or town and whatever the soil might be (as long as it is not waterlogged).

The native habitats of the various species of this large family are pretty widespread. Many were brought to Europe from China and Japan; others were carried from central Asia by plant explorers; a few valuable species originated in South America and at least one, *B. chinensis*, hails from Russia. The latter was first cultivated in gardens in 1808. The name berberis comes from the Arabic word for berries. There is one species which is native to the British Isles (or possibly was naturalized a long time ago). This is the common barberry, *B. vulgaris*, which grew widely in hedgerows until it was discovered that it acted as a host plant to the wheat fungus disease, black rust. Since then farmers have so effectively attacked it that it has become very scarce.

While dealing with the origins of the various species, there is one group of very valuable and colourful berberis that came into being as the result of a crossing between *B. aggregata* and *B. wilsoniae* that was made in the Royal Horticultural Society's gardens at Wisley. It produced a hybrid, *B. × carminea*, which in turn has given rise to a number of clones, several of which will be described later. These cultivars are categorized as the Carminea group.

Apart from the wide height range, berberis also come in a range of shapes – rounded, pyramidal, domed, compact, prostrate – all of which are valuable for giving interest and variation in a garden. Similarly, they display between them a number of different habits, such as elegant, arching branches (often weighed down in autumn under enormous crops of berries), drooping branches, or upright growth. Some have dense growth, while most of their shoots bear sharp spines. There are some berberis that are dwarf and wide-spreading, making good ground cover, such as *B. tsangpoensis* and, in particular, *B. sieboldii*, which suckers freely and spreads rapidly.

Berberis are excellent for shrub borders and mixed beds, where the changing colours of their foliage, flowers and berries give a beautiful display. Many of them make good hedges – either dwarf for interior divisions or taller for the boundary. For the former there is little better than *B. thunbergii* Atropurpurea Nana. While excellent subjects for higher hedges are *B. Buccaneer*, *B. darwinii*, *B. julianiae*, *B. stenophylla* (which makes a tough, dog-proof hedge), and *B. verruculosa*.

Cultivation
It is doubtful whether there is any race of plants more tolerant of their environment than berberis. The evergreens flourish in sun and light shade, but to get the fullest development of the autumn tints and vivid berries, the deciduous ones are better in the sun. They are happy in industrial areas and town gardens. Some, particularly *B. Buccaneer*, *B. darwinii*, *B. × ottawensis* Superba and *B. × stenophylla* thrive beside the sea, even if there is some exposure.

Berberis grow easily and are not fussy about soil. All of them grow in clay, providing it is not so heavy that it becomes waterlogged. In such a case, take steps to improve the drainage. They will grow well in dry, acid soil and, equally, with no objection in a shallow topsoil over chalk, which will be alkaline in reaction. Their only real dislike is permanently damp soil, which would have to be drained for them. Usually this defect can be corrected by digging a trench across the ground, partially filling it with rubble and finally filling it up with some of the excavated topsoil. If this action fails, then a more drastic scheme of drainage will have to be introduced.

The deciduous species and their cultivars are best planted any time in the winter from late

Left: Berberis thunbergii Harlequin *forms a rounded and compact deciduous shrub*
Below left: Berberis darwinii *is chiefly grown for its outstanding display of abundantly-borne spring flowers*
Below: Berberis darwinii *fruiting in autumn*

autumn to mid spring (October–March), when the weather is mild and the ground not excessively wet. The evergreens should be planted either in mid or late autumn (September or October) or else from early to late spring (February–April) so that the risk of exposing them to too much severe weather is lessened. Container-grown plants, of course, can be planted at any time.

Planting distances
To get an idea of how far apart shrubs should be planted, check on the ultimate spread of each (usually from a nurseryman's catalogue). The distance that two shrubs should be planted apart can be calculated by adding their two spreads together and dividing by two.

Dig a hole large enough in diameter to allow the roots of the shrub to be spread out in it, after cutting away any extra long or broken roots. To determine its depth, examine the stem of the new shrub for a mark or stain a few centimetres above the point where the roots start to spread out. This is where the soil reached to when the shrub was growing in the nursery. Make the hole to such a depth that when the roots are spread out, this mark will once again be just at the soil surface.

Careful planting makes a lot of difference to the well-being of a shrub. When the hole is dug, work some garden compost or manure into the soil at its bottom and put in the shrub, spreading out its roots. Mix more compost or manure with some of the excavated soil and cover the roots. Gently move the plant up and down a little to remove any air pockets that might have been formed and gently firm in the soil with your heel. Put in a second layer of soil, tread that in, and then fill the hole with the remaining soil. Level the surface, but do not tread the last layer of soil down.

The method of planting each shrub for a hedge is exactly the same. In order to form a good solid hedge, the planting distance between shrubs should be 45–60cm (18–24 in). The most effective-sized plants to use for this purpose are 30–38cm (12–15 in) high. After planting, give the plants about a fortnight to settle down and then prune each shrub back by about a quarter. This will encourage them to make really bushy growth and quickly produce a solid base to the hedge.

Fortunately most berberis need very little attention in order to flourish.

About 14 days after planting check that the wind has not made them loose in the soil. If it has, tread them in firmly again. (This attention should be given to *all* shrubs at the end of each winter, because frost, wind, snow and rain are likely to loosen them in the ground.)

Hoe regularly round the shrubs in order to eliminate the weeds. In dry weather particularly, berberis must be kept well watered. Give each one about 4 lit (1 gal) of water once a week during dry weather. While the soil is still moist give it a mulch with an 8cm (3 in) layer of garden compost, farmyard manure, damp peat or spent hops. A spray with cold water in the evening is also a help, particularly for the evergreens.

Berberis need no regular pruning. It is beneficial, however, periodically to remove old branches by cutting them down to the ground or a healthy bud. This encourages the growth of new wood from the base. All cutting back should, in any case, be directed towards keeping the bush an attractive shape by shortening any lengthy, untidy shoots and to maintaining it at a size appropriate to the space allotted to it. Deciduous varieties should be pruned in early spring (February), while evergreens should be cut back soon after flowering.

Trim hedges annually to keep them in shape: evergreens after flowering, deciduous ones in early or mid autumn (August or September).

Propagation
Although all species can be readily raised from seed, the resulting plants show considerable variation as berberis hybridize freely and hybrids do not come true from seed. In consequence it is more satisfactory to propagate them by rooting cuttings or layering. Some species like *B. sieboldii* that sucker freely can be reproduced by cutting off rooted suckers and replanting them where they are to grow, preferably between late autumn and mid spring (October–March).

To raise new plants from cuttings, take heel cuttings 8–10cm (3–4 in) long from lateral shoots in early or mid autumn (August–September). Plant them in a cold frame in an equal mixture of peat and sand. The following spring plant them out in a nursery bed, where they should be allowed to remain for one or two years before being transplanted to their final positions. Often cuttings of evergreen berberis are better if they are initially rooted in small pots of J.I. No 2 and then plunged in the soil outdoors, from which position they can be planted out.

The alternative method of propagating is by layering which consists of selecting a low-growing, non-flowering, flexible shoot that can be pulled down to the ground. Make an incision behind a bud at the point where it touches the ground, bury this point in the soil, firming it well in and holding the tip upwards. Fix the bend in position by means of a stone and hold the tip vertically by tying it to a stake. A shoot should be layered in mid autumn–early winter (September–November). In about a year's time, roots will form and the shoot can be severed at a point close to the root on the nearside and planted out.

Pests and diseases
Berberis are fairly free from pests, nor are they very prone to disease, but they are sometimes attacked by honey fungus, which can be detected by the presence of honey-coloured toadstools in the vicinity and by digging the surrounding soil and finding long black threads like bootlaces. The latter give this fungus its popular name of 'bootlace fungus'. If a plant is badly affected, dig it up and burn it.

Right: Berberis aggregata *heavily laden with coral-red berries; this shrub originated in W. China*

Some varieties to choose

As can be appreciated with such a large plant family as that of the berberis, only a small number of them are readily available. The first figure given under each variety description is the ultimate height and the second figure the ultimate spread of the plant.

EVERGREEN

B. candidula	Dome-shaped shrub with dark green leaves with silvery white beneath. Bright yellow flowers, blue-black berries. 60 × 60cm (2 × 2 ft).
B. verruculosa	Compact, slow-growing shrub with dark leaves, white underneath, golden-yellow flowers and black berries. 1·2 × 1·2m (4 × 4 ft).
B. hookeri	Compact shrub with leaves, glaucous underneath. Berries green at first, turning black. 1·5 × 1·5m (5 × 5 ft). Nana is a dwarf form. 75 × 75cm (2½ × 2½ ft).
B. gagnepainii	Erect branches and black berries. Good for hedges. 1·8 × 1·4m (6 × 4½ ft).
B. darwinii	Holly-like leaves, clusters of rich yellow or orange tinged with red blooms. followed by blue berries. 2·7 × 2·7m (9 × 9 ft). Prostrata is a useful dwarf form.
B. × stenophylla	Outstanding shrub with arching branches laded with golden flowers in spring, followed by somewhat sparsely-produced purple berries. 2·7 × 3·4m (9 × 11 ft).
B. linearifolia	Erect shrub with rich orange-red blooms, followed by black berries with a white bloom. 3 × 1m (10 × 3½ ft). Orange King is an outstanding form. 1·8 × 1·2m (6 × 4 ft).

DECIDUOUS

B. wilsoniae	Dense, mound-forming shrub with sea-green leaves, giving autumn tints and coral-red berries. 90 × 90cm (3 × 3 ft).
B. sieboldii	Compact, suckering shrub with bright green leaves, borne on red stems, turning rich carmine in autumn. Yellow flowers and red berries. 1 × 1m (3½ × 3½ ft).
B. thunbergii	Compact bush with brilliant autumn foliage and bright red berries. 1·2 × 1·8m (4 × 6 ft). Atropurpurea has reddish-purple leaves that become more intense in autumn. Atropurpurea Nana is a charming dwarf form of the last named. 38 × 38cm (15 × 15 in). Erecta is an upright-growing version. 1·5m × 45cm (5 × 1½ ft).
B. aggregata	Dense shrub with yellow flowers in late summer (July) with red and orange leaves and coral-red berries in autumn. 1·5 × 1·5m (5 × 5 ft).
B. buxifolia	Dark green leaves, grey underneath, yellow flowers, purple-black berries. 1·8 × 1·8m (6 × 6 ft). Nana is a dwarf variety. 45 × 45cm (1½ × 1½ ft).
B. dictyophylla	Leaves, white beneath, are carried on white bloom-covered red stems and turn red in autumn. Yellow flowers are followed by large red berries. 2 × 1m (7 × 3½ ft).

CARMINEA GROUP

B. Buccaneer	Erect-growing shrub with large, deep red berries. 1·2 × 1·2m (4 × 4 ft).
B. Pirate King	Dense-growing bush with fiery orange berries. 1·8 × 1·2m (6 × 4 ft).

BUDDLEIA

Type	deciduous, semi-evergreen and evergreen flowering shrubs, hardy and half-hardy, with a few greenhouse varieties
Family	LOGANIACEAE
Flowering season	mainly between early summer and mid autumn (May and September)
Planting date	late autumn–early winter (October–November), or mid–late spring (March–April); from containers at any time
Mature size/shape	bushy, and rounded or upright; height 1–6m (3½ –20 ft), spread 1·5–5·5m (5–18 ft)

The buddleia genus is comprised of 100 species of deciduous, semi-evergreen and evergreen shrubs and small trees. *B. davidii* is not native to the British Isles, although found growing wild, particularly in the southern parts of Britain. The 'wild' plants are strays from cultivated gardens. Its habitat is China, from where many of the species cultivated in Western gardens originate. Of the rest, *B. asiatica* comes from the East Indies, *B. colvilei*, *B. crispa* and *B. tibetica* from the Himalayas and regions north of India. The more delicate species, *B. auriculata* and *B. salviifolia* come from southern Africa, and *B. madagascariensis* originates from Madagascar. *B. globosa* is a native of Chile and Peru. With the exception of *B. globosa* and *B. salviifolia* (that came to Britain in the 18th century), buddleia were mostly introduced during the 19th and 20th centuries. The name was given in honour of Adam Buddle, an English botanist of the late 17th century.

Some buddleia are of great value in the garden since they can tolerate almost any soil conditions, and also grow very well in hot sunshine. Many make decorative garden plants because of their profusion of flowers and long flowering span that stretches throughout summer into autumn. Some are completely hardy and easily grown, while others are half-hardy. Most of those commonly grown in gardens are deciduous, but species such as *B. globosa* and *B. asiatica* are semi-evergreen or evergreen. Generally, it seems that these varieties become less hardy in proportion to how evergreen they are. For instance, *B. colvilei*, which is tender as a young plant is semi-evergreen, and the greenhouse or conservatory species *B. madagascariensis* is evergreen.

Most of the popular species flower in summer and some continue into the autumn. *B. tibetica*,

Above: its long flowering period and fragrant blooms make B. davidii *one of the most popular buddleias grown today. Buddleias were named after the Reverend Adam Buddle (1660–1715), English botanist and vicar of Farmbridge, Essex*
Top left: Buddleia alternifolia *can grow to a height of 6m (20 ft) but is usually pruned back every year to maintain a compact, neat look*
Bottom left: the hardy, unusual B. x weyerana *is excellent for growing in exposed coastal areas*

with their strong growth and comparatively large leaves, make excellent screens, while some of the relatively tall-growing species (particularly the more delicate shrubs) are good as wall plants. Several, *B. alternifolia* and *B. colvilei* in particular, will grow into small trees. A much-valued quality of *B. davidii* is the attraction it has for bees and butterflies – giving rise to its common name of 'butterfly bush'.

Cultivation and propagation
The hardier species and their varieties grow in full sun in most gardens, but the half-hardy ones do better planted against a warm wall with a western aspect. Buddleia like good garden soil and will tolerate lime.

Plant them in late autumn and early winter (October and November), or mid to late spring (March to April), and from containers at any time. Determine the planting distance by adding the spreads of adjacent shrubs and dividing by two.

Dig a hole large enough to take the rootball comfortably, and of such a depth that the original soil mark on the main stem will be just on the surface. When the shrub is in position, cover the roots well with soil, firm in by treading, and finally fill the hole. Once planted, no special care is needed.

No regular pruning is needed, except to keep the vigorous shrubs neat and bushy – particularly *B. davidii* that can be pruned to about 8cm (3 in) from the old wood in mid spring (March). Prune those that flower on the previous year's wood, such as *B. globosa* and *B. alternifolia*, after the blooms fade.

For propagation, take heel cuttings from half-ripe, lateral shoots in late summer and early autumn (July and August), and insert them in compost in a cold frame. Plant out in their permanent growing quarters in late autumn (October) of the following year.

Buddleia are fairly free from pests and diseases.

Some varieties to choose
The following is a selection of some of the most popular buddleia grown today. The first figure given in the dimensions is the height and the second is the spread.

B. alternifolia
This species is the only one that does not have opposite leaves; instead, they are positioned alternately on either side of the shoots. Bears fragrant lilac flowers in mid summer (June). 6 × 5·5m (20 × 18 ft).

B. asiatica
An evergreen, tender shrub with scented white flowers appearing during the winter. 3 × 3m (10 × 10 ft).

B. colvilei
A half-hardy, semi-evergreen shrub, with rose-pink flowers borne on drooping terminal racemes 15cm (6 in) long, appearing in mid to late summer (June to July). *B.c.* Kewensis is a form with rose-red blooms. 4 × 2·5m (13 × 8 ft).

however, comes into bloom about mid or late spring (March or April). There are also several winter-flowering ones, particularly *B. asiatica* and *B. auriculata*, both needing protection when grown outside. The greenhouse species *B. madagascariensis* and *B. officinalis* also flower throughout the winter. The flower colour varies from white through violet and purple to red. Two notable exceptions to this are *B. globosa*, with orange-yellow globular blooms, and the hybrid *B.* × *weyerana* that has rather similar orange, ball-shaped heads just tinged with mauve. Quite a number are scented, particularly varieties of *B. davidii*, and *B. fallowiana*, and also the hybrids *B.* Lochinch and *B.* West Hill.

B. davidii and its cultivars will tolerate shallow soil on chalk and will also flourish in the polluted air of industrial towns.

Generally buddleia do not grow very big; among the largest is *B. alternifolia* that can have a height and spread of 6m (20 ft) after 20 years' growth. Perhaps the smallest is the comparatively new *B. davidii* Border Beauty, that, after 10 years, can have a height of 90cm (3 ft), after which it will hardly grow at all. Eventual size is not too important, however, because it is usual to prune back the more common species annually to a greater or lesser degree in order to maintain a neat and bushy appearance.

The more popular buddleia are grown in shrub and mixed borders because of their long flowering period. Some, such as *B. davidii* and its cultivars,

B. crispa (B. paniculata)

A smaller, half-hardy, deciduous bushy shrub with leaves covered with white 'felt' that gives a silvery appearance. Has fragrant, lilac-pink flowers with an orange eye, borne in 10cm (4 in) long, cylindrical panicles in late summer (July). 2·5 × 1·8m (8 × 6 ft).

B. davidii

A hardy, deciduous, vigorous, spreading shrub, commonly known as the butterfly bush, carrying fragrant, lilac-purple blooms in 38cm (15 in) long arching racemes from late summer to mid autumn (July to September). It has numerous cultivars, flowering at about the same period. 3 × 3m (10 × 10 ft).

B.d. Black Knight	Deep purple trusses of flowers.
B.d. Border Beauty	Crimson-purple flowers; a dwarf form of Royal Red. 90cm × 1·5m (3 × 5 ft).
B.d. Empire Blue	Violet-blue, with orange centres.
B.d. Fascination	Large, lilac-pink heads
B.d. Fortune	Lilac with orange eye, borne in long cylindrical racemes.
B.d. Harlequin	The foliage is variegated creamy white, and the flowers are reddish purple. A small cultivar.
B.d. Mayford Purple	Deep purple blooms.
B.d. nanhoensis	Slender branched, with narrow leaves and mauve flowers. A small shrub with a height and spread of about 1·5m (6 ft).
B.d. Opera	Very large, blue-purple spikes; late-flowering.
B.d. Peace	A pure white variety.
B.d. Royal Red	Enormous red-purple panicles.
B.d. Salicifolia	A low-growing cultivar with willow-like, linear leaves and purple racemes.
B.d. White Cloud	Dense panicles of white flowers.
B.d. White Profusion	White blooms borne in large panicles.

B. fallowiana

Its stems and leaves have the appearance of being covered with white wool. Bears fragrant, pale lavender-blue flowers in panicles from late summer to mid autumn (July to September). Requires a sheltered site. An attractive cultivar is *B.f.* Alba that is creamy white with an orange eye. 2·5 × 1·8m (8 × 6 ft).

B. globosa (orange ball tree)

A fast-growing, erect shrub with almost evergreen leaves. The flowers are scented, spherical, and orange-yellow and appear in early summer (May). Will grow in exposed, coastal gardens. 4 × 3m (13 × 10 ft).

B. Lochinch

Has silvery grey leaves and dense conical panicles of scented, violet-blue flowers with orange centres, appearing between late summer and mid autumn (July and September). Has a compact habit. 1·5 × 1·5m (5 × 5 ft).

B. West Hill

A shrub with a spreading habit and long, arching stems. Its flowers are fragrant, pale lavender with orange centres, in curved panicles, appearing in early autumn (August). 2·5 × 3·5m (8 × 12 ft).

B. × weyerana

A hybrid of *B. davidii* and *B. globosa*, with ball-shaped heads similar to those of *B. globosa*, but often with a mauve tint. They appear during mid to late summer (June to July). An attractive cultivar is Golden Glow, flowering later than the species. 2·5 × 2·5m (8 × 8 ft).

Buddleia colvilei, *originating from the Himalayas, is one of the more unusual species, and is tender when young, becoming half hardy as it matures. It does best if planted against a warm wall with a western aspect*

CISTUS

Type	evergreen hardy and semi-hardy flowering shrubs
Family	CISTACEAE
Common name	rock rose or sun rose
Flowering season	mainly mid–late summer (June–July)
Planting date	cistus are always transplanted from containers, and can be planted at any time in good weather. The best time is late spring–early summer (April–May)
Mature size/shape	mainly rounded, bushy and compact, some low-growing, spreading and erect; height 45cm–2·4m (18 in–8 ft), spread 45cm–3m (18 in–10 ft)
Special use	useful for hot, dry positions where the soil is poor

Cistus are very useful as flowering shrubs for small modern gardens, and comprise about 20 species. They share their common names of rock rose and sun rose with the helianthemum, a member of the same family.

Many of the cistus found in present-day gardens are natural or hand-pollinated hybrids. The species originate mainly from around the Mediterranean. *C. ladaniferus*, for example, comes from south-western Europe and North Africa; *C. laurifolius* was found growing wild right across southern Europe to central Italy; and *C. parviflorus* comes from Italy and Greece. Greece is also the habitat of *C. × skanbergii*. One very distinct, tall-growing species, *C. symphitifolius*, with magenta blooms and golden anthers, originated in the Canary Islands. Although this was first introduced to British gardens in 1799, it can only be cultivated in the mildest districts in temperate countries. Other species that have been cultivated for an even longer time are *C. salviifolius*, introduced into Britain in 1550, *C. ladaniferus* (1629), and *C. populifolius* (1656).

Cistus blooms vary in size according to species and variety, and resemble single roses. They produce characteristic, saucer-shaped, papery flowers in profusion over a period from mid to late summer (June to July) and even later. Each bloom opens its petals in the morning and sheds them again by the evening. So many fresh buds are set that there is no break in the flowering period. The flowers come in many colours, including white,

through pinks, to reddish purple. Often they are blotched or have bases in contrasting colours such as yellow, crimson and chocolate-brown. Some species and varieties have greyish leaves.

Cistus shrubs are all small and vary in size from the more low-growing and spreading types, such as *C. × lusitanicus* Decumbens, with a height of about 45cm (18 in), to *C. × cyprius*, with a maximum height of 2·4m (8 ft) after about 20 years' growth. Apart from the low-growing and

Plant cistus such as C. × purpureus (top). C. × aguilari (above) together in groups for best effect

C. ladaniferus *(above)*, C. salviifolius *(left)* and
C.×obtusifolius *(below)* are all somewhat tender
and should be grown in sheltered, sunny positions
against a wall or bank The wide-spreading variety
C.×lusitanicus *Decumbens (below left)* is hardy,
but should also be given protection from frost

prostrate forms, there are a few, such as *C. × purpureus*, that grow erect. A large number of the other species are bushy, compact and round.

They grow extremely well in a sunny position and in poor, dry soil that can be either shallow over chalk, or dry and acid. They are very wind-tolerant, being quite happy in exposed gardens in coastal districts, and can resist the bad effects of polluted air in industrial towns. Frost, however, can damage them, and it is better to plant even the hardiest ones in a sheltered position and to give them protection during very severe weather. Some species are relatively tender and should only be planted outdoors in the mildest districts, though they have a chance of surviving against a warm, sheltered wall. Young plants resist frost better than older ones, so it is a good idea to make provision for replacements by propagating from cuttings whenever possible. The colourful flowers, set off by variously-hued foliage, make cistus especially useful for shrub and mixed borders, as well as banks and walls. To get the best effect, grow a number of them together in groups.

Cultivation

As cistus do not transplant well, it is usual to plant them from containers, at any time during the year when the weather is good. It is, however, best to plant them out during late spring and early summer (April and May), so that they become well established for the current growing season.

For planting distance, add together the ultimate spread of the plants that are to be adjacent and divide by two. Dig a hole about 4cm (1½ in) wider than the rootball, and deep enough so that the plant will be at the same depth in the bed as it was in the container. Remove the shrub from the container and, without breaking the rootball, gently pull out one or two root ends at the side and bottom. Place the rootball centrally in the hole, fill in with soil and gently firm in by treading carefully. Cistus need little care other than protection from very severe frosts. Little pruning is necessary, except to cut out diseased and frost-damaged shoots and any dead wood.

Propagation

Species can be propagated from seed. Hybrids will not come true from seed, and must be propagated from cuttings.

Take heel cuttings 10cm (4 in) long, of half-ripened, non-flowering shoots of hybrids and varieties during late summer and early autumn (July and August). Insert them in cutting compost in a propagator at 16°C (61°F). When they have rooted, transplant them individually to 8cm (3 in) pots. After overwintering in a cold frame, pot them on to 10cm (4 in) pots. After another winter in a cold frame, plant them in their permanent quarters in late spring (April).

Pests and diseases

Cistus are fortunately very healthy plants, little troubled with pests, and are also not particularly susceptible to diseases.

Some varieties to choose

The first figure under each item is the ultimate height, the second is spread.

C. × aguilari	Tender shrub of erect, bushy habit, with light green leaves and large white flowers, appearing during mid and late summer (June and July). 1·2 × 1·2m (4 × 4 ft).
C. × a. Maculatus	White-flowered variety that has a ring of crimson blotches at the base of each petal.
C. × corbariensis	Among the hardiest of the cistus, this forms a low-spreading, bushy shrub with dull green leaves that have wavy margins. Flowers are white, yellow at the base of each petal, and borne from early to mid summer (May to June). 90cm × 2·4m (3 × 8 ft).
C. × cyprius	Has olive-green leaves, sticky to touch, and clusters of white flowers with crimson-maroon blotches, in mid to late summer (June to July). 2·1 × 2·4m (7 × 8 ft).
C. Elma	Tender, sturdy, bushy shrub, with very large white blooms, appearing in mid and late summer (June and July). 1·5 × 1·8m (5 × 6 ft).
C. ladaniferus	Erect, tender shrub with white flowers that have bright yellow stamens and maroon blotches at the base, borne in early to mid summer (May to June). 1·8 × 1·2m (6 × 4 ft).
C. laurifolius	The hardiest species, with leathery, dark, glaucous-green leaves and white flowers with yellow centres, appearing in mid to late summer (June to July). 1·5m × 90cm (5 × 3 ft).
C. × loretii	A shrub of dwarf habit with large white flowers that have crimson basal blotches, appearing in mid to late summer (June to July). 60 × 90cm (2 × 3 ft).
C. × lusitanicus	Dwarf hybrid with dark green leaves and white flowers, blotched pink at the base, borne in mid to late summer (June to July). 45 × 45cm (18 × 18 in).
C. × l. Decumbens	Wide-spreading variety, with a maroon spot at the base of each petal and dark green, scented foliage. 45cm × 1·2m (18 in × 4 ft).
C. × obtusifolius	Rounded, dwarf, tender shrub. Flowers are white with yellow basal stain, and appear from mid summer to mid autumn (June to September). 60 × 90cm (2 × 3 ft).
C. palhinhae	Hardy, low-growing, compact species with sticky leaves and large white flowers, appearing in early to mid summer (May to June). 90 × 90cm (3 × 3 ft).
C. populifolius	Erect with poplar-like leaves and white flowers, yellow at the base, borne in mid summer (June). 1·8 × 1·5m (6 × 5 ft). *C. populifolius lasiocalyx* has larger flowers with inflated calyces. Very hardy.
C. × pulverulentus	Dwarf shrub with sage-green leaves and rose-red flowers appearing from early to late summer (May to July). 75cm × 1·2m (2½ × 4 ft).
C. × purpureus	Upright tender shrub with grey-green leaves and rose-to-purple blooms, dark maroon at the base, appearing from early to late summer (May to July). 1·5 × 1·2m (5 × 4 ft).
C. salviifolius	A low, tender shrub with sage-like leaves and white flowers, yellow at the base, borne in mid summer (June). 45 × 45cm (18 × 18 in).
C. Silver Pink	Very hardy shrub with clusters of silvery pink flowers in mid to late summer (June to July). 75 × 75cm (2½ × 2½ ft).
C. × skanbergii	Tender, upright shrub with grey-green leaves and clear pink blossoms, borne during mid and late summer (June and July). 1·2 × 1·2m (4 × 4 ft).

CLEMATIS MONTANA

Type	deciduous, woody climber
Family	RANUNCULACEAE
Flowering season	early summer to early autumn (May to August)
Planting date	late autumn to early summer (October to May) in mild weather
Mature size	up to 12m (40 ft)

Clematis montana is an extremely vigorous, deciduous climber, easily capable of reaching 7m (23 ft) and can, on occasion, extend even higher if trained into large trees. It ascends by means of its twisting leaf stalk that surrounds twigs in the wild. In cultivation, if you want to grow it up a wall, it is best to provide a trellis or plastic netting.

The plant is native to the Himalayas and was brought into cultivation in 1831 by that enterprising traveller Lady Amherst. When E. H. Wilson visited Szechwan, a province of China, in 1900, he sent back seed of the variety *C. m. rubens*. This has purplish petal-like sepals, known as 'tepals', and flowers a little later than the type. In addition to the purplish flowers, its young stems also have a purple colour and the young leaves have a purple-bronzy tinge. The leaves are somewhat downy while the Indian plants are more or less glabrous, or smooth. Wilson also sent back the variety *C. m. wilsonii* that bears smaller white flowers that do not open before late summer (end of June or early July). There are one or two named forms as well: Tetrarose has pink flowers up to 8cm (3 in) across; Alexander, with white flowers, and Elizabeth, with pink flowers, are also fragrant.

The plant bears leaves made up of three leaflets; these are lance-shaped, slightly lobed and each about 5cm (2 in) long, although there is some variation in their size. The flowers arise from the leaf axils of the previous year's growth and come in clusters of about six; each flower is on a stalk that may be 10cm (4 in) long and is made up of four white tepals. The flowers each measure about 5cm (2 in) across, produce very freely and open in early summer (May).

The plant is easy to cultivate and thrives in any soil, flowering well even if trained against a north-facing wall. Like all clematis, it is very intolerant of root disturbance, so you should only purchase pot-grown specimens. If possible, the roots and the base of the stem should be kept in the shade. The plant looks very effective if trained up into a tree and allowed to ramble at will. In some positions, its vigour may be excessive, but you can prune it hard each summer as soon as flowering is

Left: Clematis montana rubens, *one of the best forms of this vigorous grower*
Top: C. montana *produces its mass of flowers in early summer (May)*
Above: brought into cultivation at the same time as C.m. rubens, C.m. wilsonii *bears its smaller flowers towards late summer (July)*

over and remove all flowered shoots. *Clematis chrysocoma,* which looks much like *C. montana,* with rather large pink flowers and young leaves covered with yellow down, is far less vigorous, although equally attractive; it can be recommended as an alternative in cases where *C. montana* might prove too vigorous.

Propagation by cuttings is easy, but slightly different from the cuttings of most woody plants. These are generally finished just below the node, that is to say where the leaf joins the stem. Clematis cuttings on the other hand are called inter-nodal and are cut half-way between two leaves. Cuttings should be taken in late summer (late June or early July) and the stem should be firm, although not woody. It is probably sufficient to allow only one full-grown leaf to each cutting and it is not necessary to have a growing point on your cutting; as soon as the cutting is well rooted, a shoot will arise from the leaf axil and they should then be potted separately in 8cm (3 in) pots either in a soilless mixture or in J.I. No 1, and subsequently potted on into a 13cm (5 in) pot. Once this pot is filled with roots, the plant can be placed in its final position.

CORNUS

Type	hardy, mainly deciduous, flowering and fruiting small tree, shrub, and herbaceous perennial
Common name	dogwood, cornel
Family	CORNACEAE
Flowering season	mainly between early and late summer (May to July); a few species bloom in autumn and winter
Planting date	tree species – late autumn to early winter (October to November); shrubs for bark and foliage colour – mid to late spring (March to April)
Mature size/shape	ranging from 15cm high × 60cm wide (6 × 24 in), to 6m high × 6m wide (20 × 20 ft); mainly rounded, a few prostrate, spreading and upright

Above: Cornus florida rubra *with showy, rose-pink bracts in early summer although the loveliest of flowering trees, it can be injured by a late frost*

Cornus forms a genus of about 40 species. They are mainly deciduous (a small number are evergreen) and include small trees, shrubs and herbaceous perennials, belonging to the plant family CORNACEAE. However, recently some authorities have divided this genus into several families, in accordance with certain botanical differences. These changes do not appear to have infiltrated current nurserymen's catalogues, so it is more practical to deal with the subject on the old-fashioned basis.

The meaning of the Latin *cornus* is 'horned' and the genus derives this name from the fact that its species have wood of hard, firm texture. At one time it was frequently used for making small objects that also needed to be strong. In particular, it was used for making the now almost-extinct wooden meat skewers.

Although cornus are widespread in origin, their habitat is confined to the northern hemisphere. Various species are indigenous to Siberia, Manchuria, China, Japan, Korea and North America, and at least one is native to the British Isles – the common dogwood, *C. sanguinea*. Of the cornus introduced into Western gardens, *C. mas* is probably the earliest, because it is described authoritatively as 'long cultivated'. *C. stolonifera* first reached the Western world in 1656, and *C. amomum* in 1683, followed by *C. alba, C. alternifolia, C. canadensis, C. florida, C. racemosa* and *C. rugosa*, all of which came during the 18th century. Further introductions continued periodically throughout the 19th century.

Cornus is a genus of many parts: most of the species produce flowers during the summer months, although exceptions are *Cornus oblonga*, that flowers in autumn, *C. chinensis* (not to be confused with *C. kousa chinensis*), *C. mas* and *C. officinalis*, whose clusters of yellow blooms enliven their naked twigs during the winter, and the hybrid of *C. florida* and *C. nuttallii, C.* Eddie's White Wonder, that has large white flowers during spring. It should, however, be noted that in many cases the flowers of cornus are relatively inconspicuous, although they become prominent because they are subtended by coloured bracts. The flowers themselves are normally white, yellow, or yellow-green, and are borne on the last season's growth.

In some cases, the blossom is followed later by fruit. Examples include *C. capitata* and *C. kousa*, with their red, strawberry-like fruits; *C. mas*, with bright fruits like cherries; *C. controversa* with black fruit; *C. rugosa* and *C. amomum*, both of which have blue fruits, and *C. stolonifera* with white ones. The more common cornus with evergreen leaves are *C. capitata* and *C. oblonga*. Among the deciduous plants, there are some that have yellow foliage, of which *C. alba* Aurea and *C. mas* Aurea are particularly worth mentioning.

Quite a number have variegated leaves, but perhaps the loveliest is *C. alternifolia* Argentea, regarded by some as one of the best of the silver variegated shrubs. Its parent, *C. alternifolia*, gives the richest autumn tints; others that have this quality are *C. alba*, *C. baileyi*, *C. controversa* -- the foliage of which turns purple-red – *C. florida* and *C. kousa*, with its rich bronze and crimson leaves. Still the cavalcade of beauty does not end, as we have yet to take account of those cornus that brighten beds during winter with their brilliant-coloured bark, such as *C. alba*, *C. baileyi*, *C. stolonifera* and the Westonbirt dogwood, *C. alba* Sibirica – all of them red – and *C. stolonifera* Flaviramea that is yellow or olive-green. To add to this, *C. officinalis* has attractive peeling bark.

Cornus shrubs are rounded, sometimes erect-growing or spreading in habit. After about 20 years, they reach 2·5–6m (8–20 ft) high, and some 2–6m (6–20 ft) in spread. An exception is *C. canadensis*, strictly a herbaceous perennial, but often listed among the shrubs; this is prostrate and has a height of 15cm (6 in) and a spread of 60cm (2 ft).

They are as tolerant of various environments as they are versatile in the qualities they possess. All cornus will flourish in clay. A chalky subsoil is tolerated by *C. mas*, while both *C. alba* and *C. stolonifera* and their cultivars, together with *C. baileyi*, will thrive on a damp site. Both *C. alba* and *C. stolonifera* and all their cultivars are also suitable for planting in industrial towns and, together with *C. baileyi*, they will withstand cold and exposure.

With all their virtues, it is evident that cornus are eminently suited to shrub and mixed borders although some, such as *C. kousa chinensis*, with their rich autumn foliage and colourful fruits might be effectively grown as a specimen in the lawn. Owners of comparatively small gardens should not be deterred from growing cornus because of their eventual size, especially those with coloured bark; it is the practice to cut these back to within a few centimetres of the ground in spring.

In addition, the prostrate *C. canadensis*, that also tolerates deep shade, is a charming and most effective ground cover plant.

Cultivation

It is important to position tree species in a sunny situation: this helps to mature their wood. Exceptions are those species grown for their colourful bark and foliage; these require to be in moist soil, either in sun or semi-shade. Cornus are happy in any good garden soil. *C. mas* and its cultivars will grow in chalky soil; but in the case of other more popular cornus, this should be avoided.

Plant the tree species in late autumn or early winter (October or November); however, those strong-growing bushy shrubs grown for the colour of their bark and foliage are best planted in mid or late spring (March or April). Container-grown plants may be planted any time, provided the ground is wet and is kept so after planting.

Right: silver variegated Cornus alternifolia *Argentea*
Below: Cornus nuttallii *flowering in early summer; named after the English botanist Thomas Nuttall in 1835*
Overleaf, left: Cornus kousa chinensis *bearing strawberry-like fruits; this Chinese type is larger and superior to its Japanese counterpart*
Overleaf, right: Cornus canadensis *prefers a peaty or woodland soil; strictly a herbaceous perennial but usually classified as a shrub*

Planting distance is determined in the usual way by halving the sum of the ultimate spreads of plants that are to grow in juxtaposition.

Before planting, dig a hole that is wide enough to take the rootball without disturbing it too much and that allows the roots to spread out after planting. It should be deep enough so that, after planting, the soil line indicating the level at which it was previously planted is level with the soil surface. If you need to stake it, put a stake into the soil between the loose roots without damaging them. Replace the soil and firm it by gentle treading.

Normally cornus need little attention, except those grown for bark or foliage colour that should be watered well during dry spells. Generally, cornus only need pruning to control their shape and size. Cut to the ground in late spring (April) those that you want to grow for their bark.

Propagation
Species may be raised from seed taken in early and mid autumn (August and September). Sow them in seed compost and then place them in a cold frame. When large enough, pot them up and then transplant into a nursery bed later. They should grow here for two or three years before being planted out; sometimes seeds will take 18 months to germinate.

Cornus may also be raised from 10cm (4 in) long, half-ripe cuttings taken in late summer or early autumn (July or August). They are placed in growing compost and put in a propagator. After rooting, plant them in 8cm (3 in) pots in potting compost and leave to overwinter in a cold frame; then place them in a nursery bed and plant them out two or three years later.

Suckers can be planted in early winter (November). Cornus may also be propagated by layering long shoots in mid autumn (September) and severing them a year or two later.

Some varieties to choose
In the following selections, the dimensions given under species and variety descriptions refer to ultimate height and spread respectively.

C. alba (red-barked dogwood)	Suckering foliage plant of upright habit with red stems in winter; often autumn tints. Inconspicuous flowers followed by white or blue-tinged fruits. 3 × 3m (10 × 10 ft).
C. a. Elegantissima	Has white-margined and mottled leaves.
C. a. Sibirica	Has brilliant crimson shoots in winter.
C. a. Spaethii	A good golden-variegated form.
C. alternifolia Argentea	Very beautiful, silver-variegated foliage; spreading. 3 × 4·5m (10 × 15 ft).
C. canadensis (creeping dogwood)	Herbaceous perennial with star-like, white flowers in mid summer (June), followed by vivid red fruits. Excellent ground cover. 10 × 60cm (4 × 24 in).
C. controversa	Has white flowers during mid and late summer (June and July). Blue-black berries. 4·5 × 4·5m (15 × 15 ft).
C. florida rubra	Leaves turn orange and scarlet in autumn. Inconspicuous flowers subtended by rosy pink bracts in early summer (May). 4 × 6m (12 × 20 ft).
C. kousa	Elegant shrub bearing insignificant purple-green flowers with white bracts in mid summer (June); strawberry-like fruits ripening in mid autumn (September). Autumn tints. 3 × 3m (10 × 10 ft).
C. k. chinensis	Has large bracts and crimson autumn foliage.
C. mas (cornelian cherry)	Large shrub producing yellow flowers in early spring (February). Red edible fruits. Autumn colours. 3 × 2·5m (10 × 8 ft).
C. m. Aurea	Has yellow leaves.
C. m. Elegantissima	Yellow and pink variegated foliage.
C. nuttallii	A handsome species with large white, flushed pink bracts in early summer (May). Strawberry-like fruits. Yellow autumn foliage. Needs a warm position. 5·5 × 3m (8 × 10 ft).
C. stolonifera	Suckering shrub with dark red winter stems and white fruits. 2·5 × 2·7m (8 × 9 ft).
C. s. Flaviramea	Has yellow or olive-green winter shoots.

COTONEASTER

Type	evergreen and deciduous flowering and fruiting shrubs
Family	ROSACEAE
Flowering season	mid summer (June)
Fruiting season	early autumn to late winter (August–January)
Planting date	late autumn to early spring (October–February); from containers, anytime
Mature size/shape	prostrate to 7m (23 ft); spreading, round or erect shrub

Above: Cotoneaster microphyllus, *a low-growing evergreen that originated from the Himalayas, in flower during early summer*
Overleaf: C. × Hybridus Pendulus, *a low-growing shrub, grafted onto a stem to make a small, weeping tree*

The cotoneaster genus contains a little over 50 species of shrubs all of which – with the exception of a comparatively few rarities – are obtainable without much difficulty. Among them are some of the most indispensable of hardy ornamental shrubs and even small trees. There is a cotoneaster for almost every site in the garden no matter what its environment. Large, medium, small and prostrate ones are available, evergreens and semi-evergreens, and varieties suitable for a warm, sunny position or a cold exposed garden, be it inland or on the coast. In tree form as standards and half-standards they are invaluable because they are almost the only evergreens available at this size.

Although they are an extensive and diverse race, most cotoneasters nevertheless have a strong family likeness. They all have hawthorn-like white or pinkish flowers that are either flattened or cupped in shape and often carried in clusters, mainly in mid summer (June). These blossoms are most attractive to bees, although almost insignificant compared with what, in most cases, follows them. The foliage often acquires the most beautiful rich autumnal colourings and, most striking of all, the branches become laden with attractively-coloured berries of different sizes and shapes, which can be scarlet, orange-red, purplish-red, yellow, pink-tinged yellow, crimson or black. It is in these lovely berries that the real glory of cotoneasters is to be found.

With some exceptions, the native habitat of these various species is the Far East – mainly China – while a few hail from places farther to the west – the Himalayas, Assam, Tibet, Burma, East Turkestan and Afghanistan. There are one or two species that are thought to have originated in areas still farther to the west: *Cotoneaster orbicularis* from the Sinai Peninsular and *C. lucidus* from the Altai Mountains in Mongolia – which would indeed be a testimony to its hardiness. Among the earliest to be raised successfully in Britain was *C. tomentosus*, now a very rare shrub indeed; it was taken from the European Alps in 1759.

C. simonsii, *C. horizontalis* and *C. microphyllus* can be found growing wild in the British countryside, but these are probably escapees from cultivated gardens, through birds eating the seeds and later spreading them in their droppings. There is, however, one species – *C. integerrimus* – which seems to be native to Britain. It was found growing wild on Great Orme Head above Llandudno in North Wales in 1783, but there are records of it growing in gardens in the 17th century, so even this might be a stray.

Understandably, there have been numbers of cultivars raised in Britain, but two of particular interest are *C. St Monica*, which was found in a convent garden in Bristol, and *C. splendens* Sabrina, which was raised in a garden in Somerset.

Apart from their attraction in any garden, the species have characteristics and variations that make them most valuable. They range in height from about 5–8cm (2–3 in) above the ground up to an ultimate height of about 4–5m (15 ft), with a few small trees reaching 6m (20 ft) tall. Among them there is a wide range of habits, such as prostrate, spreading, erect, arching, pendulous and so on, that make them indispensable in any planting scheme. The trailing forms make excellent ground cover and also help to suppress the growth of weeds. Some species and their cultivars, particularly the evergreens and semi-evergreens, are excellent for hedge-making and with their rich autumn tints and colourful berries they give a most pleasing ornamental effect on the boundary of the plot or as a division between two sections of the garden. Probably they are best of all used in a shrub or mixed border where their colour will prolong some of the fading glory of the summer.

Several species and hybrids, for instance *C. buxifolius vellaeus, C. franchetii, C. horizontalis, C. lacteus, C. salicifolius* Autumn Fire, *C. salicifolius rugosus* and *C. simonsii*, make excellent wall plants. Because of their tolerance of a wide range of conditions, the aspect of the wall does not disturb them at all; they are therefore particularly valuable for growing against a north wall.

Cultivation

On the whole, cotoneasters are so robust and undemanding that they will survive and flourish in almost any soil and conditions. Most are tolerant to the environment of an industrial area and by the same token they all grow well in town gardens, where the smaller ones are especially acceptable because of space restrictions. There are some, such as *C. simonsii*, that can be planted in full shade and still prosper. On the other hand, all of them will grow well in both partial shade and sun. Many of these most accommodating shrubs and trees also grow well in coastal areas, where they will stand up to a certain amount of exposure.

As far as their soil requirements are concerned, any planting guide will tell you that cotoneasters will grow well in 'ordinary' garden soil. But if your soil is out of the ordinary, you may need a little more guidance.

All species will grow in clay soil providing it is well drained and there is no possibility of it becoming waterlogged. As this is the risk with very heavy clay, it is important to prepare such soil very thoroughly before planting this shrub. Dig it well, to a depth of one spit, removing the topsoil so that the subsoil can be broken up to ensure good drainage. Mix the excavated topsoil with sand or grit to lighten it and help the free passage of water through it, and then replace it. This should stop water remaining on the surface in wet weather.

All species are quite happy in dry acid soils. They will flourish in a shallow soil covering a chalky subsoil, which will almost certainly be alkaline in reaction. There is just one place where a cotoneaster should not be planted, and this is on a damp site: the best course is to choose some other plant that likes the conditions. The alternative (particularly as many other choice plants also dislike a permanently damp soil) is to drain the land either by digging a trench across the site, almost filling it with rubble and replacing the topsoil, or, if the condition is very serious, you may have to resort to a more elaborate scheme involving laying drainage tiles.

Above left and above: evergreen C. conspicuus *Decorus in flower and fruit*

When and how to plant

It is only natural that the space to be allowed between cotoneasters and their neighbouring shrubs in a border depends upon the ultimate size they are likely to reach in maturity. The correct planting distance can be calculated by adding the spans of two shrubs that are to be planted alongside each other and dividing the sum by two.

Soak the rootball well before planting. Dig a hole wide enough to allow the roots to be well spread out, and of such a depth that the previous soil level will be at the surface of the soil in the new quarters. Mix a little garden compost or manure into the soil at the bottom of the hole and put the plant in position. Place a layer of similarly-enriched soil over the roots and tread it firmly in with your heel. Then add a further layer of soil, tread it in and finally fill up the hole, levelling off the soil surface.

For planting as a hedge *C. franchetii, C. frigidus, C. henryanus, C. lacteus, C. simonsii, C. wardii* and *C. × watereri* all make excellent berried hedges. They are planted as described above for bushes in shrubberies, the first two at 45cm (18 in) and the remainder at 60–90cm (2–3 ft) apart respectively.

For use as wall plants, those suitable should be planted about 40cm (15 in) in front of the wall and trained back to it, because very often the soil at the base of a wall keeps excessively dry.

Generally speaking cotoneasters need little attention, but do keep the soil around them free from weeds with regular hoeing. In dry weather they appreciate being watered and mulched with an 8cm (3 in) layer of garden compost, manure or damp peat. The evergreens particularly like being sprayed with water during the evening.

No regular pruning is necessary. When the large-growing shrubs have outgrown their allotted space they can be pruned back: evergreens in late spring (April) and deciduous ones in early spring (February). Trim back evergreen hedges as necessary immediately after flowering by cutting out the more vigorous shoots and side growths. Prune back the current season's shoots to the berry cluster nearest to the tip of the branch. Hedges composed of deciduous cotoneasters should be trimmed in early or mid autumn (August or September).

Propagation

Fruiting cotoneasters can be propagated by removing the seeds from the ripe berries in autumn and sowing them in pans of J.I. seed compost or a soilless seed compost and placing them in a cold frame. They normally take about 18 months to germinate. After pricking out the seedlings, first into trays or pots and then into a nursery bed, allow them to grow on for 2–3 years before transplanting them.

Remember that only seeds from species will come true; cultivars must be propagated by cuttings. Take heel cuttings of ripe evergreen shoots, about 10cm (4 in) long, in early or mid autumn (August or September), and of semi-mature deciduous shrubs in late summer or early autumn (July or August). Plant them out in a nursery bed in the following late spring or early summer (April or May) and then leave them for 2–3 years before planting out in their final positions.

An alternative method is to layer shoots in late autumn or early winter (October or November) that will root within a year.

Pests and diseases

Apart from being infested with greenfly and scale insects in the summer, cotoneasters are fairly free from pests. Possibly the most frustrating are birds, that steal their berries in wintertime. Being members of the ROSACEAE family, cotoneasters are subject to possible infection with fireblight, which blackens the flowers and kills the branches. Other diseases that might possibly affect them are honey fungus disease and silverleaf.

Above and below: tall-growing evergreens C. Exburiensis and C. Rothschildianus, both are from the Watereri group

Some varieties to choose

Of the total number of species of fruiting cotoneasters and their varieties that exist, a very large proportion are readily obtainable from good nurseries, but the less common ones may be difficult to find in garden centres. The following list will help you to choose the best cotoneasters and their cultivars for your purpose. Many of these shrubs have fruits in varying shades of red, and any exceptions are indicated. Of the dimensions given, the first is the ultimate height, the second the ultimate spread.

PROSTRATE OR LOW-GROWING (EVERGREEN)

C. congestus	Attractive, densely-foliaged shrub, which forms mounds of small bluish-green leaves; red berries. 30cm × 2·7m (12 in × 9 ft).
C. dammeri	Very prostrate, trailing shrub, ideal for covering banks and ground cover; sealing-wax red berries. 5cm × 1·8m (2 in × 6 ft).
C. Donald Gem	Low, rounded, spreading bush with greyish leaves and long-lasting berries. 23cm × 1·5m (9 in × 5 ft).
C. microphyllus	Dwarf glossy-foliaged, spreading shrub; large, round scarlet berries. 5cm × 2·4m (2 in × 8 ft).
C. microphyllus cochleatus	Charming, slow-growing, creeping shrub with bright green leaves and scarlet berries. 2·5cm × 1·8m (1 in × 6 ft).
C. salicifolius Autumn Fire	Rather taller-growing, pendulous *semi-evergreen* shrub. Produces abundant quantities of bright orange-red berries. 30cm × 3·6m (12 in × 12 ft).
C. salicifolius Repens	Prostrate plant with very narrow leaves and small red berries, 30cm × 2·7m (12 in × 9 ft).
C. Skogholm	Vigorous, trailing hybrid with rather dark foliage and coral-red berries. 25cm × 1·8m (9 in × 6 ft).

PROSTRATE OR LOW-GROWING (DECIDUOUS)

C. adpressus	Dwarf, wide-spreading shrub, excellent for the rockery; bright red berries. Leaves turn scarlet in autumn. 40cm × 1·5m (15 in × 5 ft).
C. horizontalis Variegatus	Small, cream variegated leaves becoming suffused with red in autumn; red berries. 45cm × 1·8m (18 in × 6 ft).

MEDIUM-GROWING (EVERGREEN)

C. buxifolius vellaeus	Low, arching, spreading habit, with small leaves of frosted grey; bright red berries. 1·2 × 3m (4 × 10 ft).
C. conspicuus Decorus	Somewhat low-growing shrub, good for covering banks. Profuse red berries. 75cm × 2·7m (2½ × 9 ft).
C. Hybridus Pendulus	Prostrate, moderately low shrub; red berries. When grafted to a tall stem makes a beautiful weeping tree. 60cm × 3·6m (2 × 12 ft).

MEDIUM-GROWING (DECIDUOUS)

C. adpressus praecox	Vigorous, arching shrub with extra large, orange berries and brilliant autumn tints. 90cm × 1·8m (3 × 6 ft).
C. horizontalis	Branches in herringbone pattern. With its red berries and autumn colour it is invaluable for north- and east-facing walls and banks. 60cm × 3m (2 × 10 ft).

TALL-GROWING (EVERGREEN) − RED BERRIES

C. Aldenhamemsis (Watereri group)	Wide-spreading shrub with long, fan-like branches that bear bright red berries. 3·6 × 4·6m (12 × 15 ft).
C. Cornubia (Watereri group)	Vigorous, *semi-evergreen*. Its large red berries are so profuse that they weigh down its branches. 4·6 × 3·6m (15 × 12 ft).

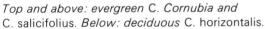

Top and above: evergreen C. Cornubia and
C. salicifolius. Below: deciduous C. horizontalis.

TALL-GROWING (EVERGREEN) − RED BERRIES *continued*

C. conspicuus	Graceful, wide-spreading, arching branched species with abundant bright red berries. 2·1 × 2·4m (7 × 8 ft).
C. henryanus	Large, spreading evergreen or *semi-evergreen* with long, dark green corrugated leaves and crimson berries. 6 × 3·6m (20 × 12 ft).
C. John Waterer (Watereri group)	Large, *semi-evergreen* shrub with bunches of red berries. 6 × 7·6m (20 × 25 ft).
C. lacteus	Large, oval, leathery leaves with a grey, hairy underside. Its red berries last long after mid winter (December). 3 × 2·4m (10 × 8 ft).
C. pannosus	Long, slender, arching branches, and sage-green leaves. Its berries are small, rounded and deep red in colour. 2·4 × 1·8m (8 × 6 ft).
C. salicifolius	Tall and graceful, bearing heavy crops of small bright red berries. 3·6 × 3·6m (12 × 12 ft).
C. salicifolius flocossus	Graceful, with small, polished, shining green leaves, white underneath, and masses of small red berries. 2·7 × 2·7m (9 × 9 ft).
C. salicifolius rugosus	Larger flowers than usual and red berries. 6 × 6m (20 × 20 ft).

TALL-GROWING (EVERGREEN) − YELLOW BERRIES

C. frigidus Fructuluteo (or Xanthocarpus)	*Semi-evergreen* with large clusters of creamy-yellow berries. 3 × 3·6m (10 × 12 ft).
C. Rothschildianus (Watereri group)	Wide-spreading habit. Creamy-yellow berries, borne in large bunches. 3 × 2·4m (10 × 8 ft).
C. salicifolius Fructuluteo	An interesting form with yellow berries. 3·6 × 3·6m (12 × 12 ft).

TALL-GROWING (EVERGREEN) − APRICOT BERRIES

C. Exburiensis (Watereri group)	Recognizable by its apricot-yellow berries, that become pinkish in winter. 3 × 2·4m (10 × 8 ft).

TALL-GROWING (EVERGREEN) − SALMON-PINK BERRIES

C. Inchmery (Watereri group)	This shrub produces clusters of big berries, yellow turning salmon-pink. 3·6 × 3·6m (12 × 12 ft).

TALL-GROWING (DECIDUOUS)

C. bullatus	Handsome, corrugated leaves, becoming richly tinted in autumn. Large, red berries produced early. 2·4 × 1·5m (8 × 5 ft).
C. bullatus Floribundus	A form with larger clusters of flowers and berries than C. bullatus. 2·4 × 1·5m (8 × 5 ft).
C. Firebird	Spreading shrub with dark green leaves and dense clusters of large orange-red berries. 1·8 × 2·4m (6 × 8 ft).
C. franchetii	*Semi-evergreen* or deciduous with sage-green foliage and orange-scarlet berries. 2·1 × 1·8m (7 × 6 ft).
C. simonsii	*Semi-evergreen*, sometimes deciduous, erect shrub with large scarlet berries. 2·7 × 2·7m (9 × 9 ft).
C. wardii	Erect-growing, with dark glossy green leaves, white underneath. Berries are top-shaped and orange-red. 2·4 × 1·5m (8 × 5 ft).

SELECTION FOR WALL PLANTS
C. conspicuus Decorus, *C. Cornubia, C. divaricatus, C. franchetii, C. henryanus, C. horizontalis, C. microphyllus, C. salicifolius* Autumn Fire, *C. salicifolius flocossus, C. salicifolius rugosus, C. simonsii, C. wardii.*

SELECTION FOR HEDGING
C. franchetii, C. frigidus, C. lacteus, C. simonsii, C. wardii.

CRATAEGUS

Type	deciduous flowering and fruiting shrubs and trees
Family	ROSACEAE
Common names	hawthorn, may or quickthorn
Flowering season	early–mid summer (May–June)
Planting date	any time in winter when the weather is good; from containers at any time
Mature size/shape	wide-spreading, occasionally erect; height and spread 4·5–6m (15–20 ft)
Special use	the berries and blossoms are used to make home-made wines

blossoms are followed by bunches of orange-scarlet fruits or haws that, combined with the brightly-coloured autumn foliage of some species, put up a superb display in autumn.

The other characteristic of most crataegus – an unpleasant one – is that their branches are armed with long, sharply-pointed spikes or thorns.

The more commonly-grown crataegus are excellent when planted as specimens in lawns; with their attractive blossoms, richly-coloured berries and, in some cases (autumn tints) they maintain interest for most of the year. They are also good plants for a shrub border, and can be grown in the dappled shade at the edge of a wide-spreading tree canopy. *C. monogyna* has long been proved to make just as good a hedge in the garden as it does in a field or hedgerow. It is quick-growing and once established forms an impenetrable barrier to man and beast.

Cultivation

As a group, crataegus will thrive in any normal garden soil. They do best in open ground, in a sunny position, but they are not averse to partial shade. They can be counted among the hardiest and most adaptable plants in the garden, being quite happy in industrial areas and tolerant of atmospheric pollution. Crataegus are equally

Crataegus is a genus containing 200 species of small, deciduous trees and shrubs, about half a dozen of which are in popular cultivation. They are collectively known by the common name 'thorn'. The name comes from the Greek word for hawthorn, that was itself derived from 'kratos' – strength – and was an allusion to the strength and hardness of hawthorn wood.

Two crataegus are native to Britain; these are *Crataegus monogyna* (common hawthorn, may or quickthorn) that is more commonly found, and *C. oxyacantha*, also popularly known as hawthorn or may. *C. monogyna* has been used very extensively for hedging in the British countryside, and its flowers and berries are still made into home-made wine. Most of the other species found in cultivation in Western gardens originate from the United States and Canada. A few have been cultivated for many centuries: *C. pedicellata* was first introduced into Britain in 1683, *C. intricata* in 1730 and *C. crus-galli* (the aptly-named cock-spur thorn) in 1691. The odd one, compared with these Western species, is *C. chlorosarca* that comes from Japan and is usually thornless.

In general, these plants have an ultimate height and spread of approximately 4·5–6m (15–20 ft). Since they respond quite well, on the whole, to being cut back, they are capable of being kept under control easily.

In most cases crataegus bear clusters of white, five-petalled flowers, with a characteristic haw-thorn scent, during early or mid summer (May or June). Some species and varieties have pink or red blooms. The popular common name of 'may' probably arises from the fact that the flowers are exceptionally prolific in early summer (May). The

Right: the old country saying 'ne'er cast a clout til may be out' refers to the blossoms of C. monogyna *(common hawthorn, may or quickthorn) – not, as is often supposed, to the month of May. Below right:* C. oxyacantha *with its bright, shiny fruits borne in autumn; below:* Crataegus prunifolia *thrives in partial shade or sun and tolerates polluted or exposed conditions*

amenable to exposure and severe winds in coastal districts, but it is wise to give the young shrubs protection for some time after planting. Another characteristic that makes crataegus so valuable in the garden is their almost unequalled ability to resist both excessive dryness and exceptionally moist conditions.

Plant crataegus at any time during the winter, provided there is not a severe frost and the soil is not excessively wet. If the plants arrive from the nursery when such conditions are prevalent, place them in a frost-free shed until better weather returns. They will be quite safe in their polythene or waterproof paper packing for two or three weeks. If, after this time, they still cannot be planted, undo the wrapping and keep the shrubs watered. If the ground is too soggy for planting, heel them in (in a dryish, sheltered spot) until conditions improve. Plant container-grown crataegus at any time of the year, provided that conditions are suitable.

As these shrubs usually grow quite quickly, allow a good space between each – at least 2·5m (8 ft) all round. Fortunately, they can be controlled in size quite easily by regular pruning back. If you are planting a hedge of *C. monogyna*, space each plant 30cm (12 in) apart. The best results are obtained if they are 30–38cm (12–15 in) in height when planted. Immediately after planting *C. monogyna* for a hedge, cut the plants back to about 10cm (4 in) from the ground, to encourage bushy growth.

For a bare-root crataegus it is important that the hole is large enough for the roots to spread out, and of such a depth that the original soil mark on the main stem will be just on the surface of the soil in its new position. As you fill in the hole, firm the soil well with your foot. It is a good idea to incorporate some garden compost or well-rotted manure in the soil at the bottom of the hole.

If the shrub is containerized, dig the hole so that its diameter is about 10cm (4 in) greater than the rootball, and of such a depth that the surface of the soil in the container will be just within the bed when the shrub is planted. Before planting, carefully remove the container by cutting off the bottom and making a vertical slit in its side with a sharp knife. Place the shrub centrally in the hole and fill in with well-firmed soil.

Crataegus are easy to grow and need little attention, other than having the soil immediately around them kept free of weeds by hoeing. No regular pruning is required, but hedges of *C. monogyna* are best trimmed between late summer and mid spring (July and March).

Propagation

Species are raised from berries that are picked as soon as they are ripe. The seeds take at least 18 months to germinate. After bruising the flesh of the berries slightly to facilitate rotting, sow them in small pots of seed compost, and then place them outside in a plunge bed. A thin layer of gravel on the surface of the compost prevents it being panned by heavy rain.

Alternatively, *C. intricata*, *C. pedicellata*, *C. × lavallei* and *C. prunifolia* can be budded in late summer (July), or grafted in early to mid spring (February to March) onto rootstocks of *C. crus-galli* or *C. oxyacantha*. Cultivars of *C. monogyna* and *C. oxyacantha* are budded or grafted onto rootstocks of *C. monogyna* in spring.

Pests and diseases

The most troublesome pests are caterpillars, and these should be picked off as they appear. If the infestation is serious, spray with a systemic insecticide such as fenitrothion.

In common with other members of the ROSACEAE family, crataegus are subject to fireblight that blackens and shrivels the flowers and causes the branches to die back and the leaves to turn brown and wither. To treat, cut back to clean wood – wood that does not show red beneath the bark. If much of the tree is infected, dig it up and burn it. In all cases, burn the infected wood to prevent the spread of the disease. Honey fungus is another disease that is fatal to crataegus. In the case of infection, dig the plant up and burn it.

Powdery mildew is a less deadly disease that can attack crataegus. It manifests itself by the presence of a white deposit on the leaves and, in very bad cases, by distortion of the tips of the shoots. Treat by cutting out infected growth. Another fungus disease is rust; it forms yellow or orange swellings on the young shoots, leaves and fruits at the beginning of summer. If the plant is seriously affected, spray with thiram or zineb.

Below: C. oxyacantha, one of the two species native to Britain, is often used to form rootstocks for other species. It bears scented flowers in early summer (May)

Some varieties to choose

Although the following varieties are sometimes sold as trees, they can quite frequently be obtained in bush or feathered (branched) form. Of the dimensions given, the first figure is the ultimate height and the second is the ultimate spread. *C. coccinea*, though still listed as such in many catalogues, has now been divided by botanists into two separate species – *C. intricata* and *C. pedicellata*. It is the latter two names that are used in this list.

C. crus-galli (cockspur thorn)
This shrub is characterized by its vicious thorns, often up to 8cm (3 in) long. Its white flowers, appearing in mid summer (June), are followed by long-lasting red fruits. 4·5 × 5·4m (15 × 18 ft).

C. × grignonensis
Bears flowers that appear quite late, and are followed by large, bright red fruits. Both leaves and berries remain till winter. 6 × 5·4m (20 × 18 ft).

C. intricata
Often included in catalogues as *C. coccinea*. It has reddish-brown fruits. 4·5 × 4·5m (15 × 15 ft).

C. × lavallei (*C. carrierei*)
This species is almost thornless. Its leaves remain green until mid winter (December), and its white flowers, borne in mid summer (June), are followed by orange-red haws. 4·5 × 3m (15 × 10 ft).

C. monogyna (common hawthorn, may, quick-thorn)
Fragrant white flowers are borne in early summer (May), and masses of crimson fruits appear in autumn. It has several most attractive ornamental cultivars. 7·5 × 4·5m (25 × 15 ft).

C. oxyacantha
Bears clusters of sweetly-scented white flowers in early summer (May), and crimson fruits in autumn. There are several attractive hybrids, including Paul's Scarlet that has double, scarlet flowers. 4·5 × 5·4m (15 × 18 ft).

C. o. Rosea Flore Pleno	Double pink variety.
C. o. Toba	Double white flowers turning pink, and glossy leaves. 5m (15 ft).

C. pedicellata (scarlet haw)
Often included in catalogues under *C. coccinea*, this shrub has thorny branches that carry clusters of white flowers in early summer (May), followed by bunches of scarlet fruits; these are often accompanied by red leaves in autumn. 4·5 × 4·5m (15 × 15 ft).

C. prunifolia
This shrub bears 5–8cm (2–3 in) wide clusters of white flowers in mid summer (June), followed by scarlet fruits and leaves that are autumn-tinted. 4·5 × 4·5m (15 × 15 ft).

CYTISUS

Type	hardy, deciduous, evergreen and semi-evergreen flowering shrubs
Family	LEGUMINOSAE
Common name	broom
Planting dates	from containers in mid–late autumn (September–October) or mid–late spring (March–April)
Flowering season	late spring–late summer (April–July)
Mature size/shape	prostrate, spreading and bushy with erect or arching branches; height 8cm–4·5m (3 in–15 ft), spread 45cm–3m (18 in–10 ft)

The genus cytisus contains between 25 and 30 species of principally deciduous and semi-evergreen flowering shrubs, with a few evergreens. It is closely related to the genera genista and spartium – all three, in fact, belong to the family LEGUMINOSAE. A few species are tender and require greenhouse cultivation, but most are generally hardy. *Cytisus (candicans) monspessulanus* (Montpelier broom), however, is liable to be damaged by severe frost.

Cytisus species originate mainly from the areas surrounding the Mediterranean; exceptions to this are *C. grandiflorus* (woolly-podded broom) and *C. (multiflorus) albus* (white Spanish broom) that come from Portugal, *C. nigricans (C. carlieri)* that grows wild in central Russia and *C. ratisbonensis* that is a native of the Caucasus and Siberia.

The numerous hybrids and varieties that are available nowadays are of garden origin and have been developed mostly during the 20th century, although a number of species were introduced to Western gardens much earlier. The most outstanding of those introduced into Britain are *C. nigricans* that arrived in 1730, *C. monspessulanus* (1735) and *C. ratisbonensis* (about 1800).

In many species the foliage is somewhat insignificant and appears on the branches for only a few months of the year. Some, such as *C. battandieri*, *C. ardoinii* and *C. × praecox* (Warminster broom), have silvery or greyish leaves.

The flowers of cytisus, that are sweet-pea-shaped and usually produced in extreme abundance, appear mainly between late spring and late summer (April and July). Primarily, the species have flowers in various shades of yellow, cream or white, but many hybrids bear flowers that combine these colours with crimson, mauve-pink,

cerise-red, orange-yellow, chocolate and salmon-red. Occasionally a cultivar appears that is self-coloured, such as *C.* Johnson's Crimson that has clear crimson blooms. Some cytisus are scented – examples of these are *C. battandieri, C. purgans* and *monspessulanus.*

Cytisus are, on the whole, fairly modest growers. After about 20 years' growth they range in size from the prostrate, rock-growing shrubs *C. decumbens* and *C. demissus* at about 10cm (4 in) high, to the tallest, *C. battandieri*, that reaches 4·5m (15 ft), with nearly as great a spread. In shape they vary from prostrate and spreading to bushy and upright. Some have arching branches.

These shrubs make excellent and colourful garden plants. Their variation in size gives them a wide range of uses in shrub or mixed borders. For instance, the taller ones can be used as background and the prostrate types in forward positions.

A number of cytisus, such as the low-growing, spreading *C. decumbens, C. demissus* and *C. scoparius prostratus*, are very good plants for the rock garden. *C. decumbens, C. scoparius prostratus, C. beanii* and *C. × kewensis* are excellent as ground cover. In addition, cytisus are effective as wall plants – in particular *C. battandieri*, and *C. monspessulanus* and its hybrid *C.* Porlock.

Cytisus × praecox bears creamy-white flowers during late spring and early summer (April and May), and makes an ideal border shrub or a small specimen bush

Cultivation

In general, cytisus are quite happy in ordinary, well-drained garden soil, but they prefer it to be on the poorer side rather than too rich. All cytisus will succeed in clay, provided it is near-neutral in reaction and most species are also lime-tolerant. Neither *C. albus* nor *C. scoparius* (common broom), however, will survive long in poor, shallow chalky soil, nor tolerate extremely acid conditions. Many cytisus are very happy grown in gardens by the sea and quite a few will tolerate the polluted air of industrial areas.

It is best to obtain container-grown plants because cytisus do not like to be disturbed once they have been planted. Container-grown cytisus can be planted at any time during the year, but the best results are obtained if this is done in mid–late autumn (September–October) or mid–late spring (March–April).

Determine the space to allow between neighbouring shrubs by adding together their ultimate spreads and dividing by two. Remove the rootball carefully from its container by cutting round the edge of the bottom and down the side.

Dig a hole that is a little larger in diameter than the rootball and of such a depth that the top of the rootball is level with the surface of the soil in the bed. With as little disturbance as possible, tease out a few roots at the side near the surface. Then place the rootball centrally in the hole and fill in with soil. Firm well by treading in and fill the hole completely with more soil. Once planted, cytisus are easily grown and need little attention.

For pruning purposes, cytisus can be divided into two types – those that flower on the previous year's wood, and those that flower on the current year's wood. The former are pruned by cutting back the stems by two-thirds immediately after flowering, and the latter by cutting the shoots back hard in the spring before growth begins. On no account cut back hard into the old wood – mature plants, particularly those of *C. scoparius* and its hybrids, do not respond well to such treatment.

Cytisus are not much affected by diseases, but can develop swellings on the stems that are due to gall mites. Remove the galls as they appear.

Propagation

Species are easily raised from seed. Propagate named varieties from 8–10cm (3–4 in) long, lateral shoot, heel cuttings taken in early–mid autumn (August–September). Insert these in rooting compost in a cold frame. When they have rooted, pot on the small plants into growing compost, in 8–10cm (3–4 in) pots and plunge them outdoors. Finally, plant them in their permanent quarters in mid–late autumn (September–October).

For a magnificent display of cytisus in early summer (May), plant low-growing species such as C.×kewensis (right) and C. purpureus (above right) Far right: cytisus are exceptionally versatile plants for the garden because of their variation in height C. battandieri (above) reaches 3m (10 ft), while C.×beanii (below) grows only 90cm (3 ft) high

Some varieties to choose

The dimensions given are first the ultimate height, and secondly the spread, after about 20 years' growth. Unless otherwise stated, the cultivars are approximately the same size as the species.

C. (multiflorus) albus (white Spanish broom)
A bushy, erect shrub with arching branches and grey-green leaves. Bears white flowers in late spring and early summer (April and May). 1·8 × 1·8m (6 × 6 ft).

C. ardoinii
A mat-forming, alpine shrub with grey-green leaves and bright yellow blooms that are borne in late spring and early summer (April and May). 8 × 30cm (3 × 12 in).

C. battandieri
Has silvery leaves and golden yellow, pineapple-scented blossoms borne during early and mid summer (May and June); has a tree-like habit. 4·5 × 3m (15 × 10 ft).

C. × beanii
A dwarf shrub that bears golden yellow flowers in early summer (May). 50 × 90cm (20 × 36 in).

C. decumbens

A prostrate-growing shrublet with bright yellow blooms borne in early and mid summer (May and June). 10 × 45cm (4 × 18 in).

C. demissus

A prostrate shrub suitable for the rock garden, with exceptionally large yellow-and-brown flowers that are borne in early summer (May). 10 × 45cm (4 × 18 in).

C. × kewensis

An attractive hybrid that has a prostrate habit, and an abundance of pale yellow flowers in early summer (May). 45cm × 1·2m (18 in × 4 ft).

C. nigricans (C. carlieri)

An erect-growing shrub with yellow flowers that first appear in mid summer (June) and continue blooming until mid autumn (September). 1·2m × 90cm (4 × 3 ft).

C. Porlock

A large, bushy shrub, bearing butter yellow, very strongly-scented flowers that appear in late spring and early summer (April and May). It needs wall protection in cold areas. 3 × 1·2m (10 × 4 ft).

C. × praecox (Warminster broom)

A pendant bush with arching branches that bear masses of rich cream flowers during late spring and early summer (April and May). Its cultivar C. × p. Allgold has rich, sulphur yellow flowers. 1·8 × 1·8m (6 × 6 ft).

C. purgans

Bears rich yellow, scented blossoms during late spring and early summer (April and May). This is a usually leafless, erect-growing bush. 1·2 × 1·2m (4 × 4 ft).

C. purpureus (purple broom)

A low-growing shrub that has lilac-purple flowers appearing in early summer (May). 45cm × 1·5m (18 in × 5 ft).

C. ratisbonensis

A small shrub with yellow flowers sometimes stained red, that grow along arching branches during early and mid summer (May and June). 1·5 × 1·5m (5 × 5 ft).

C. scoparius (common broom)

An upright-growing species with erect, bright green branches in winter. It produces rich yellow blossoms during early and mid summer (May and June). This species produces many very beautiful and colourful clones, some of which are given below. 2·5 × 2·5m (8 × 8 ft).

Andreanus	Yellow and chocolate-red blooms.
Burkwoodii	Rich crimson-red blooms.
Cornish Cream	Cream-coloured blossoms.
Donard Seedling	Purple-rose and orange blooms that are flushed pink.
Firefly	Yellow and bronze-crimson blooms.
Golden Sunlight	Rich yellow flowers.
Goldfinch	Purple, yellow and red blooms.
Hookstone Purple	Intense purple blooms.
Johnson's Crimson	Clear crimson flowers.
Killiney Red	Bright red flowers; a compact and low-growing shrub.
Killiney Salmon	Near-orange flowers.
Lady Moore	Rich red, buff and rose blooms.
Lord Lambourne	Unusual, bi-coloured flowers in cream-yellow and maroon-crimson.
Marie Burkwood	Pale rose flowers.
Mrs W. A. Slocock	Maroon and gold blooms.
Sulphureus (or Pallidus)	Deep cream blooms, tinged red in bud.
Windlesham Ruby	Ruby-red blooms; a bushy shrub.
C. scoparius prostratus	A dwarf, spreading shrub with large yellow blooms that open in mid summer (June).

DAPHNE

Type	hardy, deciduous and evergreen shrubs
Family	THYMELAEACEAE
Flowering season	certain species are in flower every month of the year
Mature size	up to 1.5m (5 ft) high, 60–100cm (2–3¼ ft) spread

The daphne genus is composed of 70 species of showy, sweetly-smelling shrubs that are usually small and suitable for a rock garden or the front of a shrub border.

The plant name 'daphne' is commemorative of Daphne, the daughter of the river god of Greek mythology, who was supposedly turned into a laurel bush to escape from the attention of Apollo, but the name itself may come from an Indo-European root word meaning 'odour'.

Daphne mezereum is found growing naturally in England from Yorkshire southwards, but not in Devon or Cornwall, and in Europe from Scandinavia to Spain and northern Greece. It prefers a calcareous (chalk or limestone) soil and the shade of woodlands, requires no pruning and flowers freely in early and mid spring (February and March) before the leaves appear. Its scented, rosy-purple flowers are followed by red, poisonous berries, while the variety *D.m.* Alba has white flowers and yellow berries; *D.m.* Grandiflora has larger flowers than the type that are produced throughout the winter.

Two evergreen species of daphne, *D. pontica* and *D. laureola*, have flowers that are not nearly so attractive as those of *D. mezereum*. Apart from Europe, *D. laureola* is also found in Asia Minor, the Azores and North Africa.

There are many shorter species, ranging from 15 to 45cm (6 to 18 in) high, that flower later in the year and are ideal for the rock garden. Some good ones include *D. alpina*, *D. blagayana*, *D. cneorum*, *D. collina* and *D. retusa*.

Daphne is propagated by sowing seed in autumn in boxes containing equal quantities of soil, peat and sand. These will germinate naturally in spring, or early spring (February) if brought into a warm greenhouse. Most types can be propagated by layering in the usual manner (see Week 12), but some rarer types can be grafted in spring to *D. mezereum*, if deciduous, or to *D. laureola*, if evergreen. Most daphnes will grow freely in colder climates, although some require temperate conditions.

Above right: Daphne retusa. *a slow-growing, alpine, evergreen ideally suited to the rock garden*
Right: Daphne mezereum Alba *(mezereon), a deciduous species bearing sweetly-scented flowers*

DEUTZIA

Type	deciduous flowering shrubs
Family	PHILADELPHACEAE
Planting date	late autumn–early spring (October–February); from containers at any time
Flowering season	early–late summer (May–July)
Mature size/shape	mainly rounded, but some with erect or arching branches; height 90cm–2·4m (3–8 ft), spread 90cm–2m (3–6½ ft)

The genus deutzia, that contains about 50 species of easily-grown deciduous flowering shrubs, was named after Johan van der Deutz, Dutch friend and patron of Carl Thunberg, the Swedish botanist and pupil of Linnaeus.

Many species of deutzia were discovered growing wild in China and Japan, but others, such as *Deutzia staminea*, come from the Himalayas. Quite a few species were introduced to Western gardens in the early years of this century, though a few came earlier. *D. scabra* was introduced to Britain in 1822, *D. gracilis* in 1840 and *D. purpurascens* in 1888. Many of the most attractive hybrid clones were raised at a rather later date, and owe their cultivation to the hybridist Lemoine of Nancy, France.

The leaves of deutzia are green, but several have foliage that is grey or white on the under surface. The brown bark on the stems – a very attractive feature – eventually peels off. The white, pink or purple flowers are prolific and the inflorescences vary from type to type, being carried in clusters, panicles, corymbs or racemes. The flowers themselves appear in different shapes – hawthorn-like, star-like, long-petalled, bell-shaped, single or double. The most magnificent is the Formosan *D. pulchra*, with racemes of white flowers that are reminiscent of the drooping heads of lily of the valley. The flowers of some deutzia, such as *D. maliflora* Avalanche, *D. compacta* and its forms, varieties of *D. × elegantissima*, and *D. sieboldiana* are sweetly perfumed. Deutzia flower between early and late summer (May and July).

These plants are modest growers: the compact shrub *D. × rosea* has a height and spread of some 90cm (3 ft) after about 20 years' growth, while the erect-growing *D. scabra* can reach a height of 3m (10 ft) and a spread of 2m (6½ ft). They mostly form neat, rounded bushes, but a few – *D. scabra* and *D. × elegantissima* for example – have erect branches, while *D. × kalmiiflora* and *D. × rosea* are arching in habit.

Above: the fragrant, massed blooms of Deutzia × elegantissima *Fasciculata*

Cultivation

Because they are easy to cultivate, deutzia can be grown successfully in both town and country gardens, and be incorporated into the smallest planting scheme. They come into flower quickly and are excellent for shrub and mixed borders. All species and varieties will grow happily in any well-drained garden soil, but they will also succeed on clay or on a shallow soil over chalk. Many types are invaluable in industrial towns because they can withstand a polluted atmosphere.

Deutzia will thrive in both full sun and light shade, such as is found in woodlands and shrubberies: under such shade, plants with rather stronger flower colouring retain their tints better. Although the vast majority of deutzia are hardy, try to avoid planting them in open positions without some protection – particularly in colder districts or in frost pockets, or where late spring frost is likely to damage the young shoots.

Right: Upright-growing deutzias Contraste and Magicien (below right) make ideal background plants for a mixed border Far right: compact D.×rosea Carminea has an attractive arching habit

Plant bare-root deutzia at any time between late autumn and early spring (October and February), provided there is no frost and the ground is not soggy. Those from containers can be planted at any time, as long as the ground is sufficiently moist. Water the deutzia well before removing it from its container, and again after planting if the weather is dry.

Determine the distance to be allowed between neighbouring deutzia or other plants by adding together the ultimate spreads of adjoining plants and dividing the sum by two.

Deutzia need little care after planting, except for annual pruning. Prune by reducing the old flowering shoots immediately after blooming, so as to thin the shrub, then cut the remaining shoots back to within a few centimetres (or inches) of the old wood.

Fortunately, as a rule most deutzia are little troubled by pests and diseases.

Propagation

To propagate these plants, take 8–10cm (3–4 in) long cuttings of semi-ripe, lateral shoots in late summer and early autumn (July and August) and insert them in rooting compost in a cold frame. Transplant the rooted cuttings into nursery rows the following late spring or early summer (April or May) and then plant them out the following autumn into their permanent positions.

Alternatively, take 25cm (10 in) long hardwood cuttings of lateral shoots in mid autumn (October). Insert them in a nursery bed and plant them out permanently a year later.

Some varieties to choose

The dimensions given for each shrub in the list below refer to its ultimate height and spread. Unless otherwise indicated assume that the cultivars of any species are about the same size as the parent.

D. discolor Major

In mid summer (June) bears flowers 2–3cm (1 in) across, that are white, and tinted pink on the outside. 1·5m × 1·5m (5 × 5 ft).

D. × elegantissima

Upright-growing, bushy shrub producing 5–8cm (2–3 in) wide, fragrant, star-shaped, pink to pale rose-purple blooms during early and mid summer (May and June). 1·5 × 1·5m (5 × 5 ft).

D. × e. Fasciculata   Bright rose-pink blooms.

D. gracilis

Carries racemes of white, star-like blossoms in mid summer (June). 1·2 × 1·5m (4 × 5 ft).

D. × hybrida

This species is the head of a group of hybrids that all bloom during mid and late summer (June and July). They are all 1·8m (6 ft) high, with a spread of 2·5m (8 ft).

D. × h. Contraste — Loose panicles of lilac-pink flowers. The outside of the petals is a rich wine purple.

D. × h. Joconde — Large, rose-purple blooms.

D. × h. Magicien — Large mauve-pink, tinted white and purple flowers.

D. × h. Mont Rose — Panicles of rose-pink blossoms.

D. × h. Perle Rose — Soft rose-pink blooms.

D. × kalmiiflora
Bears clusters of starry flowers, white inside and deep rose-pink on the reverse, during mid summer (June). 1·8 × 1·5m (6 × 5 ft).

D. longifolia Veitchii
Considered to be the finest of the *longifolia* shrubs. Its lilac-pink tinted flowers open in mid and late summer (June and July). 1·2 × 1·5m (4 × 5 ft).

D. × magnifica
Has rough, grey-green leaves and unusual, double, pompon-like flowers that open in mid summer (June). 2·4 × 1·8m (8 × 6 ft).

D. × maliflora
Strong-growing shrub producing large corymbs of white, purple-shaded flowers in mid summer (June). 1·8 × 1·8m (6 × 6 ft).

D. × m. Avalanche — Has slender, arching branches laden with fragrant white flowers in mid summer (June).

D. monbeigii
Characterized by dull green leaves with white undersides. Its flowers are small, star-shaped and white, and appear in mid summer (June). 1·8 × 1·5m (6 × 5 ft).

D. pulchra
Magnificent hardy shrub, characterized by racemes of white blooms, resembling the drooping heads of lily of the valley, and appearing in mid summer (June). 1·8 × 1·5m (6 × 5 ft).

D. × rosea
Compact, rather smaller shrub with arching sprays of rose-pink flowers borne in round clusters in mid and late summer (June and July). 90 × 60cm (3 × 2 ft).

D. × r. Campanulata — White flowers with contrasting purple calyces. 1·5m × 90cm (5 × 3 ft).

D. × r. Carminea — Rose-pink blooms.

D. scabra
Tall, erect shrub carrying large panicles of white blooms during mid and late summer (June and July). It has attractive brown bark that peels off. 2·4 × 1·8m (8 × 6 ft).

D.s. Candidissima — Double white flowers.

D.s. Codsall Pink — Purple-pink blossoms.

D.s. Plena — Double white blooms suffused rose-purple.

D. setchuenensis
Slow-growing species, not quite hardy enough for the coldest parts of Britain. It has brown, peeling bark and produces small, starry white flowers in mid and late summer (June and July). 1·8m × 90cm (6 × 3 ft).

D.s. corymbiflora — Bears a profusion of white flowers and is a broader-leaved form.

There is a deutzia for almost any size of garden. Erect D. scabra Candidissima *(top) reaches 2·4m in height, while arching* D. × rosea Campanulata *(above) is considerably more compact*

ESCALLONIA

Type	evergreen flowering shrubs, with a few deciduous exceptions
Family	SAXIFRAGACEAE
Planting date	late autumn–late spring (October–April); from containers at any time
Flowering season	early summer–early winter (May–November)
Mature size/shape	mainly rounded and bushy, some with erect-growing or arching branches; height 30cm–4·5m (12 in–15 ft), spread 1·2–2·5m (4–8 ft)

The escallonia genus contains about 60 species of evergreen and deciduous shrubs or trees, and was named after Señor Escallon, a Spanish traveller in South America.

All escallonia species come from South America, usually Brazil and Chile. Of the more popular species still grown today, *Escallonia rubra* was the earliest to be introduced to European gardens; it arrived in 1827, and was followed by *E. illinita* in 1830, *E. laevis* in 1844 and *E. macrantha* in 1848. With the exception of Exoniensis and Langleyensis, the many hybrids are almost certainly of 20th century origin. The beautiful 'apple blossom' series is of Irish garden origin, and the cultivar *E. macrantha* Bantry Bay was discovered growing in a rock crevice on Garnish Island in Bantry Bay.

There is only one deciduous species, *E. virgata* (or *E. phillipiana*), that generally features in present-day catalogues; it is hardy, but will not tolerate a chalky soil. Most evergreen escallonia are slightly tender and, in some inland positions in Britain, must be given wall protection. They grow quite satisfactorily in southern and western areas of England and Scotland, and in coastal districts everywhere.

Escallonia have attractive, dense foliage made of fairly small, light to deep green, shiny leaves. Many of the more popular ones bear foliage that is aromatic when crushed – C. F. Ball for example. In general, the flowers are small and tubular with widely expanded, rounded lobes, and are usually carried in panicles up to 10cm (4 in) long, that are lateral or terminal according to the species or hybrid concerned. They range in colour from white through blush- and rose-pink to cherry red. Some cultivars, Donard Gem in particular, have sweetly-scented blooms. Many of the present-day escallonia have a long flowering season, extending from mid summer to late autumn (June to October), and even early winter in the case of *E.*

macrantha. On the other hand, the flowering period of the comparatively new race of escallonia, known as the 'apple blossom' series, is from early to late summer (May to July).

The smallest of these fairly modest-growing shrubs is *E. rubra* Woodside, that after 20 years will not exceed 60cm (24 in) in height, but has an appreciably larger spread. On the other hand, its parent, *E. rubra*, towers to a height of 4·5m (15 ft) with a spread of 1·8m (6 ft). Many escallonia are somewhat rounded and bushy in shape, but they often have erect branches. Others, with arching branches – including Donard Seedling, Edinensis, Langleyensis and Slieve Donard – are sometimes called the 'cascade escallonias'.

Although the escallonia genus does contain quite a number of species, only a comparatively few true species are offered for sale today by nurserymen. The principal ones are *E. macrantha* and *E. rubra*. The reason for this lack of species is the tremendous number of hybrids – in many cases superior to the species – that have been raised from the hardier types.

Most escallonia flourish in ordinary, well-drained garden soil, and are lime-tolerant and drought-resistant – qualities making them particularly valuable in seaside gardens, where the proportion of sea-sand in the soil makes it not only less water retentive, but possibly alkaline because it contains the shells of many dead minute sea creatures. In addition, *E. macrantha*, Red Hedger and Crimson Spire are very resistant to high winds and salt-laden spray – again making them excellent for seaside gardens, or wind-exposed gardens in the milder districts. All escallonia will tolerate the conditions existing in industrial areas.

Escallonia can make excellent wall plants; the hybrids C. F. Ball, Donard Seedling, Slieve Donard and Iveyi are particularly good for this purpose. Some of the tall escallonia with upright growth, such as the hybrid Newryensis and the species *E. punctata* (*E. sanguinea*), make excellent

Donard Star (above) and Donard Seedling (top) grow well in polluted areas. Slow-growing Apple Blossom (above left) is worth persevering with for its unusual shape. Iveyi (left) needs wall shelter, while Pink Pearl (far left) makes a fine hedge

wind-breaks. Lastly, provided the conditions are correct for them, escallonia are excellent for hedging. Good choices for seaside hedges are Red Hedger, Crimson Spire, *E. macrantha* and Pride of Donard. For inland districts, try C. F. Ball and Edinensis as well.

Care and cultivation

Plant bare-root escallonia in open weather from late autumn to late spring (October to April); those in containers can be planted at any time.

Determine planting distance by adding together the ultimate spreads of plants that are to be neighbours and dividing the sum by two. For hedges, space the plants about 45cm (18 in) apart. Dig a hole of a sufficient diameter to take the rootball and allow space for the roots to spread, and deep enough for the original soil mark on the main stem to be at the soil surface. Replace some of the soil and firm well round the root by treading, then add the rest of the soil to fill the hole. Plant hedges in the same way.

No regular pruning is needed, but it is wise to remove the spent flowers after blooming and to trim back established hedges at the same time. Newly-planted hedges should be reduced by one quarter immediately after planting to encourage bushy growth.

Escallonia are generally free from pests, but they might be attacked by silver leaf disease. This causes die-back of the branches and the leaves often turn a silvery colour. Treat by cutting back to clean wood, and paint the wound with a proprietary sealant.

Some varieties to choose

The first dimension given in the following list is the average height, and the second is the spread.

SPECIES

E. macrantha	Fine, glossy, aromatic, deep green leaves and crimson flowers, borne from mid summer to late autumn (June to October). 3×1.8m (10×6 ft).
E. rubra	Glossy green leaves, and red flowers produced in loose panicles in late summer and early autumn (July and August). 4.5×1.8m (15×6 ft). *E. r.* Woodside is a dwarf rock shrub with crimson flowers. 30–60cm (12–24 in) high.

HYBRIDS

Apple Blossom	Slow-growing plant, with pink and white flowers borne mid summer – late autumn (June – October). 1.5×1.5m (5×5 ft).
C. F. Ball	Upright shrub with dark green leaves and crimson blossoms between early summer and late autumn (May and October). 2.4×1.5m (8×5 ft).
Crimson Spire	Erect-growing, with very dark foliage and crimson flowers blooming from mid summer to late autumn (June to October). 1.8×1.8m (6×6 ft).
Donard Brilliance	Bushy, pendulous shrub with shiny green leaves and rose red blooms, appearing mainly during mid summer (June). 1.8×1.8m (6×6 ft).

Donard Gem
Bears sweetly-scented pink blooms that open during mid and late summer (June and July). 1·2 × 1·5m (4 × 5 ft).

Donard Radiance
Shining, deep green foliage and large, rose red blooms flowering from late summer to mid autumn (July to September). 2·1 × 1·5m (7 × 5 ft).

Donard Seedling
Arching branches carrying dark green leaves and apple-blossom pink flowers that appear in mid and late summer (June and July). 2·1 × 1·8m (7 × 6 ft).

Donard Star
Compact shrub with rose pink flowers borne during mid and late summer (June and July). 1·8 × 1·5m (6 × 5 ft).

Donard White
White flowers, pink in bud, blooming from mid summer (June) to autumn. 1·5 × 1·5m (5 × 5 ft).

Edinensis
Shrub with cascading habit and bright green foliage. Bears rose pink blooms in mid and late summer (June and July). 4 × 4m (13 × 13 ft).

Glory of Donard
Large, deep carmine flowers produced in mid and late summer (June and July), with dark green leaves. 1·8 × 1·8m (6 × 6 ft).

Gwendolyn Anley
Small, very hardy, bushy shrub bearing flesh pink blooms from mid summer until mid autumn (June to September). 90cm × 1·8m (3 × 6 ft).

Ingramii
Rose pink flowers, borne between mid summer and early autumn (June and August). Fast-growing. 1·2 × 1·8m (4 × 6 ft).

Iveyi
Vigorous, rounded shrub with glossy, dark green leaves. Has white flowers in late summer and early autumn (July and August). Needs wall protection in colder areas. 3 × 2·5m (10 × 8 ft).

Langleyensis
Hardy shrub with rose pink flowers carried on arching branches in mid and late summer (June and July). 1·8 × 1·8m (6 × 6 ft).

Peach Blossom
Clear, peach pink flowers, appearing during mid and late summer (June and July). 2·5 × 1·5m (8 × 5 ft).

Pink Pearl
Soft pink, stained bright rose pink flowers, blooming in mid and late summer (June and July). 1·5 × 1·5m (5 × 5 ft).

Pride of Donard
Large, brilliant rose red, somewhat bell-shaped flowers, hanging in racemes between early and late summer (May and July). 1·8 × 1·5m (6 × 5 ft).

Red Hedger
Erect-growing shrub with glossy, mid green leaves. Produces bright crimson flowers steadily between mid summer and late autumn (June and October). 1·8 × 1·8m (6 × 6 ft).

Slieve Donard
Compact, very hardy shrub with long arching sprays, laden with apple-blossom pink blooms during mid summer and early autumn (June and September). 2·4 × 1·5m (8 × 5 ft).

St Keverne
Medium-sized shrub with arching branches, carrying large panicles of apple-blossom pink blooms during mid and late summer (June and July), and sometimes longer. 1·5 × 1·5m (5 × 5 ft).

Peach Blossom is one of the most attractive hybrid escallonia, both for flowers and foliage. To keep it looking at its best and to prolong the flowering period, remove the blooms as they fade

EUCALYPTUS

Type	evergreen flowering trees and shrubs
Family	MYRTACEAE
Common name	gum tree or ironbark tree
Flowering season	late spring to early winter (April to November) according to species
Planting date	mid to late summer (June to July); always from containers
Mature size/shape	4·5–116m (18–375 ft) high × 1·5–11m (5–35 ft) spread; usually sparsely-branched, pyramidal head on tall bare trunk
Special uses	affording partial shade; providing foliage for flower arrangements; as seedlings in summer bedding schemes; commercially to yield eucalyptus oil

This unusual genus is composed of between 600 and 700 species, varieties and hybrids of evergreen trees and shrubs. All eucalypts come originally from Australia and Tasmania, but have adapted well to conditions in most other parts of the world.

It is difficult to find a plant family that shows a greater variety in size when fully grown. Heights range from not more than 3m (10 ft) for low-growing shrubs and scrub plants, to the tallest known broad-leaved tree in the world, *Eucalyptus amygdalina regnans*, that reaches 116m (375 ft) and rivals the giant California redwoods. Nevertheless many are fast-growing and can become too big for some gardens. Often they are stooled, that is, cut back yearly 2·5cm (1 in) from the base.

Eucalyptus is beautiful in outline, pyramidal with sickle-like leaves on a bare, slender trunk. Foliage has excellent shape, colour and texture. More generally their leaves are silvery-grey to blue-green in colour. The shape of the mature leaves on many of the species is like a sickle, often at the same time with an intriguing, almost indescribable, twist. What is most interesting is that their juvenile leaves are completely different – in size, shape, colour, arrangement and mode of attachment to the stem – from adult leaves. So attractive are these juvenile leaves that it is quite common to cut back more mature branches regularly in order to encourage their growth. All the foliage has an aromatic fragrance that, at the low concentration at which it is exuded, is quite refreshing.

Another outstanding quality of many eucalyptus trees is the colour of their barks, that adds great beauty and interest to a garden. In the first place most species have twigs and branches with white or cream-coloured bark. As the wood matures, the smooth outer bark on their trunks and branches is cast annually. This shedding usually commences after they are four or five years old. At first new pale cream or white bark is revealed, but later this darkens to give a striking mottled effect.

It is not always appreciated that eucalypts flower quite prolifically after they are about four years old. The flowers are mostly white, with white or cream-coloured filaments, about 1–3cm ($\frac{1}{2}$–1 in) long, and sweetly scented.

Because of the climatic variations of their native habitat, eucalypts can become fairly readily adapted to almost any weather conditions – ranging from areas of tropical rains to the dryness of the desert and even freezing alpine regions, though the degree of adaptability does vary with the species. What is more, many of them are remarkably easy about where they will make themselves at home. All other conditions being equal, all of those available will flourish on clay soil, many of them are happy at the seaside, most

Many eucalyptus species shed their outer bark annually, adding an attractive mottled appearance to the garden even in winter

are able to resist pollution and so can be made to adorn industrial towns, and there is at least one, *E. parviflora*, that will tolerate chalky soil.

Among the earliest to be introduced into gardens from the wilds, in 1829, was the Tasmanian blue gum, *E. globulus*. It is a beautiful tree with blue-green leaves that are almost silvery when young. It can reach noble proportions.

Unfortunately, many of the species that flourish in temperate zones will grow too large for small gardens. They can, however, be very effective in larger gardens, where they give an exotic air that cannot be paralleled by any other plant. They may be grown as specimen trees, pruned shrubs and stooled plants, which normally only produce juvenile foliage. Planted in a woodland garden they give excellent partial shade to rhododendrons and other sylvan shrubs and plants.

Their foliage is excellent for flower arrangements. In winter, when dormant, the leaves will remain fresh for several weeks. Equally as lovely are the young summer shoots that will last fresh for several days if the ends are scalded.

The less hardy species when young make excellent foliage plants in summer bedding schemes. They can also be very beautiful if grown indoors as house plants.

Cultivation and propagation

Eucalypts should be given full sunshine, and sheltered from freezing winds and gales that are likely to cause root disturbance. They prefer an acid or neutral, well-drained soil that is moderately fertile and fairly moist, but not waterlogged – and certainly not dry.

It is important *not* to plant a eucalyptus in soft, freshly-dug soil, because 'root-rock' is almost certain to kill it. The position should be prepared some time before, well firmed and allowed to consolidate thoroughly before planting.

Eucalypts must be planted when small, no more than 15–30cm (6–12 in) tall and from pots. The best time to plant is in mid or late summer.

The distance between eucalypts and neighbouring trees varies from 3–5·5m (10–18 ft) according to species. As the trees are mainly bare lower down, shade-loving shrubs may be put closer.

On no account must the roots of eucalypts be disturbed. Dig a hole that is no greater in diameter than the pot from which the eucalyptus is removed, but about 5cm (2 in) deeper so that the swollen root is well under the soil. Water the plant in well and then stake firmly. As the tree grows rapidly both in height and girth, the stake should be changed periodically for a longer one, each time moving it a little farther away from the trunk to allow for growth. Young plants should remain staked for up to six years.

Protect the basal stem of young trees against frost with straw or sacking during the first winter, though otherwise they need very little attention. Eucalypts do not need pruning, unless you want to have their juvenile foliage or stooled shrubs.

New trees can be propagated from seeds sown 3mm ($\frac{1}{8}$ in) deep in pots of sandy soil in a minimum temperature of 18°C (65°F). Sow them between early and late spring (February and April).

Pests
Mature trees are normally unaffected, but young shoots and juvenile foliage are susceptible to suckers (blue gum psyllid), which can be cured by spraying dimethoate, formothion or malathion.

Some varieties to choose
The following is a selection of some of the most useful and readily-available eucalypts. The dimensions given after the species listed correspond to height and spread respectively after 20 years unless otherwise stated.

E. coccifera (Mount Wellington peppermint)	A wind-resisting sub-alpine species with oval-shaped green or blue-green juvenile leaves. The adult leaves are lance-shaped and green-glaucous in colour. Its trunk is mottled pale grey or white when newly exposed. Flowers in early and mid summer (May and June). 11 × 8m (35 × 25 ft).
E. dalrympleana	Attractive fast-growing species, which is among the hardiest. Its juvenile leaves last for two or three years and are ovoid and blue-green; the pendulous adult leaves are light green. Young shoots and foliage are bright orange and scarlet, with pink or red bark on the stems. The bark on the branches and trunk is white patchwork, becoming light brown. 14 × 3m (45 × 10 ft) after 10 years.
E. glaucescens	Very hardy. It has round juvenile leaves of brilliant blue-green that become glaucous and oblong and sickle-shaped when they mature. When young the adult leaves are sometimes tinted pink. The bark eventually becomes reddish-brown and shreds to expose white to grey. 8 × 4m (25 × 12 ft).
E. gunnii	One of the hardiest species. Its sickle-shaped adult leaves are sage green while the juvenile foliage is rounded and of a striking silver-blue colour. It makes a fine large tree or it may be pruned annually to form a bush. 14 × 4·5m (45 × 15 ft) after 10 years.
E. parviflora	This exceptionally hardy species will tolerate chalk soils. May be grown as a tree or stooled to form a bush. Its juvenile leaves, which are ovate, are green or sub-glaucous. They are carried on branching shoots giving a feathery foliage. These ultimately give way to long, narrow, blue-green adult leaves. 9 × 4·5m (30 × 15 ft).
E. pauciflora (cabbage gum)	Has lance-shaped, thick and glossy green or glaucous leaves that are up to 20cm (8 in) long, with glossy, dark red to orange-yellow twigs. Can be stooled. 11 × 6m (35 × 20 ft).
E. perriniana (round-leaved snow gum)	Juvenile leaves are blue-grey; after about two years these become long and pendulous. New leaves have an attractive lavender-purplish hue. Its glaucous or green bark shreds after about four years to give brown blotches. A more modest grower at 5·5 × 2m (18 × 6 ft) after three years.
E. pulverulenta	Another rather modest grower. Both its juvenile and adult leaves are glaucous and covered in a brilliantly silvery-white bloom. Its white bark eventually peels to reveal cream to light brown patches. Most spectacular grown as a stooled specimen. 5·5 × 1·5m (18 × 5 ft) after four years.
E. urnigera (urn-fruited gum)	This hardy tree has juvenile and adult leaves of dark green. Its pale green or cream bark eventually becomes blotched with red-brown. The cream flowers are followed by urn-shaped, glossy green fruits. 5·5 × 3m (18 × 10 ft) after four years.

Far left, above: characteristically pyramid-shaped mature Eucalyptus gunnii
One of the most striking features of eucalypts is the contrast between adult and juvenile foliage: far left, adult, and left, juvenile, foliage of E. gunnii
Above left: juvenile foliage of the hardy E. coccifera

EUONYMUS

Type	deciduous and evergreen shrubs and small trees
Common name	spindle tree
Family	CELASTRACEAE
Planting date	evergreens: mid–late autumn (September–October); late spring–early summer (April–May) deciduous: late autumn–mid spring (October–March); from containers at any time
Flowering season	throughout the summer
Mature size/shape	bushy, prostrate, trailing and climbing; height 30cm–4·5m (12 in–15 ft), spread 90cm–3m (3–10 ft)

The euonymus genus consists of 176 species of deciduous and evergreen foliage shrubs. The name euonymus – meaning 'of good name' in Latin, and deriving originally from the Greek name for the plant, 'euonymon dendron' – was an ironic reference to the plant's poisonous nature.

Two species – *Euonymus europaeus* (common spindle tree) and *E. latifolius* – are native to Europe; the former is a native of Britain, where it is commonly seen growing in the hedgerows. All the other species are Asian in origin; *E. alatus* (winged spindle tree), *E. japonicus* and *E. fortunei* come from China and Japan, while *E. sachalinensis (E. planipes)* and *E. yedoensis* are native to north-east Asia and Korea respectively, as well as Japan.

For thousands of years, long before the invention of the spinning-wheel, thread for woollen cloth was spun by twirling a stick – called a spindle – that was made from the stems of *E. europaeus*. Its wood was also used for making clothes-pegs, knitting-needles and meat skewers; for the last use it was given the country name of 'skewer-wood'. Because of the many uses for the wood, euonymus has been grown in cottage gardens for many centuries.

Most of the species cultivated today were introduced to Britain within the last two centuries. Among the earliest to arrive, in 1730, was the European species *E. latifolius*. Other species still popular today came later – *E. alatus* in 1860, *E. yedoensis* in 1865, *E. sachalinensis* in 1892 and *E. fortunei* in 1907.

Euonymus flowers, generally greenish or purplish in colour, are insignificant. The evergreens bear shiny leaves that are green, purple or greyish-green, or variegated silver, gold or white, while the deciduous species are characterized by rich

autumn colouring. Some euonymus also bear distinctive fruits – coloured white, scarlet, rose-pink and crimson – that persist long into the winter. These are poisonous and should not be eaten. To ensure good cross-pollination for fruit production, plant several euonymus in a group.

The deciduous species are hardy, but the evergreen forms are somewhat tender and need to be grown in fairly mild localities if they are to do really well. Nevertheless, the evergreens thrive in coastal areas, where they are able to resist salt-laden winds. They are also quite at home in the chalky soil that is sometimes found in seaside gardens. *E. fortunei* and *E. japonicus*, along with their many cultivars, will flourish in industrial areas. *E. fortunei* and its cultivars, as well as *E. japonicus robustus*, although preferring milder conditions, certainly tolerate cold, exposed positions. *E. fortunei* will also grow well in deep shade – an extremely useful characteristic that is invaluable for sombre areas of the garden and for clothing north and east walls.

Above: the fruits of Euonymus latifolius *are poisonous – so be careful that children do not pick or eat them*
Top right: slow-growing E. alatus; *it is famous for its magnificent autumn colouring (far right)*
Right: to ensure fruiting on E. europaeus Red Cascade, *plant several specimens close together so that cross-pollination can take place*

Many of the species and their cultivars are modest-growing enough to be accommodated in small gardens. One of the largest of the more popular euonymus, the deciduous *E. yedoensis*, grows to a height of about 4·5m (15 ft), with a spread of 2·5–3m (8–10 ft); next in size come *E. latifolius*, *E. japonicus*, *E. alatus* and *E. fortunei* (when grown against a wall) – all having an approximate height of 3m (10 ft) and a spread of 1·8m (6 ft). Quite a number of cultivars of *E. fortunei* are very modest-growing; the largest is *E. f.* Carrierei with a height of 90cm (3 ft) and spread of 1·8m (6 ft), while *E. f.* Kewensis, *E. f.* Vegetus, *E. f.* Coloratus and *E. f.* Emerald 'n Gold vary in height between 30–60cm (12–24 in). Some members of this species appear to have both trailing and climbing forms. Another small euonymus of compact habit is *E. japonicus* Microphyllus (Myrtifolius).

Both the evergreen and deciduous species of euonymus are almost essential plants for a shrub or mixed border. With their shiny green or variegated leaves they can provide an excellent contrast to flowering or other foliage plants. Some, such as *E. fortunei radicans*, a trailing and climbing shrub, are excellent grown against north-facing walls. Such shrubs are also good for ground cover, particularly where it is sunless. Others, such as *E. fortunei* Kewensis, that is low-growing and prostrate in habit, are most valuable for forming small hummocks or covering bare stretches of rock garden.

Where the climate is reasonably warm, the evergreen species *E. japonicus* can be used to make a hedge. This is particularly the case in coastal districts, where this euonymus is undoubtedly the most commonly-used hedging plant due to its tolerance of salt-laden winds.

E. fortunei Variegatus (Gracilis) is often grown as a tub plant, while *E. japonicus* Ovatus Aureus (Aureovariegatus), the most popular of the golden euonymus, is frequently grown indoors as an ornamental house plant.

Cultivation and propagation

Generally, euonymus will grow in partial shade or sun. The evergreens will tolerate quite a lot of shade, but, as they are not quite so robust as the deciduous euonymus, should be given some shelter. The variegated forms are rather less hardy than any of the others, and therefore appreciate the protection of a wall or bank, or the shelter of overhead trees. Euonymus will flourish in any ordinary garden soil.

Plant the evergreens in mid and late autumn (September and October), or late spring to early summer (April to May), deciduous shrubs between late autumn and mid spring (October and March), and container-grown types at any time. Determine the distance to be allowed between shrubs by adding together the spreads of adjoining plants and dividing the sum by two. For a hedge, allow 38–45cm (15–18 in) between each plant; the shrubs for this purpose should not be taller than 30cm (12 in). When you have planted a hedge, pinch out the growing points to encourage bushing, and repeat this process as necessary during the first year.

Dig a hole large enough to take the rootball and allow the roots to spread. After placing the rootball in position, fill in the hole with soil and firm gently by light treading. No regular pruning is necessary for specimen shrubs, but any thinning should be carried out in early spring (February). Clip hedges in late spring (April), and trim further in early or mid autumn (August and September).

Aphides and scale insects are the most common pests to attack euonymus. If the infestation of either of these becomes serious, spray with malathion, taking care to spray the undersides of the leaves. Leaf spot disease, indicated by brown spots on the leaves, can cause serious disfigurement; if this occurs, spray with captan. Powdery mildew often affects E. japonicus, and all infected shoots should be cut out and burnt. Spray with dinocap if this disease is serious. Euonymus are also liable to attack from honey fungus which can cause rapid death of the plant.

To propagate euonymus, take 8–10cm (3–4 in) long heel cuttings in early and mid autumn (August and September), insert them in growing compost and keep in a cold frame until they have rooted. Then plant them out in rows in a nursery bed, in late spring or early summer (April or May). After one or two years transplant them to their permanent growing quarters.

Some varieties to choose

The first dimension given in the list below is the height and the second is the spread, both after about 20 years' growth. Unless otherwise stated, assume that a cultivar has about the same dimensions as its species.

DECIDUOUS

E. alatus (winged spindle tree)
Slow-growing shrub with many branches, and branchlets characterized by winged corky bark. Excellent autumn colouring. 2·1 × 2·1m (7 × 7 ft).

E. europaeus (common spindle tree)
Vigorous shrub with green stems and mid green, oval leaves. Insignificant green-white flowers are followed by numerous rose-red capsules that open to reveal orange-red seeds. 2·5 × 1·8m (8 × 6 ft).

E. e. Albus	Yields snowy-white fruits.
E. e. Atropurpureus	Leaves purple throughout spring and summer, but turn vivid red in autumn.
E. e. Fructu-coccineo	Characterized by bright red seed capsules.
E. e. Red Cascade	Arching, near-pendulous branches weighed down by a profusion of rosy-red fruits.

E. latifolius
Has brilliant scarlet autumn tints, accompanied by persistent, large, drooping, scarlet fruits containing orange seeds. 3 × 2·5m (10 × 8 ft).

E. sachalinensis (E. planipes)
Produces the most brilliant foliage tints and large, scarlet fruits in autumn. 3 × 2·5m (10 × 8 ft).

E. yedoensis
Mid green leaves that turn yellow and red in autumn. Cymes of insignificant white flowers yield to large, persistent, conspicuous, rosy-pink fruits containing orange-red seeds. 4·5 × 3m (15 × 10 ft).

EVERGREEN

E. fortunei
Very hardy, trailing evergreen that is good for ground cover or as a self-clinging climber. Its leaves are mid green. and it gives pink fruits enclosing orange seeds in autumn. It appears to exist in a prostrate (juvenile) form that grows 30–90cm (12–36 in) high, and a climbing form (adult) that reaches 3m (10 ft) if grown against a wall. The spread for both is about 1·5m (5 ft).

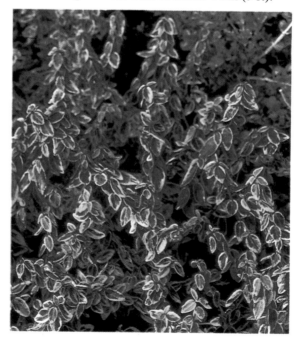

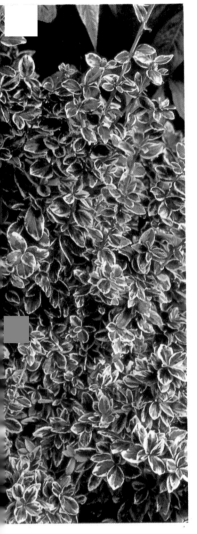

Above: E. japonicus *Ovatus Aureus needs a sunny site for its leaves to retain their colour. This variety can look particularly decorative even in winter (left) Far left: variegated* E. fortunei *Silver Queen needs the shelter of a wall or bank Below left:* E. fortunei *Emerald 'n Gold is one of the best small varieties, and its winter foliage (far left below) is especially attractive*

E. f. Carrierei	Has larger leaves than the species. 90cm–1·8m (3 × 6 ft).		Trailing form 45 × 90cm (18 × 36 in), climbing form 2·5m (8 ft) high. Small, bushy, creeping, free-fruiting form. 60cm × 2·5m (2 × 8 ft).
E. f. Coloratus	Produces deep red-purple leaves that persist through winter and turn green in summer. Height (climbing form) 2·5m (8 ft), (trailing form) 75cm (30 in), spread 1·2m (4 ft).	*E. f.* Vegetus	
		E. japonicus	Upright bushy shrub. Excellent for hedges in milder districts. 3 × 1·8m (10 × 6 ft).
E. f. Emerald Cushion	Dwarf, mounded, rich green shrub. 30 × 60cm (12 × 24 in).	*E. j.* Aureopictus (Aureus)	Leaves have a golden centre and a green margin. 1·5 × 1·5m (5 × 5 ft).
E. f. Emerald 'n Gold	Golden-variegated leaves, pink-tinged in winter. 30cm × 1·2m (12 in × 4 ft).	*E. j.* Microphyllus (Myrtifolius)	Slow-growing, compact, green bush. Similar forms are *E. j.* Microphyllus Pulchellus (Aureus) with golden leaves and *E. j.* Microphyllus Variegatus that has leaves with a white margin. All 60 × 30cm (24 × 12 in).
E. f. Emerald Gaiety	Variegated white-leaved bush. 30cm × 1·2m (12 in × 4 ft).		
E. f. Kewensis	Prostrate form with minute leaves. Suitable for rock gardens. 30 × 60cm (12 × 24 in). Will also climb.		
E. f. Silver Queen	Green leaves with a creamy-white margin.	*E. j.* Ovatus Aureus (Aureovariegatus)	A golden euonymus. 1·5 × 1·2m (5 × 4 ft).

FUCHSIA

Type	tender, half-hardy or hardy, deciduous flowering shrubs
Common name	fuchsia
Family	ONAGRACEAE
Flowering season	early summer to late autumn (May–October), sometimes longer
Planting date	outdoors: mid spring to mid summer (March–early June); repotting, as necessary, mid spring to mid autumn (March–September)
Mature size/shape	30cm–2m (1–6½ ft), mostly bushy; some prostrate, sprawling or semi-climbing to 4m (13 ft)

Fuchsias were named after a German physician, Professor Leonhart Fuchs (1501–1506), who is chiefly remembered for an early 'herbal' illustrated by unusually beautiful woodcuts. He never saw the plants called after him as he died long before the first fuchsia was discovered.

History and development
Although fuchsias were known and grown in Britain in the late 18th century, the fuchsia story, so far as gardeners are concerned, really began in the 1820s when a species called *Fuchsia magellanica* was introduced from Chile. It was far hardier and more variable than *F. coccinea* that was already in cultivation. Some forms were quite stiff and angular in branching, others more slender and lax. The flowers too, though fairly small, varied in colour and shape, some having short oval sepals, while others were short and narrow. One of these natural variations, *Fuchsia magellanica* Gracilis, is still a popular shrub for planting outdoors as are some other forms and hybrids. But what was important about the Magellan fuchsia was that it could be interbred with other species and was able to pass on to its offspring a greatly extended capacity for variation.

Very soon gardeners had crossed it with *F. coccinea* producing quite a showy shrub, which was christened *F. globosa* because of its much rounder flowers, particularly when in bud and half open.

The next and really vital step occurred in 1838 when Theodore Hartweg went to Mexico at the behest of the Horticultural Society (it had not yet acquired the prefix 'Royal') to look for new plants in the mountains. He discovered 'a most beautiful broad-leaved fuchsia'. It was sent home, named *Fuchsia fulgens*, and within a few years had been crossed with *F. magellanica*, *F. coccinea* and *F. globosa*. This resulted in a completely new race of man-made fuchsias, different from any of the parent species, with greatly increased flower size and diversity in colour, shape and plant habit.

Almost at a stroke, what we think of today as garden fuchsias were born. Although they have been developing ever since, nearly all the elements on which this advance was based were already there by the mid 1840s. Some early varieties are still grown and admired; for example the Chillerton Beauty, introduced in 1847, is still one of the dozen or so best fuchsias for planting out of doors.

Hybrids
As time went by, other species were introduced into the breeding programme, most notably *F. triphylla*, an especially elegant West Indian species that has passed on its long, slender, almost tubular flowers and its relative tenderness to fine garden hybrids such as Gartenmeister Bonstedt and Thalia.

Since *F. magellanica* was fairly hardy and *F. fulgens* distinctly tender, with *F. coccinea* occupying an intermediate position, it is not surprising that subsequent garden hybrids display a widely-ranging sensitivity to cold. In Great Britain, a few are purely greenhouse plants, many are half-hardy (can be planted outdoors in summer but need protection in winter), and some are hardy enough to be grown outside in most places though they may be killed during exceptionally severe winters.

Left: broad-leaved
Fuschia fulgens,
brought from Mexico in
the mid 19th century
Below: Fuchsia
triphylla *Thalia, a*
West Indian species
with slender tubular
flowers
Below right: Fuchsia
procumbens, *a tender*
prostrate species,
quite different from
the garden races
Bottom right: the
arching Mrs Popple,
one of the hardier,
long-flowering varieties
Below, far right:
aptly-named Mission
Bells variety is
strong and vigorous

Gardeners have been captivated by man-made hybrids on account of their great variety in form and colour. Some have single flowers, some semi-double, others fully double. A few varieties, such as Bon Accord, have quite small upward-facing flowers and, at the other extreme, giants such as Texas Longhorn have pendant flowers fully 15cm (6 in) across. The colour range is from white, palest pink and lavender, to salmon, scarlet, crimson and purple; colour in sepal and petal often contrasts and is sometimes different from the tube.

But it is not so much the colours themselves as their many different combinations, plus the variety of flower form and plant habit, that have made it possible for breeders to go on producing new cultivars for over a century, without yet appearing to have exhausted the resources of the fuchsia. This is well-illustrated by the long descriptive trade catalogues devoted exclusively to the plants. Some estimates put the present number of fuchsias at over 2,000.

Some tender species

Today about a hundred tender species are known, all from Central and South America, New Zealand and Tahiti. The flowers attract bees and humming-birds for pollination, and some are most beautiful, though not as a rule very showy, and they are quite different in character from the garden races. Not many are grown in gardens though *Fuchsia procumbens* is sometimes seen as a pot plant; this is prostrate and has small, upturned, purplish and green-tipped flowers and bright red berries. *F. arborescens* has larger leaves with clusters of narrowly-tubular flowers rather like those of a lilac; it can grow to the size of a tree and is occasionally seen trained on the back wall of a heated conservatory. *F. cordifolia*, a straggly bush with scarlet, green tipped flowers, will also train on a wall, either outside in a warm sheltered spot, or in a frost-proof greenhouse.

Flowering season

Fuchsias have an exceptionally long flowering season and some varieties would bloom all the year round if the temperature never dropped below about 13°C (35°F) and there were no more than twelve hours of darkness. These are mostly what the scientists call 'long day' plants, meaning that their flowering-mechanism is triggered by long days and short nights, in contrast to chrysanthemums, that are typically geared to short day and long night flowering.

Modern research, giving a fascinating insight into plant behaviour, has shown that fuchsias in the greenhouse can be made to flower earlier than normal. This is achieved by illuminating them for an hour or so in the middle of the night,

thus breaking a long night into two short ones.

But in practice, most gardeners are prepared to settle for a five- to six-month flowering period from early summer to late autumn (May to October), involving little artificial heat even for the more tender varieties, and with no interference in normal day lengths.

Some of the hardier varieties, such as Margaret and Mrs Popple, will flower for that length of time outdoors or, if the weather is mild, may even go on flowering until Christmas. Others tend to bloom in a succession of flushes, or periods of flowering, rather like modern roses.

By their profusion and continuity of display in both garden and greenhouse, fuchsias are un-excelled by any other easily-grown plant.

Cutting and propagation
The plant can be propagated readily by cuttings 5–8cm (2–3 in) long, prepared from young shoots at any time from spring to early autumn (March–August). The cuttings root quickly in a propagator filled with sandy or peaty compost or even in a pot placed inside a polythene bag. Once well-rooted, they should be potted singly in small pots with John Innes No 2 or loamless/soilless compost, and then moved on to larger pots as necessary. Cuttings of half-hardy fuchsias should be taken from half-ripe wood and rooted in the late summer to mid autumn period (July–September). The young plants may be kept going slowly during the winter in a temperature above 9°C (48°F).

Pinching and training

Varieties of a sprawling or weeping habit, such as Cascade, Mrs Marshall, Marinka and Golden Marinka, are excellent for hanging baskets or window boxes. Many of the upright varieties can be trained quite easily to form pyramids; those slightly arching in habit also make fine standards (branched heads on bare but sturdy stems) and some kinds, with very long stems, can be spread out on trellis work or wires fixed beneath the greenhouse rafters.

If you want bushy fuchsias, you should pinch out the tip of each rooted cutting when the plant is 15–20cm (6–8 in) high. This will make it produce several sideshoots more rapidly than it would do if left to grow naturally, and these sideshoots can themselves be pinched when 15–20cm (6–8 in) long, to make them branch again.

Alternatively, if you want to form a standard, do not pinch the cutting but encourage it to grow straight up, removing all sideshoots back to one leaf and tying the main stem to a cane to keep it as straight as possible. Then, when the desired height has been reached, usually between 75–100cm (2½–3 ft), remove the tip of the stem and allow the sideshoots to develop freely from the uppermost buds. This will produce the bushy head mentioned above.

Fuchsias are easy to pinch and train and you can form other shapes quite readily, including what are known as pyramids (though they are really cones), and espaliers that have an erect central stem with branches trained in horizontal tiers.

Left: Fuchsia cordifolia, *a greenhouse species*
Below left: Golden Marinka, *with its unusual and attractive variegated foliage*
Below: Mrs Marshall, *a sprawling variety much used in hanging baskets and window boxes*

Planting out, pruning and winter care

From late spring (April) onwards, half-hardy fuchsias should be grown without artificial heat and, for the last few weeks before being planted outdoors in early or mid summer (May or June), they are better in a frame than in a greenhouse. By autumn, they can be lifted, repotted and returned to a frost-free greenhouse where they are allowed to rest and will drop their leaves.

Hardy varieties can be planted outside from mid spring to mid summer (March–June), and are best placed with their uppermost roots at least 5cm (2 in) below the soil level. In cold districts you can ensure protection by spreading a 5cm (2 in) layer of peat over the roots in early winter. Then, even if frost kills the top growth, as often happens, the plant will probably throw up new stems straight from the roots in the following spring.

In any case, you should prune all fuchsias in mid spring (March), shortening straggly stems and removing weak or damaged ones. Do not prune back in autumn as the old wood provides further protection to the root stock.

In winter, even the most tender fuchsias will survive as long as the temperature never falls below 7°C (45°F) and many will grow in unheated or almost unheated greenhouses.

Plants that have been trained as standards, or pyramids, or other interesting shapes, are valuable and should be kept going from year to year by being sheltered in the greenhouse during winter.

Watering and feeding

Fuchsias like all reasonably fertile soils and will grow in light or shade although they flower most freely in the sun. If they are under glass, you may have to shade them a little in hot weather, to prevent their leaves and flowers from being scorched. They need plenty of water while in full growth during spring and summer, but in winter, when days are dull and temperatures are low, keep the soil just moistened.

The plants require moderate feeding when growing from early summer to early autumn (May–April) so add a little liquid fertilizer to the water every 10–15 days. But do not use more than is recommended by the maker's instructions, for the soft foliage of fuchsia is easily damaged by over-feeding.

Pests and diseases

The plant can also be severely damaged by capsid bugs which are insects so small and active that they frequently escape detection. The injury they cause is distinctive; leaves distort and flower production falls off rapidly. Greenfly also attacks fuchsias and both pests can be controlled by the occasional spraying with an insecticide containing diazinon, BHC or malathion. Whitefly can be found on fuchsias, especially those under glass, and should be controlled with the same sprays.

Fuchsias are seldom subject to disease though grey mould may damage the plants in winter if temperatures are too low and the soil and atmosphere too moist.

HAMAMELIS

Type	hardy, deciduous shrub
Common name	witch hazel
Family	HAMAMELIDACEAE
Flowering season	mid winter–early spring (December–February)
Planting date	late autumn–mid spring (October–March); from containers, anytime
Mature size	1·8–3m (6–10 ft) high, 1·8–2·5m (6–8 ft) spread

The name hamamelis is said to come from *hama* and *mela*, the Greek words for together and fruit, because flowers and fruit can sometimes be found side by side on the same plant. It was discovered in China by the plant collector Charles Maries in 1878 but was relatively unused in Britain for about 20 years after this.

These deciduous plants need not be pruned, although if the side branches are cut back in the formative years a small 'trunk and tree' effect is produced, rather than the natural bush shape. The plants will withstand cold conditions and even the flowers will not be damaged by a touch of frost. A light, loamy soil suits them best, with an addition of peat or leaf mould at planting time.

Propagation is easiest from seed but they often do not germinate for two years. Sow seed in boxes of soil, peat and sand mixture. The Chinese and Japanese varieties of hamamelis are often grafted onto *Hamamelis virginiana* to give them a vigorous root-stock, as cuttings of these varieties are difficult to root. Grafting should be done under glass in the spring.

Hamamelis japonica from Japan has slightly-fragrant yellow flowers. The variety *H. j. arborea* is more vigorous and has darker-coloured flowers, while *H. j. zuccariniana* has lemon-yellow flowers that do not appear until mid spring (March).

Hamamelis mollis from China is often said to be the most beautiful. It has a primrose-like fragrance with golden-yellow flowers that proliferate from mid winter to early spring (mid December to mid February). *H. m.* Pallida, a recent variety, produces large, sulphur-yellow flowers in clusters.

Hamamelis virginiana, the American witch hazel, flowers in the autumn before the leaves fall, and as the flowers are altogether smaller than their Asian counterparts, they are not easily seen. The bark and leaves of this plant are the source of a medicinal oil used in the preparation of bay rum.

There are now several new forms and hybrids. Successful varieties include *Hamamelis × intermedia* Diane, a red-flowered cultivar, and *H. × i.* Jelena with large, coppery flowers and spreading habit; the leaves of both colour well in autumn.

Above: Hamamelis japonica arborea, *a tall-growing variety, flowering in spring*
Below: Hamamelis mollis, *most popular of witch hazels, in flower during winter*

HEBE

Type	hardy and semi-hardy evergreen flowering shrubs
Family	SCROPHULARIACEAE
Flowering season	mainly mid–late summer (June–July)
Planting date	mid–late autumn (September–October), or late spring–early summer (April–May); from containers at any time
Mature size/shape	mainly rounded, prostrate and erect-growing; height from 5cm–2·5m (2 in–8 ft), spread from 15cm–2·5m (6 in–8 ft)

These plants used to be included by botanists in the genus veronica, but in recent years the shrubby types have been separated from the annual, perennial herbaceous, and rock plants, and placed in separate genus – hebe – consisting of about 100 species of evergreen flowering shrubs. They are grown mainly for their decorative flowers and shapely foliage, and were given their name in honour of Hebe, the Greek goddess who was cup-bearer to the gods on Mount Olympus.

Some of the species originate in South America, but most come from New Zealand, which has a predominance of coastal areas. This has tended to make hebe develop as excellent plants for the seaside. They are exceptionally tolerant of high winds and salt-laden gales – one form, *H. × franciscana*, is regarded as the most wind-and-salt tolerant of all seaside shrubs. Unfortunately, these characteristics have the disadvantage of making hebe somewhat on the tender side, because the climate tends to be warmer in coastal districts than inland. It is therefore important to consider most hebe as half-hardy plants likely to thrive best in warm, sheltered gardens. Wherever they are planted they must always be sheltered from severe frost. In Britain many of the more delicate species and cultivars that do not thrive inland are quite happy if planted along the south and west coasts, even in exposed places.

The flowers are mostly coloured blue, lavender, mauve, purple, lilac, pink and red, with a few white exceptions. They are usually crowded in racemes or spikes that vary in length from one plant to another; the smallest is about 2·5–5cm (1–2 in) in length increasing to 15cm (6 in) long in the case of *H. salicifolia*. In addition there is great variation in the size of the flowers in the racemes or spikes.

Above: the summer-flowering Hebe *Great Orme is very resistant to seaside winds.* H. salicifolia *(right) can reach a height of 2·5m (8 ft)*

79

Hebe have a long flowering period that begins in early summer and continues until late autumn (May to October), and frequently much later. For instance, *H. × franciscana*, a very compact, rounded hybrid, produces its dense racemes of bright violet-blue, scented flowers intermittently throughout the year.

The foliage of hebe is a valued asset in the garden because it is often dense enough to make an excellent screen. The leaves are usually lanceolate or ovate, and very variously coloured, ranging from dark green through violet-purple, coppery-red and grey, and including the golden foliage of *H. loganioides*, the silver-edged leaves of *H. × andersonii* Alba Variegata and the sulphur-yellow, variegated ones of *H. × andersonii* Aurea Variegata. Some forms – called 'whipcord' hebe – have closely overlapping, scale-like leaves, resembling the foliage of cupressus (cypress).

The largest in size is *H. salicifolia*, with a height and spread of 2·5m (8 ft); at the other end of the scale there is the tiny, cushion-forming cultivar *H. buchananii* Minor with a height of 5cm (2 in) and spread of 15cm (6 in).

Hebe are most valuable in a shrub or mixed border, and prostrate and low-growing cultivars such as *H. Carl Teschner*, *H. carnosula* and *H. pinguifolia* Pagei make very good ground cover plants. The dwarf hebe used for this purpose are generally hardy and can therefore be grown in town gardens. The more tender species and cultivars usually have to be given wall protection when grown in inland gardens.

Another more unusual function of hebe is making informal hedges. For rather taller hedges, almost any variety of *H. speciosa* is suitable. For a hedge up to about 90cm (3 ft) or so high, choose *H. Alicia Amherst*, but if one twice this height is required, plant *H. Midsummer Beauty*. *H. brachysiphon* (*traversii*) will make an attractive 1·2m (4 ft) high hedge, and *H. anomala* is suitable for a hedge no taller than 60cm (2 ft).

Cultivation and propagation

All hebe should be planted in full sun, and they need some protection where exposure to frost is likely. They thrive in any well-drained soil, even chalk, and can be planted in industrial areas.

Plant bare-root hebe during mid and late autumn (September and October), or in late spring and early summer (April and May); container-grown plants can be established at any time. Determine the planting distance between two hebe shrubs by adding their respective ultimate spreads and dividing by two.

To propagate, take 8cm (3 in) cuttings of non-flowering shoots in late summer and early autumn (July and August) and plant them in a compost mixture suitable for cuttings in a cold frame (preferably in a frost-free position). The following late spring (April) pot the rooted cuttings into 8cm (3 in) pots and place them outdoors. Plant out the hardy species and cultivars permanently in mid autumn (September), and the more tender ones the following spring.

Some varieties to choose

In the following selection the first figure given is the height and the second is the spread after about 20 years' growth. When this is not shown for any cultivar, assume that its dimensions are similar to those of the species. All those listed are hardy in coastal areas.

Hardy

H. albicans
Rounded shrub with glaucous leaves that make it an excellent foliage plant. Its white flowers appear in mid to late summer (June to July). 60 × 60cm (2 × 2 ft).

H. brachysiphon (*traversii*)
Rounded shrub with dark green, narrowly oval leaves. It bears masses of white flowers in mid to late summer (June to July), and is excellent for hedging. 1·5 × 1·5m (5 × 5 ft).

H. Carl Teschner
Dwarf shrub of compact habit, admirable for ground cover. Its profusely-produced flowers are violet-blue with a white throat and are carried in short racemes. They appear in mid and late summer (June and July). 30 × 75cm (12 × 30 in).

H. Edinensis
Dwarf plant with tiny, bright green leaves, excellent for a rockery. It seldom flowers. 38 × 38cm (15 × 15 in).

H. Great Orme
Compact, bushy, upright shrub with dark green lanceolate leaves. It produces long, tapering racemes of pink flowers between early and late summer (May and July). Resistant to salt-laden winds. 90 × 90cm (3 × 3 ft).

H. pinguifolia Pagei
Grey-foliaged, low, bushy shrub that makes a very good ground cover and rock garden plant. Its profuse, short spikes of white flowers open during early and mid summer (May and June). 20 × 90cm (8 in × 3 ft).

Moderately hardy

H. armstrongii
One of the 'whipcord' species of hebe, with a dwarf, spreading, cupressus-like growth. Its foliage is the colour of old gold and is borne on olive green stems, and it produces white flowers from mid summer to early autumn (June to August). 75 × 75cm (2½ × 2½ ft).

H. Bowles' Hybrid
Pretty, low-growing shrub with crowded mauve-coloured racemes borne between early summer and mid autumn (May and September). 60 × 45cm (24 × 18 in).

H. × franciscana Blue Gem
Compact, dome-like shrub with rich green leaves and bright blue flowers that appear intermittently during the whole year. Very resistant to salt-laden winds. 1·2 × 1·2m (4 × 4 ft).

H. × franciscana Lavender Queen ✓
Tall, erect bush with medium green leaves. It produces lavender-blue flowers from late summer to mid winter (July to December), and even later. 1·8 × 1·5m (6 × 5 ft).

H. Midsummer Beauty ✓
This shrub has reddish undersides to its leaves, and its flowers are lavender-coloured, appearing continuously through the summer until mid winter (December). 1·8 × 1·8m (6 × 6 ft).

H. salicifolia ✓
Moderately large species with pale green lanceolate leaves and lilac-tinged white flowers that appear from mid summer to early autumn (June to August). 2·5 × 2·5m (8 × 8 ft). The variety *H.s.* Spender's Seedling has fragrant, white blooms.

H. Waikiki
Bushy shrub with bronze-tinted young shoots. The flowers are blue and appear in mid to late summer (June to July). 60 × 60cm (24 × 24 in).

HYDRANGEA

Type	deciduous and evergreen flowering shrubs and climbers
Family	HYDRANGEACEAE
Flowering season	mid summer–mid autumn (June–September)
Planting date	late autumn–early winter (October–November), or mid–late spring (March–April); container plants, anytime
Mature size/shape	shrubs: 75 × 75cm (2½ × 2½ ft) to 4.5 × 4.5m (15 × 15 ft); climbers: up to 7m (23 ft) high

The name hydrangea comes from *hydor* and *aggos*, the Greek words for water and a jar, after the shrub's cup-shaped fruits.

The hydrangea genus, HYDRANGEACEAE, is composed of 80 species. It is a most valuable family of flowering garden plants and contains both shrubs and climbers. There are deciduous and evergreen plants among the species but the climber *Hydrangea serratifolia* is the only popular one that is evergreen.

The shrubs are quite hardy in milder climates such as are found in the south and west of England, but in other areas the gardens must be very warm and sunny to ensure success. They make excellent shrubs for town and mild coastal districts. In severe, exposed areas hydrangeas can only be grown in a greenhouse or indoors. Generally speaking the climbing species are hardier than the shrubs.

The majority of hydrangeas produce flowers in flattened or dome-shaped heads on the ends of the previous year's growth. They are composed of flowers of two different sorts. Most are fertile but rather small and almost insignificant, yet coloured. The second kind are conspicuous with rather large, coloured sepals. These larger type of flowers are sterile and they are known as ray-florets. They occur on the outside of the head and in some cases, such as the lacecap hydrangeas, the fertile flowers grow in a ring of coloured ray-florets. There are other cultivars, particularly the mop-headed, or hortensia, group of *H. macrophylla* completely made up of sterile ray-florets.

Among the earlier species to be introduced into Western gardens was *H. arborescens* that is native to the eastern part of North America. It was first cultivated in 1736. Another hydrangea that grows wild in the United States is *H. cinerea* – introduced somewhat later, in 1908. A third, originally collected from the New World, is the evergreen climber *H. serratifolia*, this grows in a wild state in Chile. For the rest, almost all have their homes in the Far East – western China, Taiwan, South Korea, Japan and the Himalayas. *H. macrophylla*,

Below: Hydrangea serrata *Bluebird, a small, robust shrub belonging to the lacecaps group, with stout shoots, abruptly acuminate leaves, and both fertile and sterile florets*

the common hydrangea, with its numerous varieties of hortensias and lacecaps, first came from China and Japan.

The origin of one of the most distinctive and unusual hydrangeas, however, is rather a mystery. This is Ayesha, also listed as Silver Slipper, and it produces dense, flattened heads of greyish-lilac or pink, cup-shaped florets that have a slight but definite fragrance. Although it is different, it is normally classified in the hortensia group of *H. macrophylla*.

Perhaps lacking in any other quality, hydrangeas do have one exceptional ability that makes them invaluable in a garden of almost any size during the summer. This is their capacity for enlivening the scene with their bright green leaves and large, colourful flowers sometimes 30cm (12 in) in diameter, particularly in a shrub border where evergreens predominate, at a time when the picture might be starting to become a little drab because their flowering time has passed. Fortunately they vary quite widely in size, from dwarfs not exceeding 60cm, up to 4.5m or more in height (2–15 ft). So you can find one that would be suitable for almost any position.

Lacecap and mop-head cultivars make excellent informal screens and hedges and are often seen at seaside resorts; they tend to be more unusual in inland gardens. They are very resistant to wind and salt. Given the right climatic and soil conditions, there is no reason why they should not be used similarly anywhere.

They grow well in semi-shade and often do best in the dappled shelter of trees where other flowering subjects may not prosper.

The climbing hydrangeas are very valuable in a garden because of their hardiness. They are equally happy in sun or semi-shade and are useful for clothing a north-facing wall. They withstand atmospheric pollution and are therefore excellent for covering walls and fences as well as buildings in industrial areas.

The hortensia and lacecap groups of *H. macrophylla* are ideal for tub culture. In severe weather they can be brought under cover. This quality makes them suited to paved areas.

Planting

As mentioned previously, hydrangeas require fairly mild conditions. The best soil for them is good, moisture-retentive loam, previously enriched with well-rotted manure, garden compost or peat. The naturally blue *H. macrophylla* varieties will not produce good blue blooms in alkaline soil and need dressings of peat and applications of sequestrene or aluminium sulphate if they are planted in it. Pink varieties become less clear or assume purple hues in acid soil and need an additional dressing of ground limestone.

Plant hydrangeas in late autumn and early winter (October and November) or in mid and late spring (March and April). Container plants can be established at any time.

Sufficient space is afforded between a hydrangea and its neighbour if you determine the

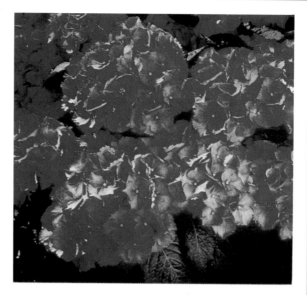

distance by adding the ultimate spread of each together and dividing the sum by two. When used for hedging, the planting distance should be 60cm–2m (2–6½ ft) according to variety.

For a bare-root hydrangea, dig a hole wide enough so that the roots, after being pulled apart gently, can be spread out in it, and of such a depth that the soil mark on the main stem, showing how far down it had been planted in the nursery, is level with the surface of the soil in its new quarters. Then place the plant into position, replace the excavated soil and firm it. In the case of a pot plant, it is advisable not to disturb the roots. The hole should be of such a depth that the soil at the top of the rootball is level with that of the bed.

For pot culture, plant in 15cm (6 in) pots of J.I. No 3 or a soilless compost. You must be careful not to use lime in the case of blue cultivars and so compost must be specially prepared for this purpose. Start the plants into growth in late winter (January) at a temperature of 9°C (48°F), keep them moist and, finally, water them well when they are in full leaf. Normally you grow hydrangeas in pots for one season after which you can plant them outdoors in a sheltered place.

Plant climbing types about 38cm (15 in) away from a wall or fence and train them back to the structure that they will climb by means of their aerial roots. You can also train them up a tree.

Cultivation and propagation

Keep hydrangeas well watered particularly during dry spells. They appreciate an annual mulch of well-rotted manure or compost in spring.

Most hydrangea species require no pruning but you should remove dead flower-heads in spring. Two exceptions are *H. arborescens* and *H. paniculata*; they should have their previous year's flowering shoots reduced to half in spring. The two or three-year-old shoots of *H. macrophylla* need to be thinned out at ground level to promote strong, new shoots.

Propagate hybrids by taking cuttings and putting them into sandy soil in a cold frame in early autumn (August).

Above, far left: low-growing Hydrangea macrophylla*;*
Above left: H. arborescens *Grandiflora, with large, globular heads of sterile florets*
Above: climbing H. petiolaris, *with large-flowered clematis*
Left: H. macrophylla *Hamburg*

Some varieties to choose

This genus contains numerous species, varieties and cultivars of which the following form a brief and easily-cultivated selection. The dimensions given after each one listed correspond to height and spread respectively.

Climbers

H. serratifolia (integerrima)	An evergreen species that grows in sun or shade. Creamy-white flowers in mid and late summer (June and July). $6 \times 2m$ ($20 \times 6\frac{1}{2}$ ft).
H. petiolaris	A strong, self-clinging species that is excellent for growing in trees and on a shady wall. It also makes a very attractive large shrub. Has flowers in corymbs composed of white, sterile florets surrounding its greenish-white fertile flowers during mid summer (July). 7m (23 ft) high.

Shrubs

H. arborescens	A small species shrub of loose growth. It has corymbs, 15cm (6 in) across, of creamy-white flowers from late summer to mid autumn (July to September). $1.5 \times 1.5m$ (5×5 ft).
H. aspera	It is massed in mid and late summer (June and July) with large heads of pale porcelain-blue flowers, surrounded by a circle of lilac-pink or white ray-florets. $2.5 \times 2.5m$ (8×8 ft).
H. involucrata	A pretty dwarf species with blue or rosy-lilac and white blooms. $1.2 \times 1.2m$ (4×4 ft).

Shrubs continued

H. macrophylla This species covers two very important groups of hydrangeas – the hortensias or mop-heads, and the lacecaps. The dimension given with each variety below is the height: height and spread can be regarded as about the same as the height.

HORTENSIAS Their florets are sterile, forming large round heads. They bloom from late summer to mid autumn (July to September). A good selection includes the following:

Altona Deep pink, almost red. 1.5m (5 ft).
Amethyst Pink or flax-blue double flowers. 1.5m (5 ft).
Ami Pasquier Crimson. 1m (3¼ ft).
Hamburg Deep pink to crimson. Deep blue, on blueing soil. 2.5m (8 ft).
Holstein Pink. Sky blue, on blueing soil. Large flowers. 1.5m (5 ft).
Kluis Superba Rosy-crimson or blue, on blueing soil. 1.5m (5 ft).
Madame Emile Mouillière White becoming pink-tinted. 2.5m (8 ft).
Maréchal Foch Rich rose or deep purple-blue, on blueing soil. 2.5m (8 ft).
Parsival Deep rosy-pink. Violet purple on blueing soil. 1.5m (5 ft).
President Doumer Deep crimson. 75cm (2½ ft).
Princess Beatrix Clear red. Compact. 75cm (2½ft).
Westfalen Rich crimson or violet. 1.5m (5 ft).

LACECAPS Have flattened corymbs of fertile flowers surrounded by a ring of coloured ray-florets, between late summer and mid autumn (July and September). The following represent a good choice:

Blue Wave Heads of blue fertile flowers surrounded by large ray-florets, coloured pink to blue. Best in semi-shade. 1.8m (6 ft).
Lanarth White Dwarf with pure white florets surrounding blue or pink fertile flowers. 75cm (2½ ft).
Mariesii Rosy-pink or blue. 1.8m (6 ft).
Tricolor Pale pink to white flowers. Green, grey and pale yellow variegated leaves. 1.8m (6 ft).
Seafoam Blue fertile flowers surrounded by white ray-florets. 1.8m (6 ft).
White Wave Bluish or pinkish fertile flowers margined by large, pearly white ray-florets. 1.5m (5 ft).

H. paniculata A large shrub with terminal panicles of white, sterile florets during early and mid autumn (August and September).
H.p. Grandiflora is a very hardy cultivar and is more frequently grown. 4.5 × 4.5m (15 × 15 ft).

H. quercifolia A medium-sized hydrangea that gives beautiful autumn tints and white flowers during late summer (July). 2 × 1.5m (6½ × 5 ft).

H. serrata An important dwarf species that, although charming in itself, has given rise to a number of beautiful small cultivars such as *H.s.* Bluebird, with blue fertile and sterile florets that become reddish-purple on chalk soil and blue on acid, and *H.s.* Rosalba with blue fertile florets and white sterile ones, quickly turning crimson. 90 × 90cm (3 × 3 ft).

H. villosa One of the most beautiful late summer-flowering species. Medium-sized, it has 15cm (6 in) long, pale purple corymbs in early autumn (August); likes semi-shade. 2.5 × 3m (8 × 10 ft).

Left: Hydrangea macrophylla *Mariesii, with large, sterile, ray-florets around insignificant fertile florets; top:* H. paniculata, *with pyramidal inflorescences Above: the eye-catching* H. villosa, *with hairy leaves and flower-stalks*

ILEX

Type	evergreen and deciduous, green and variegated, berried trees and shrubs
Common name	holly
Family	AQUIFOLIACEAE
Flowering season	late spring – early summer (April–May)
Fruiting season	early winter – early spring (November–February)
Planting date	late spring – early summer (April–May), or mid – late autumn (September–October)
Mature size/shape	height 45cm–9m (18 in–30 ft), spread 1–9m (3–30 ft). Various, from conical to weeping

To many people, holly bushes are merely plants that grow wild, with their brilliant red berries set deep among the rich green, spiny leaves providing the most lovely, colourful, welcoming decorations for our homes each Christmas. There are also moments when these same bushes, seen growing without any berries, are deadly dull. Yet when laden with fruit, particularly when it peeps through their leaves whitened with glistening snow, holly can present a beautiful sight.

However, this large genus – composed of 300 species of tender and hardy, deciduous and evergreen, trees and shrubs – provides many elegant specimens that are hardy in a temperate climate. It is doubtful whether any genus of trees and shrubs presents greater variety or is more versatile than ilex; beyond the bounds of the very popular green-leaved, red-berried species and their cultivars there are others with a wide range of leaf colorations and markings; berry tints, shapes, stem colourings and other variations give almost infinite opportunities for ringing the changes in the garden scene.

It is as well to mention at the outset that their somewhat inconspicuous white and green flowers that appear in late spring and early summer (April and May) display very little beauty and are likely to pass unnoticed. Male and female flowers are usually borne on separate trees; when these are planted side by side, the females yield masses of berries that last well into the winter until they are ultimately eaten by birds. Some cultivars, however, are self-fertile (or hermaphroditic); examples of these include *Ilex × altaclarensis* J. C. van Tol and *I. aquifolium* Pyramidalis.

are orange. The berries of *I. crenata*, *I. glabra* (the inkberry) and *I. macrocarpa*, another deciduous species, are all shiny black.

Although holly trees and shrubs are both evergreen and deciduous, the evergreen types are far more common.

Many of the holly cultivars have splendid foliage so varied in character that it is hard to do them credit in a few words. Some, such as *I. × altaclarensis* Camelliifolia, have reddish-purple hues in their green leaves when they are young. Quite a number of plants have reddish or purple stems. Among these are *I. × altaclarensis* Maderensis Variegata and *I. aquifolium* Madame Briot. There is at least one species, *I. serrata*, that is deciduous and has attractive tints in autumn.

Perhaps the most exceptional species is the Canary Island holly, *I. platyphylla*, that has dark green, leathery, short-toothed leaves, sometimes 13cm (5 in) long and 7cm (2¾ in) wide. These are closely rivalled by the large, bold leaves of *I. latifolia*. It is striking how holly leaves vary in shape. The most intriguing leaf forms are the bat's wing shapes of *I. pernyi*, rivalled only by the kite-shaped leaves of *I. cornuta* O. Spring. Most holly leaves have sharp spines but a few are spineless, or almost so, such as *I × altaclarensis* Camelliifolia and *I. aquifolium* Pyramidalis. Another curiosity in this respect is the silver form of the hedgehog holly, *I. aquifolium* Ferox Argentea, that has spines arising from the surface of the leaves. Lastly, and perhaps the most unholly-like of all, is the dwarf *I. crenata* Mariesii that is crowded with tiny round leaves.

The species and cultivars that have variegated foliage possibly constitute the crowning glory of the ilex genus. Many claim that it includes among the best of the variegated shrubs. A great number of shades and patterns have been woven on the leaves of this type of holly and the many combinations include splashings, mottling, blotching, stripes and, very often, edgings. These may consist of any of the following colours: green, pale green, gold, yellow, creamy-white, white and grey.

Hollies are very tolerant as a group. While *I. crenata*, *I. aquifolium* and their cultivars are content in dry-acid soil, all will grow in clay soil; in fact, *I. aquifolium* and its varieties are happy in both extreme acidic and alkaline conditions. One holly at least, the deciduous *I. verticillata*, with its autumnal, yellow-tinted foliage, flourishes on a damp site. Deep shade does not worry either *I. × altaclarensis* or *I. aquifolium* and their cultivars. Both the latter, together with *I. cornuta* and its hybrids, withstand atmospheric pollution in industrial towns. Exposure at the seaside is no problem to *I. × altaclarensis* and *I. aquifolium* and their cultivars; *I. × altaclarensis* Maderensis is especially resistant to strong winds.

I. aquifolium, the common holly, has a very widespread habitat throughout the world stretching from Europe to North Africa and China. It has been in cultivation since ancient times. Over the years it has been used to decorate cottages and

Above: Ilex aquifolium, *common holly, a useful and attractive evergreen that makes excellent hedging or can be grown as a specimen tree in the garden* Left: *I. a. Aureomarginata, an ornamental variety*

As far as shape is concerned it is possible to find ilex that grow as tall and wide pyramids, or miniatures, such as *I. crenata* Mariesii that makes an excellent subject for rockeries, and *I. c.* Golden Gem that grows to a height of 30–60cm (12–24 in) with a spread of 60–120cm (2–4 ft). Between these limits, there are round bushes, ones of conical and columnar shapes, and others with weeping and fastigiate habits.

In terms of size there is also a wide selection. Two of the smaller hollies have been mentioned already. At the other end of the scale are found heights of up to 9m (30 ft) and spreads of the same dimensions. Fortunately most hollies do not mind being pruned so that size can be largely controlled; although most hollies are naturally pyramidal, the shape too can be modified to a certain extent by judicious cutting back.

Much of the attraction of members of the ilex genus lies in the variously-sized coloured berries they produce that are so evident in winter. In the majority of species and hybrids they are red, but on *I. aquifolium* Amber they are bronze-yellow; *I. a.* Bacciflava's are yellow, while those of the deciduous *I. decidua* and the evergreen *I. latifolia*

mansions in the depth of winter, particularly at Christmas when so many other shrubs are leafless and colourless.

Many of the forms and cultivars grown today are of garden origins, but there are still a large number of species that have originated in widely-separated parts of the world: China, Japan, the Himalayas, North America and the Canary Isles.

With such variation and brilliance of colour, these plants are obviously of value to present-day gardens. They are fairly slow-growing and most of them can be readily trimmed, so size will not become a problem for a long time. Another great asset they possess is their ability to offer a wide range of shapes that help so much in creating a harmonious garden scene. They can be splendid when planted as specimens in a long stretch of grass. The more columnar forms make excellent markers for a gateway and might well supersede some of the conifers of similar habit. In a shrubbery, or simply a shrub border, you can use some of the brilliantly-coloured varieties most effectively to brighten up dark spots and create interest with their variety of size and shape.

Several species and their cultivars make good hedges that are easily kept in shape – and with the sharp spines of the leaves they are almost impenetrable to man and beast. *I. aquifolium* and its cultivars Argenteomarginata and Madame Briot make excellent hedges of this sort, while *I. × altaclarensis* Camelliifolia, *I. × a.* Golden King and *I. × a.* J. C. van Tol make very beautiful but less prickly ones. *I. crenata* Convexa, reaching 1·2m (4 ft) in height, makes a superb low hedge.

Cultivation

We have already referred to the tolerance shown by the ilex genus. Practically all its members are hardy so when they are established there is little fear of their meeting disaster. They will grow quite well in both sun and shade. However, it must be remembered that the variegated types need plenty of sun to colour well.

They can be grown in any ordinary garden soil but if something a bit moist and loamy can be provided the results are better.

The best times to plant hollies are late spring (late April), early summer (May), or mid to late autumn (September to October), although if the weather is good you can plant them at any time during the winter. You can, of course, plant containerized plants at any time of the year.

You calculate the distance that must be allowed between a holly and its neighbour in the normal way by adding the ultimate spread of each together and halving the sum. When planting a hedge, place hollies 60cm (24 in) apart.

It is best to plant holly (particularly the variegated forms of *I. aquifolium*) by digging a hole of such a diameter that it will take the rootball intact and of such a depth that the main stem is buried to the same extent as when it was growing in the nursery. When replacing the soil, firm it well by treading it in. When it is dry you must water the plants frequently. Always use young plants as

Left: Ilex aquifolium *Handsworth New Silver, a female clone with long, deeply-variegated, spiny leaves*
Below: Ilex × altaclarensis *Golden King, that has broad, nearly spineless leaves with bright yellow variegation*
Right: Ilex crenata *Mariesii, an unusual dwarf-growing form, compact, round-leaved and suitable for growing in a rock garden or trough*

larger ones very much resent root disturbance. If they are exposed to high winds during winter give them some protection by erecting a screen of sacking, polythene or wattle on the windward side, until they are established – after which they will need little attention. No regular pruning is required but if you want to clip holly to size and shape it, this should be done in late summer or early autumn (July or August). Hedges should be kept trimmed every year, preferably in late spring (April).

Keep a watch to check that no shoots on variegated hollies revert to green. If you find any, remove them immediately.

Holly is fairly free from disease but may be attacked by leaf miners. The larvae of this pest tunnel into the holly leaves. They should be sprayed regularly with BHC between mid summer and late autumn (June and October).

Propagation
Hollies are propagated by means of cuttings taken in early autumn (August). In addition they may be layered in late autumn (October).

Some varieties to choose
The following is a selection of the most popular of the hollies grown today. The first figure given in the dimensions is the ultimate height, and the second is the spread.

I. × altaclarensis
Has dark green leaves. Produces red berries. Has many beautiful cultivars, some of which are given below. 7·5 × 4·5m (25 × 15 ft).

I. × a. Balearica	Erect tree with almost spineless green leaves. Berries quickly. 7·5 × 3m (25 × 10 ft)
I. × a. Golden King	One of the best variegated, golden hollies. Red berries. 7·5 × 4m (25 × 12 ft)
I. × a. Hodginsii	Strong, vigorous male clone with purple stems. 7·5 × 4·5m (25 × 15 ft)
I. × a. Silver Sentinel	Erect, creamy-white and grey variegated, berry-producing tree. 7·5 × 2·5m (25 × 8 ft)
I. × a. Wilsonii	Dome-shaped tree with large clusters of red berries. 7·5 × 3·5m (25 × 11 ft)

I. aquifolium
Common holly, with an ultimate height and spread of 7·5 × 3m (25 × 10 ft); has numerous cultivars.

I. a. Angustifolia	Neat, pyramidal tree. Tiny red berries. 4·5 × 2·5m (15 × 8 ft)
I. a. Argenteomarginata Pendula	Perry's silver weeping holly has bright red berries. 3 × 4·5m (10 × 15 ft)
I. a. Aureomarginata	Has golden-edged leaves. Female trees bear red berries. 5·5 × 3m (18 × 10 ft)
I. a. Bacciflava	Has bright yellow berries. 5 × 5·5m (16 × 18 ft)
I. a. Golden Queen	Gold-margined leaves. No berries. Columnar 4·5 × 2·5m (15 × 8 ft)
I. a. Handsworth New Silver	Modest-growing tree with purple stems and grey and creamy-white colouring on leaves. Red berries. 4 × 2m (12 × 6 ft)

I. cornuta Burford Variegated
Leaves edged gold and suffused with varying shades of green. 3 × 3m (10 × 10 ft).

I. crenata
Small, slow-growing holly. Females have black berries. Excellent as a hedge. The cultivars are dwarf or modest growing. 2·5 × 2m (8 × 6 ft).

I. c. Convexa	100 × 75cm (3 × 2½ ft)
I. c. Golden Gem	45 × 100cm (1½ × 3 ft)
I. c. Mariesii	45 × 100cm (1½ × 3 ft)

I. pernyi
Has dwarf, pyramidal growth, near-triangular in shape; pale green leaves and small bright red berries. 2 × 1·2m (6 × 4 ft).

JASMINE

Type tender and hardy, deciduous, semi-deciduous and evergreen flowering shrubs and climbers

Family OLEACEAE

Planting dates hardy: late autumn–early winter (October–November) or early–mid spring (February–March); tender: early–mid spring (February–March); from containers at any time

Flowering season early summer–mid autumn (May–September) except *J. nudiflorum*–winter

Mature size/shape shrubs: height and spread from 25 × 60cm (10 × 24 in) to 2·4 × 1·5m (8 × 5 ft); climbers: 1·2–9m (4–30 ft) high

Special use perfume

Jasmine, or jessamine as they are sometimes called, are fairly popular as climbing plants, but the value of the ones that are self-supporting shrubs is not fully appreciated. This is a pity, because those sold in temperate areas such as the British Isles are hardy, whereas quite a number of the climbers are tender.

The jasminum genus is a large one, containing 300 species. The Persians called these plants 'yasmin', and the modern name is derived from the Latin version of this.

Many of the jasmine grown today originate from China. Notable exceptions to this are the shrubs *J. fruticans*, that grow wild in Mediterranean regions, and *J. humile wallichianum*, from north-east Nepal, and the climbers *J. dispersum* and *J. officinale* from the Himalayas, and *J. azoricum* that was introduced into Western gardens from Madeira. *J. officinale* has long been a favourite plant in Britain, and was grown in cottage gardens in Elizabethan times. Some of the others, however, are relative newcomers; the shrubs *J. humile revolutum* and *J. nudiflorum*, and the climbers *J. dispersum*, *J. floridum* and *J. polyanthum* were introduced to Western gardens at various times throughout the 19th century.

Jasmine flowers are tubular and often borne in terminal clusters, or emerge from the leaf joints; sometimes they form panicles. The flowers vary in

Jasminum mesnyi *with semi-double flowers (top) and* J. polyanthum *(right) are both tender climbers that can reach a height of up to 3m (10 ft)*

size from the tiny ones of the shrub *J. parkeri* to those of the tender climber *J. angulare*, that are 5cm (2 in) long. All the shrubby species have yellow blossoms; the climbers, however, are primarily white, cream and yellow, but there are exceptions such as *J. beesianum* that has deep velvet red flowers, and *J. × stephanense* with pale pink ones. The majority of the shrubs and climbers flower between early summer and mid autumn (May and September), but some, such as the tender climber *J. polyanthum*, flower from late spring to mid summer (April to June) when grown in a warm place in a mild district, and between early winter and late spring (November and April) when grown under glass.

All the shrubby species are more or less deciduous during a severe winter, but the stems maintain a green effect in most cases. The leaves of jasmine are usually trifoliate or pinnate with three to eleven leaflets. In some instances, such as the climbers *J. officinale* Aureovariegatum and *J. × stephanense*, the leaves are variegated. At least two of the more popular species, *J. fruticans* and the climber *J. beesianum*, bear black fruits after the flowers fade.

Jasmine are fairly modest growers and therefore suitable for smaller gardens. The smallest of the shrubs is the dwarf *J. parkeri*, that has a height of 25cm (10 in) and a spread of about 60cm (2 ft). One of the largest shrubs is *J. humile revolutum* that has maximum dimensions of about 2·5 × 1·5m (8 × 5 ft), after about 20 years' growth. The tender and hardy climbers range in height from *J. floridum* at

J. angulare *(above)* and J. officinale *(overleaf)* are both sweetly scented
Below: J. nudiflorum *must be pruned back hard as soon as it has flowered*

Some varieties to choose

The dimensions given for the shrubs are the height and spread after about 20 years' growth, and the ultimate height in the case of the climbers.

HARDY SHRUBS

J. fruticans	Semi-evergreen with erect growth. Has yellow flowers in terminal clusters appearing from mid summer to mid autumn (June to September), succeeded by black fruits. 1·5 × 1·5m (5 × 5 ft).
J. humile	Semi-evergreen, semi-scandent shrub. Has bright yellow flowers in terminal clusters that appear in mid to late summer (June to July). 1·2 × 1·2m (4 × 4 ft).
J.h. revolutum	Has dark evergreen leaves and relatively large, yellow, fragrant blooms borne during mid to late summer (June to July). 2·5 × 1·5m (8 × 5 ft).
J.h. wallichianum	A shrub of scandent growth, with leaves that have up to eleven leaflets. It produces pendant clusters of yellow blossoms from mid summer until mid autumn (June to September). 3 × 2·5m (10 × 8 ft).
J. nudiflorum (winter jasmine)	Winter-flowering shrub producing bright yellow flowers on naked green shoots from early winter until early spring (November to February). 3 × 2·5m (10 × 8 ft).
J. parkeri	Dwarf shrub with tiny yellow flowers. Excellent for rockeries. 25 × 60cm (10 × 24 in).

HARDY CLIMBERS

J. beesianum

Has long, pointed, dull green leaves. Although they are rather small, the scented flowers have an unusual deep velvet red colour. They open during early and mid summer (May and June), and are followed by long-lasting black berries. 3m (10 ft).

J. officinale (common jasmine)

Tall, twining climber with scented white flowers borne from mid summer to mid autumn (June to September). Plant in a sheltered position in cold districts. The form *J.o.* Affine is a greenhouse species. 9m (30 ft).

J. × stephanense

A vigorous climber with scented, pale pink flowers, borne in terminal clusters that appear during mid to late summer (June to July). Its leaves are often variegated. 6m (20 ft).

TENDER CLIMBERS

J. angulare

Has rather thick, dark, evergreen, trifoliate leaves. Its 5cm (2 in) long, scented white flowers are carried in large panicles and appear in early and mid autumn (August and September). 3m (10 ft).

J. floridum

Evergreen climber with yellow blooms that open between late summer and mid autumn (July and September). 1·8m (6 ft).

J. mesnyi (J. primulinum)

An almost evergreen climber. It has semi-double, bright yellow flowers, 5cm (2 in) long, that appear successively from mid spring to early summer (March to May). 3m (10 ft).

J. polyanthum

Vigorous twining species. Its fragrant white blooms, flushed rose on the outside, are borne in panicles and appear from late spring until mid summer (April to June) outdoors, and between early winter and late spring (November to April) under glass. 3m (10 ft).

1·2m (4 ft) to *J. polyanthum* and *J. × stephanense* at 4·5m (15 ft).

One particular value of the hardy and slightly tender species is that they will flourish in industrial areas. Some of the shrubs, such as *J. humile* and its forms and *J. nudiflorum*, are quite suitable for a north-facing wall or in a sunless position.

The shrubby species are most effective grown in mixed and shrub borders, where the more scandent types (those with a tendency to climb) can benefit from being given some support. Jasmine are also suitable for ground cover on rockeries, and the hardy climbers are invaluable for training against outside walls and fences or for clambering over trellises, arbours and pergolas. The tender types make a fine display in a cool greenhouse.

Cultivation and propagation

Outdoor jasmine thrive in any ordinary, well-drained garden soil. The more delicate ones need to be planted in a growing medium composed of equal parts of loam, peat and leaf mould, with a little sand or soilless compost. Plant bare-rooted jasmine in mild weather either in late autumn and early winter (October and November) or in early to mid spring (February to March). Most jasmine are usually supplied from the nurseries in containers, so can, in fact, be planted at any time.

Pot or plant the more tender species in a cool greenhouse border during early to mid spring (February to March). Determine planting distance for shrubby, outdoor plants by adding together the ultimate spreads of adjacent shrubs and dividing by two. For climbing species, allow a distance of 1·5–2·5m (5–8 ft) according to ultimate height and vigour.

The hardy species need little attention except that some protection might be given when the weather is very severe. Tender species planted in a cool greenhouse should be watered freely from mid spring until late autumn (March to October) and then sparingly. Train shoots to the walls or a trellis. Potted plants that have their own support will benefit from being stood outside in the sun from mid summer (June) onwards.

Cut back the flowering shoots of *J. nudiflorum* and *J. mesnyi* to 5–8cm (2–3 in) long, after they have bloomed. Prune out all old, weak wood and tie in the new growths. Thin out the shoots of *J. officinalis* after flowering, but do not cut back. No regular pruning is necessary for the other species.

Propagate greenhouse species from cuttings taken between mid spring and mid autumn (March and September); plant them in rooting compost and put them in a propagator with bottom heat of about 16°C (61°F). For the hardy species, root 8–15cm (3–6 in) cuttings in a cold frame or a sheltered border between mid autumn and mid winter (September and December).

The most serious pests that attack jasmine are aphides and mealy bugs. If infestation becomes serious, spray with malathion. Jasmine are generally free from disease, but grey mould (botrytis) might attack after frost damage.

LABURNUM

Type   hardy, deciduous spring-flowering trees and shrubs

Family   LEGUMINOSAE

Common name   golden chain or golden rain tree

Flowering season   early–mid summer (May–June)

Planting date   late autumn–mid spring (October–March); from containers at any time

Mature size/shape   mainly broad-headed, a few erect-growing, pyramidal-shaped and weeping; height 6m (20 ft), spread 4·5m (15 ft)

The laburnum genus consists of six species of hardy, deciduous flowering trees and shrubs. Of this small genus, only two species, *L. alpinum* and *L. anagyroides*, are in general cultivation. Although they are sometimes found growing on the fringe of woodlands in Britain, they are not native but strays from gardens. These two common species were introduced into cultivation from central and southern Europe between the middle and end of the 16th century. The rest grown today are of garden origin.

The timber of laburnum trees is used for turnery, decorative wood carving and inlay, and also for making musical instruments including the chanters of bagpipes. Rootstocks of the common species are used for the grafting of cytisus.

Flowering during early and mid summer (May and June), these trees and shrubs are most suitable for small gardens. Unfortunately, all parts of the laburnum are poisonous, particularly the seed in the pods. These should be collected and burned as soon as they develop, if young children are likely to play anywhere near the tree. If you have the choice, avoid planting a laburnum until your children are older.

Laburnum trees of all types are characterized by long racemes of yellow, pea-like flowers, growing in dense, hanging clusters, and pale green, bean-like seed pods appearing in autumn. The flowers have some fragrance but do not seem to attract bees particularly. There is one hybrid, *Laburnocytisus adamii* (a cross between *L. anagyroides* and *Cytisus purpureus*), that can have blooms showing three colours simultaneously – yellow, purple and a mixture of the two.

Magnificent laburnum avenue in full flower at Hampton Court. The trees have been trained over arches and provide a golden area of coolness and shade in the summer

The leaves are mostly green and trifoliate, but two notable exceptions are *L. anagyroides* Aureum, with golden leaves, and *L. a.* Quercifolium, with deeply-lobed, oak-like leaves. All laburnum are comparatively modest-growing: the trunk can reach about 30cm (12 in) in diameter, and after about 20 years' growth the tree will be some 6m (20 ft) tall. However, laburnum rarely exceed 9m (30 ft) in height during their whole life span of about 50 years. Their spread is usually 3·4m (11 ft), or a little more. They are particularly useful for screening in summer, and can be quite effective if planted at the rear of a shrub border that skirts the boundary of the garden. They start to bloom at a time when the spring-flowering camellias, cherry trees and rhododendrons are reaching the final stages of their display.

The erect-growing forms, such as *L. anagyroides* Erect, can be used as accent plants to give height to a garden. *L. × watereri* Alford's Weeping is

excellent grown as a specimen tree in the lawn. Similarly, laburnum of pendulous habit can make colourful focal points in a garden, especially if they are framed on either side by shrubs and trees with dark green foliage.

Cultivation and propagation
Laburnum are easily grown, flourishing in both sun and partial shade; they will grow in ordinary, well-drained soil, but show a preference for light soil, rarely being successful in a wet or heavy one. They can also tolerate conditions in cold, exposed gardens, in coastal areas and industrial towns.

Plant laburnum between late autumn and mid spring (October and March), or, if grown in containers, at any time. Space them about 3·7m (12 ft) apart, or the same distance from other neighbouring small trees.

Dig a hole large enough to take the rootball comfortably and allow the longer roots to spread, and of such a depth that the original soil mark on the trunk will eventually be just on the surface of the bed. Before replacing the soil, knock in a stake between the outspread roots, then replace the soil to fill the hole, firming it by gentle treading. Secure the trunk to the stake with tree ties, at points near

the ground, at the middle and at the top. Once planted, laburnum need little extra care and attention. In order to ensure regular flowering, and to maintain health and vigour, remove the seed pods after flowering. Newly-planted specimens often remain dormant until mid autumn (September). Little pruning is required.

Propagate species from seeds planted in pots in a cold frame in late autumn (October). Prick off the seedlings into trays, and then into nursery rows, and set them out in permanent quarters the following autumn. Hybrids and cultivars are propagated by being grafted in mid spring (March) on to seedling stocks of the two species cultivated.

Pests and diseases

The only pests that attack laburnum seriously are leaf-cutter bees and leaf miners, both of which damage the leaves. The trees are, however, subject

Both L. × vossii *(left) and* L. alpinum *(below left) make ideal small specimen trees*
Far left: laburnum seed pods are poisonous and should be picked and burnt as soon as they appear
Below: avenue of L. anagyroides *at the Royal Botanic Gardens, Kew*

to attack by honey fungus, indicated by failure to flower properly, premature leaf fall and die-back of branches. If the infestation is serious, you must dig up the tree and burn it.

Some varieties to choose

In the following list the first figure given is the height and the second is the spread. Any small variation of size in the varieties compared with species or hybrids is indicated; otherwise you can assume that they are approximately the same.

L. alpinum (Scotch laburnum)
A broad-headed tree that usually becomes gnarled

as it ages. Its leaves are a deep, shining green, paler beneath. Has racemes of yellow flowers 25cm (10 in) or more long, appearing from early to mid summer (May to June). It is drought-resistant. 4·8 × 4·5m (16 × 15 ft).

L.a. Pendulum	A lower, slow-growing tree that develops a dome-shaped head of stiff, pendulous branches.
L.a Pyramidale	Has erect branches.

L. anagyroides or *L. vulgare* (common laburnum)
A small tree that spreads with age. Compared with *L. alpinum*, it has shorter racemes of yellow flowers appearing in early to mid summer (May to June), with small, dull green leaves and rounder seed pods. Its racemes are about 20cm (8 in) long. 4·5 × 3m (15 × 10 ft).

L.a. Aureum (golden-leaved laburnum)	An unusual, colourful tree with soft yellow leaves borne throughout the growing season, becoming green in colour before or during autumn (August to October). As autumn nears they turn green, but they can revert to green at any time. Flowers in mid summer (June).
L.a. Autumnale	Useful cultivar with deeper green foliage than the species. Its yellow flowers, borne in racemes up to 38cm (15 in) long, appear about two weeks later than the species; often repeat-flowers in autumn. It is smaller than the species.
L.a. Erect	Has ascending branches.
L.a. Pendulum	Low-growing, elegant, weeping tree, excellent for small gardens.
L.a. Quercifolium	Has oak-shaped leaves.

L. × watereri
A hybrid of *L. alpinum* and *L. anagyroides*. It has small, glossy green leaves and long thin racemes of yellow flowers 30cm (12 in) long, appearing in mid summer (June). 4·8 × 3·4m (16 × 11 ft).

L. × w. Alford's Weeping	Vigorous, colourful tree with wide, spreading head composed of long, weeping branches. When in flower in mid summer (June), these carry pendulous racemes of yellow blooms. Makes an excellent specimen tree for the lawn.
L. × vossii (*L. × watereri* Vossii)	A profusely-flowering form with long racemes borne in summer.

LONICERA

Type	deciduous and evergreen flowering shrubs and climbers
Family	CAPRIFOLIACEAE
Common name	honeysuckle
Flowering season	early summer–early autumn (May–August) and mid winter–mid spring (December–March)
Planting date	late spring–early summer (April–May) and mid autumn–mid spring (September–March); from containers at any time
Mature size/shape	climbers: up to 6m (20 ft); shrubs: 1–3m (3½–10 ft) high × 60cm–3m (2–10 ft) spread

The lonicera genus is remarkable for its variety of types and their uses in the garden. There are altogether 200 species, some deciduous and others evergreen. Many are flowering shrubs (shrubby honeysuckles), while quite a few are climbers of varying vigour and height. The latter include *Lonicera periclymenum* (woodbine or common honeysuckle) that has been grown in cottage gardens in Britain since earliest times. The name was given in honour of Adam Lonitzer, a 16th century German botanist.

This species is one of the most widespread throughout the world – originating from such far apart places as Afghanistan, Burma, China, Iran, Japan, the Pyrenees and the United States.

Various members of the genus were first introduced into cultivation a long time ago. Possibly one of the oldest known is *L. alpigena*, that is of garden origin and has been cultivated since the 16th century. The rather tender greenhouse climber, *L. sempervirens*, was first introduced in the West in 1656; other climbers of early origin are *L. etrusca* and *L. implexa*, that first arrived in Western gardens in 1750 and 1772 respectively. Similarly, the very floriferous, vigorous shrub *L. tatarica* also arrived about the middle of the 18th century.

Two species of lonicera are tender climbing plants that, in temperate zones, will only survive in the very mildest of climates, but they are excellent for the greenhouse. One of them, *L. hildebrandiana*, is so vigorous, growing 18m (60 ft) or more in height, that only a large conservatory can house it. It is evergreen and has the largest leaf, flower and fruit of all the loniceras. The other, the aforementioned *L. sempervirens* is a semi-evergreen growing to a height of only 6m (20 ft).

*Above: early-flowering
L. periclymenum
Belgica has scented
blooms
Left: shrub honeysuckle
L. tatarica produces
red berries after
flowering
Far left: the climber
L. × tellmanniana is
ideal for covering a
sunny wall — but be
sure its roots are
shaded*

L. japonica *Halliana*
(below) and L. j. *Repens*
(below right), are
two climbing varieties
with different-coloured
but equally-scented
flowers

Lonicera flowers are mainly tubular with diverging lips, and are borne in close pairs. These pairs are often fused together (on the shrubby honeysuckles in particular) and so are the berries that follow them. This feature is characteristic of the family. In many cases, and particularly with the climbers, the flowers have a strong, sweet scent. There are at least three fairly common lonicera – *L. fragrantissima*, *L. × purpusii* and *L. setifera* – that flower during the winter.

With most species, both shrubs and climbers, the flowers are followed by berries that can be black, purplish-black, dark blue, red, coral, lilac-pink, violet or amethyst, pink suffused with yellow, and white.

It is possible to find a number of members of this large family that will tolerate some of the worst environments. The low-growing *L. pileata* will tolerate the polluted air of industrial areas and the salt-laden atmosphere of coastal districts, as well as cold, exposure, and heavy shade – making it excellent for underplanting and ground cover. *L. nitida* is another species suitable for heavy shade.

The vigorous, spreading shrub *L. involucrata* also withstands the adverse conditions of the seaside and industrial areas, and is suitable for cold and exposed gardens.

Shrubby loniceras are not generally very large-growing; the more popular ones range in size from *L. pileata* with a spread of 60–90cm (2–3 ft) and height of 1–2m (3¼–6½ ft), to *L. tatarica* with a spread and height of 2–3m (6½–10 ft). The most common lonicera shrubs are erect and rounded in shape, although there are quite a few that have a spreading habit and arching branches, among other characteristics.

As might be expected with a group of shrubs that have so many variations, their uses in the garden are manifold. The cool greenhouse climbers, *L. hildebrandiana* and *L. sempervirens* have already been mentioned as being attractive for large and medium-sized conservatories. The outdoor species described below are hardy, twining climbers, ideal for clothing walls, fences, pergolas and archways, for climbing over unsightly sheds and concealing the ugliness of objects

such as telephone poles and tree trunks. The shrubs, with variations in size and habit, are excellent for planting in mixed borders and for growing against a wall. In the border, the green, and occasionally gold, leaves and the different-textured foliage, often studded with coloured berries, can make an invaluable contribution to the appearance of an ornamental garden.

A practical use for shrubby lonicera is hedge-making. Until recently the undoubted leader in this respect was *L. nitida*, but latterly some nurserymen are recommending its variety *L. n.* Fertilis instead. This makes a very effective hedge, with its box-like glossy leaves that cover its erect branches. Nevertheless, it is hard to fault the species that, with its dense habit and small evergreen leaves, quickly makes a good hedge that responds well to clipping. Another shrubby honeysuckle sometimes used for hedging is the light-green leaved, deciduous *L. involucrata*.

Cultivation

Lonicera grow quite well in any ordinary, well-drained soil, although it is advantageous to reinforce it with well-rotted manure or compost for the climbing species. The shrubs are happy in partial shade or sun, but the climbers do better in light shade. In particular, the climbers *L.* × *tellmanniana* and *L. tragophylla* like their feet to be in the shade and their heads in the sun.

Plant the evergreen climbers during late spring or early summer (April or May) and deciduous and shrubby ones between mid autumn and mid spring (September–March). Plant container-grown ones at any time.

Calculate planting distance by adding the sum of the ultimate spread of the lonicera being planted to that of its neighbour and dividing by two. When making a hedge, the distance between each plant should be 30cm (12 in). Dig a hole large enough so that the roots can be comfortably spread out, and deep enough so that the original soil mark will be just on the surface. Firm well after the soil is replaced. After planting, train the climbers back to their support. Keep well-watered and mulch lightly with leaf mould or compost each spring.

Prune out old wood when necessary after flowering. Cut hedges back by two-thirds after planting and tip back all new growth during the first summer. Cut all new growths back halfway each year until the desired height is attained, and clip in early summer and mid autumn (May and September).

Propagation

Take hardwood cuttings in mid autumn (September) and insert in a sheltered nursery bed. Plant out a year later. Layer branches between early autumn and early winter (August and November). They can usually be severed after a year.

Pests and diseases

Lonicera are sometimes attacked by aphides that cause distortion of the foliage. They are moderately free from diseases.

Some varieties to choose

CLIMBERS

L. japonica

A strong-growing evergreen or semi-evergreen species, reaching up to 9m (30 ft) high. *L. japonica* Aureoreticulata is now more commonly grown, and has small oval leaves, netted by golden yellow veins and mid-rib, and scented yellow flowers appearing between mid summer and early autumn (June–August). *L. j.* Halliana is an attractive variety with fragrant white flowers that change to yellow, while *L. j.* Repens has leaves and shoots that are flushed purple, and scented flowers purple-coloured on the outer side.

L. periclymenum (woodbine or common honeysuckle)

The varieties *L. p.* Belgica (early Dutch honeysuckle) and *L. p.* Serotina (late Dutch honeysuckle) are nowadays more frequently cultivated than the species. The former has scented tubular blooms, purple rose on the outside and lips yellow inside, and flowers from early to late summer (May–July); the latter blooms red-purple outside, cream-white inside – from late summer to mid autumn (July–September). Both attain a height of 6m (20 ft).

L. × tellmanniana

This bears 5cm (2 in) long, trumpet-shaped flowers of golden yellow in mid to late summer (June–July), and grows 6m (20 ft) high.

SHRUBS

L. fragrantissima

A partially evergreen shrub that produces sweetly-scented, cream-coloured, bell-shaped blooms from mid winter through to mid spring (December–March), followed by red berries that ripen by early summer (May); attains a height and spread of 2m (6½ ft).

L. involucrata

A spreading, deciduous shrub with yellow flowers appearing in mid summer (June), and two red bracts that remain as the shiny black berries are forming. It has bright green leaves and reaches a height and spread of 2·4m (8 ft).

L. nitida

A dense evergreen, used for hedging; it has insignificant yellow flowers in late spring and early summer (April–May), that are followed by round, translucent violet or amethyst berries; it reaches a height and spread of 2m (6½ ft).

L. pileata

A low-growing, semi-evergreen shrub that will grow in heavy shade; it has light green foliage and bears insignificant yellow-green flowers in late spring and early summer (April–May), followed by translucent violet berries; it reaches a height of 1m (3¼ ft) and a spread of 1·5m (5 ft)

L. × purpusii

Another winter-flowering deciduous shrub that yields sweetly-scented, cream-coloured, short tubular flowers from mid winter to mid spring (December–March); height and spread 2m (6½ ft).

L. syringantha

A deciduous shrub with sea-green leaves, bearing hyacinth-scented, soft lilac-rose, tubular blooms in early to mid summer (May–June), followed by red fruits in autumn; it has a height and spread of approximately 2·4m (8 ft).

L. tatarica

A deciduous shrub with leaves that are dark green above and blue-green beneath. It produces 2–3cm (1 in) long pink flowers that clothe the branches in early to mid summer (May–June); following the flowers are red, globular berries that appear in late summer to early autumn (July August); attains a height and spread to 2·4m (8 ft).

MAGNOLIA

Type	deciduous and evergreen, hardy flowering trees and shrubs
Family	MAGNOLIACEAE
Planting date	deciduous: late autumn to mid spring (October–March); evergreen: mid–late autumn (September–October) late spring to early summer (April–May); from containers at any time.
Mature size/shape	rounded, conical, erect, wide-spreading; height 2·1–5·4m (7–18 ft), spread 1·8–2·7m (6–9 ft)

There are eighty species in the genus, Magnoliaceae, all of which are evergreen and deciduous trees and shrubs. The family includes some of the most magnificent specimen trees. Of these *Magnolia denudata* (conspicus), which is slow-growing, and *M × soulangiana* are probably the most spectacular. Magnolias were originally named after the French botanist, Pierre Magnot, (1638–1751) professor of botany and director of the botanic gardens at Montpellier.

The foliage of magnolias is usually striking. Mostly the leaves are lanceolate in shape, sometimes broadly and occasionally narrow and willow-like as is the case with *M. salicifolia*. Perhaps the most beautiful of all the foliage among magnolias is that of *M. grandiflora*, 'The Laurel-leaved Tulip Tree of North America'.

They have lovely, well-formed blossoms which might be bowl- or chalice-shaped or star-like. They are largely white or cream, sometimes stained or flushed with purple. Exceptions are *M × soulangiana* 'Rustica Rubra' with blooms of rich rosy-red and the rather less common *M. acuminata* with greenish-yellow. Some magnolias have fragrant flowers. *M. sieboldii* follows its flowering by producing the loveliest pink capsules, which open in late autumn (October) to reveal orange-coloured seeds. Many magnolias unfortunately do not flower when they are small. An exception to this is *M. stellata*.

Most magnolias are hardy, but it is advisable to plant those that flower in the spring and that may have their blooms damaged by frost and cold winds, in a sheltered spot. Those that have large leaves would also benefit by being positioned so that they are not exposed to gales. Magnolias are particularly happy growing in heavy clay, but this is not essential; many prefer a slightly acidic soil, often abhorring chalk. A few, however, will tolerate an alkaline soil, among these are *M. ×*
loebneri and *M. wilsonii*. Magnolias are tolerant of atmospheric pollution; and especially suitable for growing in industrial areas are *M. × soulangiana* and *M. × loebneri* and their cultivars.

Magnolias are either large shrubs or small trees, often short-stemmed, and assume a variety of shapes and habit-rounded, conical, erect, wide spreading and so on. In stature the more popular ones vary from *M. liliiflora*, height 2·1m (7 ft), spread 1·8m (6 ft) to *M. × loebneri*, height 5·4m (18 ft), spread 2·7m (9 ft), after about 20 years.

Historically, probably the earliest to be introduced to western gardens were *M. virginiana*, *M. grandiflora* and *M. liliiflora* during the 17th century. After that there was a long succession during the 18th and 19th centuries. Many that grace present-day gardens are of garden origin, but most of the species are variously indigenous to China, Japan, Tibet and North America.

Magnolias may be planted advantageously in almost every position in a garden, where they can be accommodated. It is, however, as specimens and wall plants that they excel themselves.

Growing conditions and soil requirements
Magnolia are happy in any good well-drained, loamy soil. If it is heavy clay it should be admixed with peat or well-rotted garden compost. Generally alkaline soil should be avoided, although there are a few varieties that will tolerate.

Above: Magnolia × soulangiana, *named in honour of the chevalier Etienne Soulange-Bodin (1774–1846), French horticulturist and raiser of this splendid hybrid*

Planting distance

Magnolias should be planted so that they will eventually touch either their own kind or other types of shrubs after a period of years. (say, 10 to 20). The space that should be allowed them to achieve this is determined by adding together the eventual spreads of neighbouring plants and dividing the total by two.

How to plant

It is better not to disturb the roots of magnolia when planting. A hole should be dug of such a depth that the surface of the new bed will be finally at the level to which it it was planted in the nursery, and wide enough to take the root-ball leaving space for soil to be packed round it. This space is filled in with soil and well trodden in. Magnolia usually need staking when they are young.

Container plants should have their container carefully removed by cutting away the bottom and slitting down the side. They should be then treated as for bare-root plants.

Cultivation

During the first few years they should be top-dressed each late spring (April) with leaf mould, peat or compost.

Propagation

Species can be raised from seeds by planting them in peaty compost in a seed pan and allowing it to stand up to 18 months to allow for germination. Seedlings are then transferred to a nursery bed.

Magnolias can also be propagated by means of heel cuttings and by layering.

Some varieties to choose

The first figure given with each item refers to height, the second to spread.

M. grandiflora EXMOUTH	Polished evergreen leaves, soft above, reddish below. Large richly fragrant, creamy-white flowers late summer to mid-autumn (July to September). 3·6m × 2·4m (12 × 8 ft).
M. liliiflora	Mid-green deciduous leaves. Red-purple, chalice-shaped flowers between late spring and late summer (April and July). 2·1m × 1·8m (7 × 6 ft).
M. × soulangiana	Deciduous, mid-green leaves. White, chalice-like blooms, stained purple at the base, in late spring (April). 3·6 × 4·2m (12 × 14 ft).
M. stellata	Slow-growing, deciduous tree with pale to mid-green leaves. White, star-shaped flowers in mid spring and late spring (March and April). 2·7 × 3m (9 × 10 ft).

Below: Magnolia grandiflora
Bottom: Magnolia × soulangiana *Lennei*
Below right: Magnolia Stellata

MALUS

Type	deciduous flowering and fruiting trees
Common name	flowering crab apple
Family	ROSACEAE
Flowering season	late spring and early summer (April–May)
Mature size/shape	height 2–7·5m (7–25 ft), spread 2·5–6m (8–20 ft); round-headed, erect, or weeping tree
Special use	fruits of some varieties used in preserves

Left: Malus *Lemoinei,* one of the erect-growing hybrids. Its attractive blooms are followed by purple-bronze fruits *Below: the fruits of* M. *Golden Hornet cling on late into the year*

The genus Malus is composed of 35 species of hardy deciduous flowering and fruit-bearing trees together with a few shrubs. To this basic number, however, has to be added a mass of cultivars and forms that in many cases are even more beautiful than their parents. When it comes to loveliness, malus may be included with prunus (ornamental cherry) as being unexcelled in floral charm by any other trees.

Among the species of flowering crabs and their cultivars there are no less than five styles of flowers, which range in colour from the white of Dartmouth to the deep wine-red of Lemoinei and they have a wonderful display of colourful fruits in the autumn. Sometimes these are like small, brightly-coloured apples, or they can resemble cherries. There are some enthusiastic gardeners who plant flowering crabs almost entirely for the enjoyment that these fruits give when the days are shortening. You can first of all enjoy the marvellous show of variously-coloured blossoms that they give in late spring and early summer (April and May) and then the autumn tints of their fruits. The fruits of many of them are also suitable for making delicious preserves.

Malus are usually small trees, and nurseries generally offer them as standards with trunks ranging from about 1·25–1·8m (3½–6 ft) in height. On the whole they are modest growers and probably the maximum height reached by any of them is the 9–11m (30–36 ft) attained after many years by *Malus tschonoskii*, which compensates to some extent for this large vertical dimension by being an erect species of pyramidal shape with an ultimate spread of 1·8–3m (6–10 ft). When grown as a bush, *M. tschonoskii* is less attractive, and certainly requires more room than many small gardens today can afford to give it. There are, however, a small number of malus that are suitable for just such a situation. One of these is the very delightful shrubby species, *M. sargentii*, which has an ultimate height of 2·5m (8 ft) and spread of 3m (10 ft).

The origin of these beautiful ornamental trees is a somewhat complex subject. The habitat of the species from which many of them are derived covers widespread parts of the world – Europe, North America, the Mediterranean region, Siberia, China and Japan. Many of the most beautiful ones grown in gardens nowadays are garden-bred.

There is, however, little doubt that the existence of wild or crab apples goes back a long way in time. They were eaten by prehistoric man, who also brewed from them a primitive form of cider. As a further confirmation of its antiquity, the crab apple is claimed to derive its name from the old Norse word 'skrab' meaning a small, rough-barked tree. The many varieties grown in present day orchards originated with these wild crab apples. Some experts believe that *M. sylvestris* was the original, while others say it was *M. pumila*; and there are some authorities who claim the two species are identical. There is, however, evidence that they are separate entities and *M. sylvestris* is most likely the original flowering crab. It is obvious from the present-day varieties that several groups of species had an influence on their development. There are the purple-leaved forms, that all have the influence of *M. niedzwetzkyana* in them. The superbly-flowered Chinese species, *M. floribunda*, can claim to be an early parent of many of the most beautiful. Another strain originated in Canada, and its descendants are classed as the Canadian crabs or rosy blooms. Another line stems from the Arnold Arboretum in the United States, where *M. × arnoldiana* was raised in 1883 to become the parent of present-day cultivars. Finally there is the Pumila group that is derived from *M. pumila* and contains some of the best producers of fruit for jelly – among them Red Sentinel, Montreal Beauty, and John Downie.

Needless to say, few gardens can afford to be without such beautiful trees. They are superb grown as specimens in a well-mown lawn and are equally as beautiful in a shrub border. Possibly one of their greatest, but almost unrecognized, assets to a garden is the variety of shapes they present – pyramidal, vase-shaped, or round-headed, with erect-growing, spreading or pendulous habits. It is doubtful whether any species offers a greater choice.

Cultivation

Malus can be planted in sun or partial shade. It is not particular about soil and will grow in any ordinary garden soil, providing it is reasonably fertile, although it has a preference for one that has been enriched with well-rotted manure or good garden compost.

Like other deciduous trees, malus should be planted when the weather is mild and the ground not soggy, from late autumn until mid spring (October–March). Trees in containers can be planted at any time. As a general guide, each tree should be planted so that there is an all-round space between itself and its neighbours on all sides equal to its ultimate spread.

In order to give the tree a good start, it should be

Left: Malus *Dartmouth*
Below: M. *Echtermeyer,*
also known as M. ×
purpurea *Pendula. Its*
fruits are purplish red

*Above: the aptly-named M. Profusion produces a mass of flowers in spring
Right: the fruits of M. Yellow Siberian often last through most of the winter*

planted carefully by digging a hole of such a diameter that its roots can spread out, and of such a depth that the existing soil mark on the trunk will be level with the new soil surface. Place the tree in the hole and spread out the roots. As it is necessary to stake a standard until it is well established, drive a stake (one that reaches the top of the trunk) into the bottom of the hole between the roots. Then mix in a small amount of bonemeal or fishmeal into the excavated soil and gradually refill the hole with it, firming it gently with your heel. When it is completed, tie the trunk to the stake at the bottom, centre and top, preferably using tarred twine with a fabric or plastic band to protect the bark.

When planting a container-grown tree, remove the container carefully without disturbing the roots; use a sharp knife to cut off the bottom and again to make a vertical slit down the side. In their early years after planting, all malus benefit from an annual mulch in late spring of well-rotted manure or compost.

No regular pruning is needed, except to remove dead and straggly branches in autumn or winter. Anything particularly unruly can be hard-pruned in late summer (July) after flowering.

It is possible to propagate species (that almost always come true) by sowing seeds, but it is not a very satisfactory method for the amateur, as such seed-raised trees take ten or more years to reach the flowering stage. A better way is to bud them in mid spring (March) or to graft them in late summer and early autumn (July and August). This is essential in the case of all hybrids and varieties to ensure faithful reproduction. Both budding and grafting should be done on seedling apple stocks or root stocks of Malling II, Malling-Merton III or Malling XXV.

Pests and diseases

Malus is rather prone to attack from pests. Aphides, particularly the woolly variety, may attack the young leaves and fruits. The presence of these aphides is shown by the branches being covered with white, waxy, woolly tufts and the growth of galls.

Capsid bugs cause distortions by piercing the young leaf buds and fruit. Fruit tree red spider mites attack the undersides of the leaves, which turn bronze, wither and drop. The fruits of malus are sometimes holed by the larvae of the codling moth and apple sawfly.

Malus is liable to much the same diseases as the ordinary apple. These include apple mildew, which is shown by a white powdery layer on new growths and leaves.

Apple scab produces brown or black scabs on the fruits. In addition, the leaves become blotched with olive green and often they fall. Small blisters also develop on the shoots; these eventually crack the bark and can be seen as ring-like scabs.

Bootlace fungus could cause the rapid death of the tree unless it is brought under control in the early stages. An application of a chemical called Armillatox may save the tree.

Some varieties to choose

In the list that follows, the first figure given under the variety description is the ultimate height and the second the ultimate spread of the plant.

M. Aldenhamensis	Small tree with loose growth and purplish leaves that become bronze-green in late summer. It has wine-red blossoms and purplish-red fruits. 4·5 × 4·5m (15 × 15 ft).
M. Chilko	Canadian tree, with large purplish-red flowers and egg-shaped, shiny, brilliant crimson fruits. 6 × 4m (20 × 13 ft).
M. coronaria Charlottae	Broad-headed tree with autumn tints. Its large shell-pink flowers are violet-scented. Has globular, green to yellow fruits. 5 × 4m (16 × 13 ft).
M. Dartmouth	Mid green leaves, white flowers and a wealth of red and yellow fruits. 6 × 3m (18 × 10 ft).
M. Dorothea	Raised at the Arnold Arboretum in USA. Its flowers are pale crimson and its fruits golden yellow. 4·5 × 4·5m (15 × 15 ft).
M. Echtermeyer	Weeping variety with purplish leaves, whose drooping branches reach the ground. Rose-pale pink flowers and purplish-red fruits. 4·5 × 4·5m (15 × 15 ft).
M. Eleyi	Dark purplish-green leaves. Its flowers are deep red-purple and are followed by conical, purplish-red fruits. 4 × 4m (13 × 13 ft).
M. floribunda Japanese **Crab**	Small tree with arching branches. Very beautiful crimson buds opening to white flowers. Small red and yellow fruits. 4 × 4m (13 × 13 ft).
M. Golden Hornet	Strong-growing erect tree with pale green leaves and white flowers, followed by persistent bright yellow fruits. 5 × 4m (16 × 13 ft).
M. hupehensis	Stiff, spreading, vigorous species with plentiful fragrant, white flowers that are pink in bud. Yellow fruits, tinted red. 7·5 × 5·5m (25 × 18 ft).
M. John Downie	White flowers, with large fruits conical in shape, bright orange and red in colour. Possibly the best. 7·5 × 6m (25 × 20 ft).
M. Lemoinei	Erect-growing. Purple leaves and purple-crimson flowers followed by purple-bronze fruits. 5·5 × 4·5m (18 × 15 ft).
M. Montreal Beauty	Large, scented, white blossoms tinged with pink. Erect habit. Huge, brilliant orange-scarlet fruits. 6 × 6m (20 × 20 ft).
M. niedzwetzkyana	Vigorous, open-branched tree, with deep green leaves, flushed purple. Flowers are purple-red and conical fruits dark purple-red. 7·5 × 6m (25 × 20 ft).
M. Profusion	Profuse wine-red flowers. Young leaves coppery crimson. Has small ox-blood red fruits. 5·5 × 4m (18 × 13 ft).
M × *purpurea*	Round-headed tree with bronze-coloured young leaves and wine-red blossoms; most attractive because they usually appear simultaneously. Crimson-purple fruits 6 × 4m (20 × 13 ft).
M. Red Sentinel	White flowers and large clusters of deep red fruits, that persist throughout most of the winter. 4 × 3m (13 × 10 ft).
M. sargentii	Delightful, shrubby species, massed with pure white flowers with golden anthers in spring, and small bright cherry-like fruits in autumn. 2 × 3m (7 × 10 ft).
M. Yellow Siberian	Mid green leaves and single white flowers, followed by cherry-like, bright, deep yellow fruits that often persist during the winter. 4 × 3m (12 × 10 ft).

Top: blossoms of M. floribunda, *a small tree with arching branches*
Above: M. Eleyi *has unusual, dark purplish-green leaves*

PHILADELPHUS

Type	hardy, deciduous, fragrant flowering shrubs
Family	PHILADELPHACEAE
Common name	mock orange
Planting date	late autumn–mid spring (October–March); from containers at any time
Flowering season	mid–late summer (June–July)
Mature size/shape	mainly rounded bushes, some with erect or arching branches; height 60cm–3m (2–10 ft), spread 60cm–4m (2–12 ft)

Philadelphus shrubs are popularly known as 'mock orange' because their flowers have a perfume similar to that of the orange blossom. They have sometimes – incorrectly – been called 'syringa' (lilac). The philadelphus genus consists of 75 species of hardy, fragrant, deciduous shrubs that are grown mainly in shrub and mixed borders.

Philadelphus are widespread throughout the world: *Philadelphus coronarius* is of central European origin, *P. argyrocalyx* is native to New Mexico, *P. insignis* to California and *P. maculatus* to Mexico and Arizona. *P. delavayi* originated in China, Tibet and Upper Burma and *P. incanus* is native to central China. Some historians claim that *P. coronarius*, the most commonly-cultivated species today, was introduced to Britain by the Romans; it was certainly grown in cottage gardens in Tudor times. Most of the other species were brought from their native habitat to Western gardens during the 19th century – the earliest probably being *P. maculatus*, the parent of many fine hybrids growing today.

The flowers of these shrubs are mostly pure white, single or double, sweet-scented and cup-shaped, varying in diameter between 13mm and 5cm ($\frac{1}{2}$–2 in). A few exceptional hybrids, raised from *P. × purpureo-maculatus*, have white blooms blotched irregularly with purple. Examples are Beauclerk, Etoile Rose and Sybille. Another popular hybrid, Belle Etoile, has white flowers flushed maroon in the centre. The flowering season for all species and varieties lasts throughout mid and late summer (June and July).

Most philadelphus have mid green, ovate leaves with prominent veins. Two attractive exceptions are *P. coronarius* Aureus, with gold young foliage, and *P. c.* Variegata, with green and cream variegated leaves.

Although philadelphus are mainly bushy shrubs, some have an erect habit, and still others have arching branches that are laden with

Top: dainty P. microphyllus *grows some 60–90cm (2–3 ft) high*
Above: P. Virginal *– a strong-growing, superb double-flowered hybrid*

blossoms during the flowering season. Usually they are modest-sized plants that can be grown in gardens where space is somewhat restricted. One of the smallest in stature is the very dainty, small-leaved species *P. microphyllus* that has a height of 60cm (2 ft) and a spread of 90cm (3 ft). Among the largest are the hybrids Belle Etoile and Burford-ensis, both growing up to 3m (10 ft) in height, with a spread of 4m (12 ft), after about 20 years.

Only a small number of the species are grown today, but there are a large number of very beautiful hybrids that are very popular. These are collected into groups that are distinguished by the appropriate parental name. Among the most common are the Lemoinei, Purpureo-maculatus, Virginalis, Cymosus and Polyanthus groups.

Cultivation and propagation

Plant philadelphus either in full sun or partial shade. They thrive in any ordinary, well-drained soil and do not object to chalk. They will even flourish in the poor conditions and polluted atmosphere of industrial areas, and help to sweeten the air with their rich, penetrating perfume. Many species will grow quite happily in cold, exposed gardens.

The best time to plant bare-root shrubs is between late autumn and mid spring (October and March); but those in containers can go in at any time. Determine the planting distance to be allowed between neighbouring shrubs by adding together their ultimate spreads and dividing the result by two.

For a bare-root philadelphus, dig a hole deep enough to take the undisturbed rootball comfortably and allow the roots to spread, and position the plant so that the original soil mark on the main stem will be on the surface of the soil.

Once planted, philadelphus are easily grown and require very little attention. Thin out old wood after flowering has finished, but retain the new young shoots because they will flower during the next season. Philadelphus are not usually troubled by pests, but can be attacked by leaf spot disease. This manifests itself on the leaves by yellow blotches with darker margins. If the attack is serious, spray with benomyl.

Propagate philadelphus by taking hardwood cuttings about 30cm (12 in) long in late autumn or early winter (October or November), and rooting them in a sheltered border. Plant these out the following year in their permanent positions.

Left: P. coronarius *Aurea is noted for its unusual foliage colour*

Some varieties to choose

The dimensions given in the list below refer to the height and spread after about 20 years' growth in both cases. Unless otherwise stated, the flowers are white or cream and fragrant, and appear in mid and late summer (June and July).

SPECIES

P. coronarius	Strong-growing, medium-sized bush, particularly good for dry soils. 2·4 × 2·1m (8 × 7 ft).
P. × lemoinei	A cross between *P. coronarius* and *P. microphyllus*, this species has produced numerous clones. It is a comparatively small shrub. 1·8 × 1·2m (6 × 4 ft).
P. microphyllus	Very dainty, small shrub with tiny leaves carried on twiggy branches. Flowers are very richly perfumed. 60–90cm × 60–90cm (2–3 ft × 2–3 ft).

Thin out the old wood after flowering to maintain shape of large-growing philadelphus like Burfordensis (above right) and smaller types like Bouquet Blanc (right)

HYBRIDS

Avalanche (Lemoinei group)	Loose-growing shrub with arching branches carrying single flowers in great abundance. Has small leaves. 1·2 × 1·5m (4 × 5 ft).
Beauclerk (Purpureo-maculatus group)	Medium-sized shrub bearing single flowers with white petals that have a maroon-cerise blotch near the stamens. 2·4 × 1·8m (8 × 6 ft).
Belle Etoile (Purpureo-maculatus group)	Compact shrub with single blooms that are white with purple blotches at the base of the petals. 3 × 4m (10 × 12 ft).
Bouquet Blanc (Cymosus group)	Moderately small shrub with double flowers carried in large, crowded clusters. Strongly orange-scented. 1·5 × 1·5m (5 × 5 ft).
Burfordensis (Virginalis group)	Magnificent shrub with erect branches. Bears large, single blooms distinguished by an outstanding boss of yellow stamens. 3 × 4m (10 × 12 ft).
Enchantment (Virginalis group)	Very vigorous, large bush, giving terminal clusters of double blooms in great abundance. 2·4 × 3m (8 × 10 ft).
Etoile Rose (Purpureo-maculatus group)	Blooms have a carmine-rose basal coloration. 1·8 × 1·5m (6 × 5 ft).
Favourite (Polyanthus group)	Moderate-sized shrub with single, very large blooms characterized by serrated petals and prominent yellow stamens. 1·5 × 1·5m (5 × 5 ft).
Manteau d'Hermine (Lemoinei group)	Dwarf shrub with double flowers borne in great profusion. 90 × 90cm (3 × 3 ft).
Silver Showers (Lemoinei group)	Upright-growing, small shrub producing abnormally large blooms in great abundance. 1·2 × 1·2m (4 × 4 ft).
Sybille (Purpureo-maculatus group)	Small shrub with arching branches loaded with single white flowers that are purple-stained. 1·2m × 90cm (4 × 3 ft).
Virginal (Virginalis group)	Strong-growing, erect shrub, considered to be the best double-flowered cultivar. 3 × 2·1m (10 × 7 ft).

POTENTILLA

Type	deciduous, flowering shrubs and sub-shrubs
Family	ROSACEAE
Common names	shrubby cinquefoil
Flowering season	late spring–early winter (April–November)
Planting date	late autumn–mid spring (October–March) when the weather is good; from containers at any time
Mature size/shape	prostrate, mound-shaped, bushy and erect-growing, height 30cm–1·5m (12 in–5 ft), spread 90cm–2·1m (3–7 ft)

The potentilla genus is a large one, containing about 500 species of plants. It belongs to the family ROSACEAE – a relationship that many potentillas, particularly the shrub types, demonstrate by their rose-like single or semi-double blooms. It derives its name from the latin *potens*, meaning 'powerful' – a reference to the reputed medicinal properties of the plant. The genus is made up of herbaceous perennials, hardy annuals, deciduous flowering shrubs and sub-shrubs. From a garden point of view the hardy annuals are of little interest, but the others, being fairly modest-growing and blooming profusely and continuously over a long period, are extremely valuable for a small garden.

Many of the shrubby potentillas grown nowadays are garden-originated varieties of *P. fruticosa* – a species that is widespread throughout the Northern Hemisphere. Of the other shrubby types, *P. arbuscula* is native to the Himalayas, the dwarf shrub *P. salesoviana* to Siberia, and the prostrate sub-shrub *P. tridentata* to the eastern part of North America.

Shrubby potentillas

The shrubby potentillas are all modest growers, ranging from an ultimate height of 30cm (12 in) and spread of 90cm (3 ft) for *P. fruticosa mandshurica*, to a height of 1·5m (5 ft) and spread of 2·1m (7 ft) for *P. f. grandiflora* Jackman's Variety. Some are prostrate in form, while others have an erect habit. Most are very amenable to being clipped back, particularly cultivars of *P. fruticosa* and some should be cut right down every mid spring to keep them bushy.

The vast majority of shrubby potentillas have yellow flowers, but a few types bear cream or white blooms. In more recent years there have been some interesting breakthroughs in colour. Among the new cultivars *P. fruticosa* Daydawn is peach-pink;

P. f. Tangerine is bright yellow to coppery red (according to the general temperature and whether it is grown in sun or shade); *P. f.* Sunset is deep orange to brick red; and *P. f.* Red Ace, the very latest available, is bright vermilion-flame.

With a few exceptions, the shrubby potentillas bloom from early summer to early winter. They are exceptionally hardy and will grow both in sun and partial shade. Although they are shade tolerant, there is no doubt that they flower best when grown in full sun. They flourish in light, well-drained soil and are reasonably drought-tolerant.

These potentillas are excellent for shrubberies in small gardens. They are bushy in shape, with tiny leaves coloured sage green, silver, dark green, and grey-green, and are smothered with brightly coloured flowers that persist over a long period. Some make very good ground cover.

Several of the shrubby potentillas can be grown to great effect as deciduous, informal, flowering hedges. Suitable forms for this purpose are *P. fruticosa grandiflora* Jackman's Variety, that makes an excellent 90cm (3 ft) high hedge; *P. f.* Katherine Dykes, that grows to 1·2m (4 ft) high; and *P. f.* Primrose Beauty, reaching 75cm (2½ ft).

Care and cultivation

Plants from all kinds of containers can be planted out at any time of the year, provided they are not allowed to dry out. All potentillas are generally free from pests and diseases.

Shrubby potentillas Plant these shrubs out in good

Below: keep Potentilla fruticosa mandshurica *in good bushy shape by clipping the stems back every spring*

weather, at any time from late autumn to mid spring. Determine the planting distance to be allowed between neighbouring shrubs by adding together their ultimate spreads and dividing the sum by two.

Dig a hole large enough to take the rootball comfortably and allow the roots to spread out, and of such a depth that the original soil mark on the stem will be just on the surface of the bed. Replace the soil after positioning the shrub and firm in by gentle treading. The shrubby species need little attention, except that it is advantageous to prune back the tall types to the ground each spring, to encourage bushing. After blooming has finished, remove the tips of the flowering shoots.

Propagation
Divide and replant long-lived herbaceous perennial varieties in late autumn or mid spring. Raise the short-lived types from 8cm (3 in) cuttings taken in late spring; insert them in cutting compost and keep them in a cold frame. Plant them out in a nursery bed when they have rooted, and transplant them to their permanent positions in the garden in mid autumn.

Propagate shrubby species from 8cm (3 in) long, half-ripe heel cuttings taken in mid autumn. Plant them in a cold frame, then put the rooted cuttings in a nursery bed; transplant them to permanent quarters in the following late autumn.

Some varieties to choose
The dimensions given for the shrubby potentillas refer first to the height and secondly to the spread.

Left: P. fruticosa arbuscula

P. arbuscula	Sage-green leaves, and yellow flowers that appear from mid summer to late autumn. 60cm × 1·5m (2 × 5 ft).
P. a. Beesii	Mound-forming, with silver foliage. 45cm × 1·5m (18 in × 5 ft).
P. a. rigida	A dwarf compact plant with bristly stems covered in striking papery stipules and small pretty leaves that have three leaflets. It has bright yellow flowers mid summer to mid autumn. 60 × 60cm (2 × 2 ft).
P. Elizabeth	A cross between *P. arbuscula* and *P. fruticosa mandshurica*. Dome-shaped bush with canary-yellow blooms flowering from early summer to late autumn. 90cm × 1·2m (3 × 4 ft).
P. fruticosa	Dense bush with yellow flowers borne from early summer to mid autumn. 1·5 × 1·5m (5 × 5 ft). It has numerous forms and cultivars; all of those listed below have yellow flowers unless otherwise stated.
P. f. glabra	Has red stems, and white flowers produced between mid summer and late autumn. 60 × 60cm (2 × 2 ft).
P. f. grandiflora Jackman's Variety	Flowers from mid summer to mid autumn. 1·5 × 2·1m (5 × 7 ft).
P. f. Katherine Dykes	Blooms from early summer to late autumn. 1·5 × 1·8m (5 × 6 ft).
P. f. mandshurica	Forms mats of greyish foliage and bears a continuous show of white flowers from early summer to late autumn. 30 × 90cm (12 in × 3 ft).
P. f. Tangerine	Mound-shaped shrub with pale coppery-yellow blooms if grown in partial shade or cool weather, otherwise yellow. They appear from mid summer to mid autumn. 60cm × 1·5m (2 × 5 ft).
P. f. Red Ace	New cultivar with vermilion-flame blooms, produced early summer to early winter. 60cm × 1·2m (2 × 4 ft).
P. salesoviana	Dwarf shrub with hollow, reddish-brown stems and white, pink-tinged blooms flowering in mid and late summer. 45 × 60cm (18 × 24 in).

PRUNUS

Type	deciduous and evergreen flowering shrubs and trees
Family	ROSACEAE
Flowering season	late winter to mid summer (January to June)
Planting date	early–mid autumn (August–September); from containers at any time
Mature size/shape	round, round-headed, conical, pyramidal, flat-headed, narrow-headed and dome-shaped; height 60cm–12m (2–40 ft), spread 60cm–11m (2–36 ft)
Special uses	cherrywood pipes and walking sticks are made from *Prunus mahaleb* blackthorn walking-sticks are made from the wood of *Prunus spinosa*, and the fruits of the same plant are used for preserves, wine-making and flavouring gin

The prunus genus is comprised of 430 species, and a wider range of these are grown today than of any other flowering tree species. For convenience, the genus is divided into five sections – almonds, peaches, plums, cherries and cherry laurels. Here we look at the largest section – flowering cherries – before going on to consider the remaining four.

Two ornamental cherries are native to Britain: *Prunus avium*, commonly known as gean, mazzard or wild cherry, is found throughout the British Isles, while the rather smaller *P. padus* (bird cherry) grows wild in Scotland and Wales. Some flowering cherries, such as *P. conradinae* and *P. serrula*, have come from China, while *P. cornuta* (Himalayan bird cherry) originates in the Himalayas. *P. incana* (willow cherry) and *P. prostrata* come from Europe, *P. subhirtella* (spring cherry) and *P. sargentii* from Japan, and *P. serotina* from the eastern part of North America, Mexico and Guatemala. Many of the most beautiful ornamental cherries are of garden origin.

Flowering cherries have been grown in Japan for a very long time, particularly *P. incisa* (Fuji cherry) and the small, slender shrub, *P. japonica*. These Japanese cherries form a large section of the prunus genus, and are usually treated as a separate

P. sargentii is ideally suited to a garden with limited space. It bears single blooms (right, above) and has blazing autumn foliage (right)

group. Some cherries have been cultivated in Western gardens for several centuries. *P. fruticosa* (ground cherry) was first introduced to Britain in 1587, *P. serotina* in 1629, *P. mahaleb* (St Lucie cherry) in 1714 and *P. glandulosa* Sinensis (Chinese bush cherry) – a favourite in Victorian and Edwardian gardens – in 1774.

These prunus are almost entirely deciduous, but a notable exception is *P. ilicifolia* (holly-leaved cherry), that has leathery leaves with spreading spines. Some forms, such as *P.* Pandora and *P. sargentii*, produce bronze-red young leaves that make a delightful foil to the buds in spring. Quite a few, including the two last-named, have foliage that turns brilliant yellow, orange and crimson in autumn. *P. incisa*, that has been used for centuries by the Japanese for bonsai, *P.* Okame, and *P. serotina* are notable for this quality.

All the ornamental cherries bear masses of blooms shading from white to purplish-pink or, in the case of the Japanese cherry *P.* Ukon, pale yellow. Most flower from mid spring to early summer (March to May), though a few flower at other times of the year: *P. subhirtella* Autumnalis (autumn cherry) blooms intermittently from early winter to mid spring (November to March), and *P. conradinae* produces its flowers during early spring (February).

Some ornamental cherries have attractive-coloured bark; these include the British wild cherry, *P. avium*, that has a grey trunk turning mahogany-red. This bark peels off and becomes deeply fissured with age. Possibly the most delightful of those with coloured bark is *P. serrula*, that has glistening, polished, red-brown mahogany-like new bark.

These trees are quite varied in size. Possibly the smallest is the dwarf *P. prostrata* (rock cherry), that forms a gnarled hummock not exceeding 60cm (2 ft) in height and some 1·8m (6 ft) in width. The largest is *P. avium* that has been found growing in Britain to a height of 30m (100 ft), but most of the ornamental cherries grown in modern gardens do not exceed 6m (20 ft) in either height or spread.

Among the different shapes found in this section of the prunus genus are round, round-headed, conical, pyramidal, flat-headed, narrow-headed and dome-like. Some are spreading with ascending or horizontal branches, while others are weeping, arching, twiggy or erect-growing. One of the loveliest of the erect-growing forms is the Japanese cherry *P.* Amanogawa, with a height of up to 7m (23 ft) and a spread of just over 2m (7 ft). Some species are pendulous: *P.* × *yedoensis* Ivensii, that has long, twisted branches and slender drooping branchlets, is a good example.

Quite a number of ornamental cherries, including the Japanese ones, can tolerate industrial atmospheres – a quality that is of great use in individual gardens and overall town designs alike, because with them considerable colour can be imparted to otherwise drab surroundings. Another advantage of these prunus is that they will all grow on clay soils.

The great value of the ornamental cherries is that they supply masses of blooms in spring when many other trees and shrubs are just stirring from their winter rest. They are effective planted as specimens in the lawn or when grown in shrub borders. In placing such trees in a garden layout, it is vital to remember that their shape and size is perhaps more important than the colour of their flowers. The blooms are transient, whereas the other factors are constant throughout the year. The columnar, erect-growing cherries, such as Amanogawa, *P.* × *hillieri* Spire, and Umineko, make excellent accent points in a garden design, and are more colourful than the conifers that are often used to obtain this effect.

Some of the ornamental cherries, particularly the Japanese forms, are so heavily foliaged that they make dense screens in summer, while others make excellent deciduous hedges. For this purpose the best choice is either the small-growing purple-leaved *P.* Cistena that reaches a height of 1·8m (6 ft) and has rich red leaves in autumn, or *P. incisa*, that is also magnificently tinted during autumn.

Cultivation

The majority of ornamental cherries are hardy and are easy to grow in an open, sunny position. There are, however, several that are suitable only for growing in the mildest areas. One of these is *P. campanulata* (Formosan cherry). All cherries will thrive in any ordinary, well-drained soil, but they prefer one that contains a little lime. The Japanese cherries are particularly suitable for planting in shallow soil over chalk.

Plant all cherry trees in early or mid autumn (August or September), while the soil is still warm. If the weather is mild, you can plant right through the winter. Those grown in containers can be planted at any time provided they are well-watered.

Determine the planting distance between prunus in the usual way by taking the ultimate width of the prunus to be planted, adding it to that

Far left: Prunus Pandora, *with a maximum height of 10m (33 ft), makes an excellent flowering specimen tree*
Left: the almond-scented P. × yeodensis *is smaller at 8m (26 ft)*

of its neighbour and dividing by two. For a hedge, plant each prunus 60cm (24 in) apart.

Ornamental cherries are shallow-rooting plants, therefore it is important that the soil in which they are to be planted is not cultivated too often nor dug too deeply. The prunus should not be planted too deeply either. Dig a hole of such a diameter that the roots can spread out in it. When the hole is refilled, firm the soil by treading it well. At the time of planting, especially in exposed, windy positions, insert a stake into the soil and tie the young tree to it until it has become established.

Once planted, prunus need little attention apart from watering, and mulching with well-rotted manure or garden compost when needed. While the prunus are still young, take care to see that they are not loosened at their roots by high winds, and that their ties are secure.

No regular pruning is needed for these trees, but if it is necessary to cut any wood, do so in the summer because this reduces the risk of infection from silver leaf. Cherry hedges should be trimmed after flowering.

Propagation
The species are best increased from seeds sown outdoors immediately after they have been collected. Japanese cherries can be budded in late summer (July) and grafted in mid spring (March), using *P. avium* as the rootstock.

To propagate other flowering cherries, take 8–10cm (3–4 in) long heel cuttings from semi-ripe

Ornamental cherries are quite varied in height, so you should be able to find one to suit your garden, whatever its size and shape. P. avium Plena *(right) reaches a height of 12m (40 ft), while* P. glandulosa *(top right) grows only to 1.5m (5 ft) The popular, double-flowered Japanese cherry,* P. Sekiyama *(below), is medium-sized at about 7m (23 ft) high with a similar spread*

shoots of the smaller-flowered types such as *P. conradinae* and *P. incisa* in late summer (July). Insert these in a soilless cutting compost and place them in a propagating case giving a bottom heat of 16–18°C (61–64°F). When rooted; pot the cuttings into 8cm (3 in) containers of potting compost and place them in a cold frame for the winter. After winter is over plant them in a nursery bed. In a year or two, plant them out in their permanent growing quarters.

Pests and diseases
Birds, and bullfinches in particular, eat the flowering buds in winter. Aphides, cherry blackfly and mealy bugs can infest the leaves, and caterpillars feed on them. Treat by spraying with the appropriate proprietary insecticide.

Flowering cherries can be attacked by silver leaf – this is a fungus that causes the leaves to turn a silvery colour. You can minimize the risk by not cutting any wood away during winter – this should be done in the summer, when the wound is likely to heal quickly.

Some varieties to choose
In the list of ornamental cherries given below, the first dimension is the ultimate height and the second is the ultimate spread.

P. avium (gean, mazzard, wild cherry)
Has grey bark that turns mahogany-red, and bears white flowers in late spring and early summer (April and May). Its autumn foliage is crimson. 12 × 9m (40 × 30 ft).

P. conradinae Semiplena
An early-flowering spring cherry that produces its semi-double, soft pink blooms in early and mid spring (February and March). 8 × 4·5m (26 × 15ft).

P. glandulosa Sinensis
Has double, bright pink flowers borne during late spring (April). It has a bushy, round habit and likes a warm, sunny position. 1·5 × 2·4m (5 × 8 ft).

P. × hillieri Spire
An erect tree with masses of soft pink, single flowers borne during late spring and early summer (April and May). It has rich, autumn-tinted foliage. 8 × 2·4m (27 × 8 ft).

P. incisa (Fuji cherry)
A bushy tree, bearing flesh-pink flowers in great profusion during mid and late spring (March and April). 3·7 × 6m (12 × 20 ft).

P. Kursar
Has a somewhat upright habit and clusters of deep rose-pink flowers on short stalks. It has orange autumn tints. 8 × 6m (26 × 20 ft).

P. Okame
A small tree that has masses of carmine-rose flowers blooming throughout mid spring (March). It has good autumn tints. 6 × 6m (20 × 20 ft).

P. Pandora
Has ascending branches that bear masses of shell pink blossoms during mid and late spring (March and April). It has rich autumn tints. 10 × 10m (33 × 33 ft).

P. sargentii
Rounded tree with dark chestnut-brown bark and single, pink blooms borne in mid spring (March). It has glorious autumn tints. 9 × 6m (30 × 20 ft).

P. subhirtella Autumnalis (autumn cherry)
Has semi-double, white flowers, borne intermittently from early winter to mid spring (November to March). 6 × 8m (20 × 26 ft).

P. × yedoensis (Yoshino cherry)
An early-flowering tree with arching branches and a profusion of almond-scented, bluish-white blooms borne during mid and late spring (March and April). 8 × 11m (26 × 36 ft).

JAPANESE CHERRIES

P. Amanogawa
Columnar tree that produces fragrant, shell pink flowers during late spring (April). 7 × 2·1m (23 × 7 ft).

P. Asano
Small tree with ascending branches that carry thick clusters of deep pink, double flowers during mid and late spring (March and April). 8 × 6m (26 × 20 ft).

P. Horinji
Small, upright tree with soft pink flowers set in purplish-brown calyces, blooming during late spring (April). 5·5 × 3m (18 × 10 ft).

P. Shirotae
Beautiful cherry with fragrant, snow-white blooms carried in long, drooping clusters during late spring and early summer (April and May). 6 × 10m (20 × 30 ft).

P. Sekiyama (Kanzan)
Popular cherry, with purplish-pink flowers borne during late spring and early summer (April and May). 7 × 7m (23 × 23 ft).

P. Shimidsu Sakura
Small tree with pure white blossoms appearing in early summer (May). 4·5 × 6m (15 × 20 ft).

P. Ukon
Spreading tree with semi-double, greenish-yellow, occasionally flushed pink flowers that are borne in late spring (April). 5·5 × 7m (18 × 23 ft).

The exceptionally attractive Japanese ornamental cherries will grow quite happily on clay or chalk, and in areas of industrial pollution. The scented, columnar, P. Amanogawa (right), and the fragrant P. Shirotae (top) are among the most popular

OTHER ORNAMENTAL PRUNUS

The deciduous ornamental almonds, peaches, apricots and plums, together with the flowering cherries shown earlier, are among the world's most popular and decorative flowering trees and shrubs. The cherry laurels (a group of evergreen shrubs), though not comparable as far as flowers are concerned, are yet very attractive for garden purposes – either as lawn specimens or as hedges.

Although several of these ornamental prunus were introduced to Britain as long ago as the 17th century, *Prunus spinosa* (blackthorn or sloe) has the strongest claim to being a native of Britain. This might be because of the long period over which it has been cultivated, but it has certainly naturalized to the extent that it is a common plant found in hedgerows throughout Britain. This species is found all over Europe and in North Africa and western Asia. Most of the others that are not of garden origin come from China and Korea – even *P. armeniaca* (common apricot) that now grows wild in southern Europe. *P. cerasifera* (myrobalan, cherry plum) comes from the Balkans, the Caucasus and western Asia, and *P. (amygdalus nana) tenella* (dwarf Russian almond) is native to south-eastern Europe, western Asia and Siberia.

P. laurocerasus (common or cherry laurel) is a native of eastern Europe and Asia Minor and was introduced to Britain in 1576; *P. lusitanica* (Portugal laurel) grows wild in Spain and Portugal and was introduced to gardens in 1648.

Deciduous ornamental prunus

Possibly the greatest virtue of the deciduous prunus is the prettiness of their single, semi-double or double white, pale pink, rose-pink, salmon-pink, rose-red, cherry-red and crimson blossoms. Many flower on bare branches long before their own leaves appear, and before many other deciduous trees start to show any signs of life after their winter dormancy.

Above left: peach trees make a spectacular display at blossom time.
Prunus persica *Klara Meyer is an excellent example*

The first to flower, *P. davidiana* (Chinese peach), has single rose-coloured blooms, borne on bare branches, opening in late winter (January) and continuing into mid spring (March). *P. mume* (Japanese apricot) flowers in early spring (mid February), producing clusters of pale pink flowers; the next to open is *P. cerasifera* that crowds its thin branches with masses of white flowers. The majority of the other prunus (apricots, almonds, peaches) bloom during mid and late spring (March and April).

Some of these prunus yield fruits that are not only picturesque but also edible. *P. cerasifera* bears red or yellow 'cherry plums', the wild apricot, *P. armeniaca*, produces red-tinged apricots and the hybrid *P. cerasifera* Trailblazer gives bright, cherry-red plums during early and mid autumn (August and September). In addition, the Manchurian apricot *P. mandshurica*, a small, somewhat uncommon tree, bears pink blossoms and rounded yellow fruits.

The best known of all the flowering plums, however, is the blackthorn, *P. spinosa*, that abounds in the British countryside. Its small, damson-like, black fruits are familiar to most people. They are used in making preserves, wine and sloe gin.

The common almond, *P. dulcis* (*P. amygdalus* or *P. communis*), produces, later in the year, almond-green, soft velvety fruits. Unfortunately it does not usually produce good fruits in Britain, since it needs the warmer climate of southern Europe. One of the best of the edible cultivars is *P. dulcis* Macrocarpa.

The foliage of some of the deciduous prunus is quite attractive, the leaves mainly having a purple tinge. Among the ornamental plums, *P. × blireana* has leaves of a metallic coppery-purple; some of the cultivars of *P. cerasifera* also have purple-tinged leaves. Perhaps the most interesting of these is *P. c.* Pissardii (Atropurpurea); the young foliage is dark red turning to deep purple. The ornamental peach *P. persica* Foliis Rubis has rich purplish-red leaves when it is young, turning to bronze-green on maturity. The dwarf shrub *P.* Cistena (purple-leaf sand cherry) is another prunus with rich red foliage; *P. (triflora) salicina* (Japanese plum) has leaves that change to bright red in autumn.

The ornamental prunus are not exceptionally large trees; they take some years to reach their full size. Typical among the larger ones is the almond. *P. × amygdalo-persica*, with a height and spread of 6–8m (20–26 ft), while at the other end of the scale, *P. spinosa* has a height and spread of 3–4·5m (10–15 ft). Of the dwarfs, the almond *P. tenella* has a height and spread of not more than 60cm–1·2m (2–4 ft), and *P.* Cistena a maximum height and spread of 1·2–1·5m (4–5 ft).

Generally, all these trees look their best planted in a shrub border, along the boundary of the garden or, in the case of the more modest growers, as specimens in the lawn. The dwarfs, such as *P. tenella* and *P.* Cistena, are excellent shrubs for island beds and narrow borders. In addition, some prunus make very attractive, comparatively modest-growing, colourful hedges and screens. *P. cerasifera* and its purple-leaved cultivar *P. c.* Pissardii, *P. spinosa* Purpurea and *P. s.* Rosea are recommended for this purpose.

The cherry laurels

Both *P. laurocerasus* and *P. lusitanica* are evergreen and they both have dark green leaves and small white flowers that, with the exception of one or two varieties, are not particularly outstanding. The leaves of *P. lusitanica* have red stalks and, in some cultivars, are reddish as they unfold. After flowering, *P. laurocerasus* yields red fruits that turn black; the fruits of *P. lusitanica*, also red, become dark purple. A particular virtue of *P. lusitanica* is that it is quite happy in shallow chalk soil, whereas *P. laurocerasus* is not. Both are excellent for hedging.

Because *P. laurocerasus* is so frequently seen growing as a clipped hedge, it is not always realized that it can reach a height of 4·5–6m (15–20 ft) and a spread of 6–10m (20–30 ft). *P. lusitanica* is a rather more modest grower, with a maximum height and spread of 4·5–6m (15–20 ft).

P. laurocerasus is grown mainly for its outstanding value as a hedging and screening plant. This value is appreciably enhanced by its tolerance of shade. One variety, the almost prostrate *P. i.* Zabeliana, makes excellent ground cover. When allowed to develop freely both the species and its cultivars make beautiful specimen trees.

Cultivation

The deciduous prunus thrive in any ordinary, well-drained soil, but prefer one that contains a trace of lime. The soil must not be too dry or water logged, nor cultivated too frequently or very deeply, because prunus are mostly shallow-rooting plants. Neither *P. laurocerasus* nor *P. lusitanica* is very particular about soil, provided it is fertile and well-drained, except that the former does not thrive on shallow chalk soil.

Plant all types of prunus in early autumn (August), or throughout the winter during mild spells. Provided you water generously, you can plant them out from containers at any time.

Calculate the planting distance by adding together the spreads of the proposed adjoining trees and dividing by two. For hedges, *P. cerasifera* and its cultivars should be 60cm (2 ft) apart, *P. spinosa* 38cm (15 in), *P. laurocerasus* 75cm (2½ ft), *P. lusitanica* 60cm (2 ft) and *P.* Cistena 60cm (2 ft) apart.

Plant all types in a hole large enough in diameter to allow the roots to spread out, and of such a depth that the soil mark indicating the original depth will be at the surface of the soil in the new position. Replace the soil with gentle treading in. In windy positions, insert a stake at the same time as you plant, particularly for trees. After planting a hedge, cut back all shoots by one-third to promote a good bushy growth.

Apart from mulching and watering in order to

Prunus persica *Klara Meyer, an ornamental peach, follows its showy, double blooms with juicy, edible fruits*

prevent the roots drying out, hardly any attention is needed. Little pruning is required, but you can clip back deciduous hedges at any time, unless you are growing them for the flowers. In this case prune after flowering. Prune laurels with secateurs, not shears, in late spring (April).

Fortunately, these prunus are fairly free from pests, except that greenfly and blackfly might be troublesome. Treat by spraying with the appropriate proprietary insecticide, used according to the manufacturer's instructions. These prunus are also fairly free from disease, except for the risk of silver leaf that can be avoided by always cutting back in the summer when the wound will heal rapidly. The ornamental peaches are liable to be affected by peach leaf curl. Treat by spraying just before bud-burst with lime sulphur, liquid copper fungicide or captan. Repeat the treatment a fortnight later and once again at leaf-fall.

Some varieties to choose
The first dimension given is the average height and the second is the spread. Unless otherwise stated, assume that the cultivars are approximately the same size as their parents.

ORNAMENTAL ALMONDS
P. × amygdalo-persica Pollardii
Vigorous hybrid between a peach and an almond. Rich pink blooms 5cm (2 in) across, opening in mid and late spring (March and April), before any leaves appear. 6–8m × 6–8m (20–26 ft).

P. (amygdalus or *communis) dulcis* (common almond).
Erect tree, producing clear pink flowers in clusters on bare branches in mid and late spring (March and April). 7 × 7m (23 × 23 ft).
P. d. Alba   White flowers.
P. d. Praecox   Pale pink flowers, in early spring (February).
P. d. Erecta   Variety with columnar habit.
P. d. Roseoplena   Double, pale pink flowers.

P. (amygdalus nana) tenella (dwarf Russian almond)
The best variety of this species is *P. t.* Fire Hill that is a dwarf plant with rose-crimson blooms borne during late spring (April). 90 × 90cm (3 × 3 ft).

ORNAMENTAL PEACHES
P. davidiana (Chinese peach)
Small, erect tree that needs a sheltered position because it produces its white or rose-coloured flowers from late winter to mid spring (January to March). 8·5 × 7m (28 × 23 ft).
P. d. Alba   White blossoms.

P. persica (common peach)
Smallish, bushy tree or large shrub with pale pink flowers and fleshy, juicy fruits. 6 × 6m (20 × 20 ft).
P. p. Cardinal   Glowing red, semi-double blooms.
P. p. Crimson   Weeping habit, crimson
Cascade   blossoms.

Above: P. dulcis *(common almond) needs constant warm weather to produce good fruits*
Left: the fruits of P. spinosa *(sloe) have many culinary uses*
Top left: P. lusitanica *(Portugal laurel)*
Far left: P. cerasifera *Pissardii (cherry plum) makes an ornamental hedge*

P. p. Iceberg	Semi-double, pure white blooms.
P. p. Klara Mayer	Double, peach-pink flowers and edible fruits.
P. p. Russell's Red	Carmine-red flowers.

ORNAMENTAL APRICOTS

P. mume (Japanese apricot)
Small tree with almond-scented, pink flowers, some borne in late winter (January), others during late spring (April). 6 × 6m (20 × 20 ft).

P. m. Alphandii	Semi-double pink blooms.
P. m. Beni-shi-don	Deep madder-pink blossoms.
P. m. Pendula	Weeping habit, with pale pink flowers.

ORNAMENTAL PLUMS

P. × *blireana*
Beautiful small tree with metallic coppery-purple foliage and double, fragrant, rose-pink blossoms opening in late spring (April). 5 × 4·5m (16 × 15 ft).

P. cerasifera (myrobalan, cherry plum)
The species has a height and spread of 7m (23 ft).

P. c. Pissardii	Deep purple leaves; an excellent hedging plant.
P. c. Trailblazer	Larger-leaved variety.
P. c. Pendula	White-flowered, weeping tree with bronze leaves.

P. Cistena (purple-leaf sand cherry)
Dwarf shrub characterized by deep red leaves, white flowers and black-purple fruits. A good hedging plant. 1·5 × 1·5m (5 × 5 ft).

P. spinosa (blackthorn, sloe)
Spiny, bare branches packed with small white flowers during mid spring (March) and succeeded by blue fruits. 4 × 4m (13 × 13 ft).

P. s. Plena	Double-flowered form.
P. s. Purpurea	Excellent purple-leaved form.

CHERRY LAURELS

P. laurocerasus (common or cherry laurel)
Characterized by dark, shiny evergreen leaves. In late spring (April) it bears small white flowers followed by red, subsequently black, fruits. It is very tolerant of shade and rain drips from trees. 5·5 × 8m (18 × 26 ft).

P. l. Otto Luyken	Compact, low-growing form.
P. l. Rotundifolia	Bushy variety.
P. l. Variegata	Variety with creamy-white, variegated leaves.

P. lusitanica (Portugal laurel)
Evergreen, with dark green leaves on red stalks. It has long racemes of white flowers in mid summer (June), followed by small red fruits that turn dark purple. 5·5 × 5·5m (18 × 18 ft).

P. l. Angustifolia	A neat, slightly smaller cultivar.
P. l. azorica	A large evergreen shrub.
P. l. Variegata	Attractive variegated form.

PYRACANTHA

Type	evergreen flowering and fruiting shrubs
Common name	firethorn
Family	ROSACEAE
Flowering season	early and mid summer (May and June)
Planting date	best mid and late autumn (September and October) and then late spring and early summer (April and May); container-grown: any time
Mature size/shape	2·4–4·2m × 2·4–4·2m (8–14 ft × 8–14 ft) round, sometimes erect

The pyracantha genus popularly known as firethorn, is one of the groups within the ROSACEAE family and is composed of 10 species of hardy evergreen shrubs. The reason for their popular name will be fully appreciated by anybody who has seen some of the species during the winter, almost on fire with their brilliant display of red berries, or who has attempted to pluck a branch to brighten up a floral arrangement and jabbed their thumb on one of the vicious spikes that cover the shoots. Pyracantha are unrivalled for their many uses and values in the garden; they have a cheerful, tidy appearance and add brilliance during the winter when things are getting a bit dull and a lot of the neatness has gone from the outdoor surroundings of the house. They are all relatively quick-growing, which is a great asset in these days of small gardens, where often there is an urgent need to cover ugly walls or fences, or for screens to obscure some neighbouring eyesore or to increase privacy.

The species all have great similarities. Of these the most obvious are the masses of very attractive, hawthorn-like, white or creamy-white blossoms that they bear in mid summer (June) and the plethora of brilliantly-coloured small berries, about 6mm ($\frac{1}{4}$ in) in diameter, that they produce during autumn and winter. The colours to be found among the berries of the different species and their cultivars are red, coral-red, orange, yellow and creamy-yellow. It is unfortunate that because these winter colours are so outstanding only the most discriminating of gardeners fully appreciate the great quality of the firethorns as flowering shrubs. For beauty, abundance and perfume there are few evergreens to surpass them. When their branches are heavy with the myriad clusters of flowers nestling among their foliage – that sets them off so well – it is difficult to find a more beautiful sight in any garden.

Pyracantha are closely related to cotoneasters, producing much the same type of bloom and in many instances the same massive display of coloured berries. They are, however, distinguished from them by having thorny branches. Incidentally, the main differences between the various firethorns are largely found in their foliage. The leaves can be large, small, narrow, oval, broadly rounded at the apex and so on.

Most of the pyracantha species that adorn gardens at the present time originated in China. *Pyracantha atalantioides* was brought from that country in 1907 by the botanist and explorer E. H. Wilson, while another – *P. rogersiana* – was introduced from the same part of the world in 1911 by George Forrest. Exceptions are *P. crenulata*, whose habitat is in the Himalayas, and the very beautiful *P. coccinea*, that was discovered growing wild in southern European countries and Asia Minor and first brought to northern Europe round about 1629. In fact there are records that show that firethorn was quite well-established in English gardens from the early 17th century.

It can be imagined that a race of plants giving such a wonderful display of beauty and colour through more than one season cannot fail to have numerous uses in a garden. They are seen growing against walls so often that it is frequently accepted they are exclusively wall plants. This is certainly

Below: P. Orange Glow has very long-lasting berries

one of the purposes for which they are eminently suitable, particularly as many of them are indifferent to the aspect of their background. In addition to this quite valuable use they make excellent specimen shrubs, for with their solid mass of coloured berries from autumn onwards, there is little else in the garden to rival them. A single bush might be placed as a focal point in the corner of a rich green sward of neatly-mown grass, or you might grow one in a shrubbery border where the brilliance of its colourful berries and the clear greenness of its evergreen foliage would enliven the sombreness of its neighbours in winter. One in particular is highly recommended for this last task: *P. rogersiana* Flava follows its masses of creamy-white flowers in early summer with cascades of brilliant chrome-yellow berries as the summer gives way to the cooler days of autumn.

Another invaluable use of several species is for making hedges that, with the very vicious, long spines of the plants, become almost impenetrable. Perhaps the best for this job are Orange Glow, which is very dense, *P. rogersiana* and Watereri. Several of them, such as *P. atalantioides* that grows 4·5–5·4m (15–18 ft) high, make good screens.

To grow pyracantha against a wall, train the sideshoots horizontally along strands of wire, 15cm (6 in) or less apart, fixed to vine eyes driven into the wall. After a time these sideshoots knit together to form a solid mass of green at least 1·5m (5 ft) either side of the main stem. This characteristic affords an excellent, economical way of making a hedge in a small garden. You erect a post and wire fence with strands of wire 10–15cm (4–6 in) apart, either in the open or against an existing wooden fence, and plant the pyracantha at intervals along it. If you train the sideshoots carefully along these wires and cut out all shoots growing backwards and forwards as soon as they appear, it is surprising how quickly a good hedge can be made. When the shrubs are first planted to achieve this object, cut them back by about a quarter to encourage basal growths that should be trained horizontally as soon as possible to secure a good solid base to the hedge.

A pyracantha hedge has several virtues. The first is that it is quite inexpensive because it is only necessary to plant one bush about every 2·5m (8 ft) instead of every 45–60cm (18–24 in) as with a conventional hedge. With the cost of shrubs this is quite a consideration. The second important thing is that such a hedge does not take up much space, because it can be kept clipped back to a depth of under 30cm (12 in). Thirdly, as the hedge has been created by far fewer shrubs than is more conventional, the demand on the plant foods in the soil is much lower. Once again, this is invaluable in a small garden, because it does not become unduly impoverished and allows for other ornamental shrubs to flourish. You must remember, however, that it takes rather longer to get a good hedge this way, but the extra patience required is well compensated.

Right: espalier-trained pyracantha

Above: The very compact
P. watereri *makes a
fine hedge and is equally
useful for screening
an odd wall*

Cultivation

Pyracanthas are hardy and can tolerate almost any conditions; they are even quite happy to be planted in seaside areas. When they are mature they are pretty tolerant of exposure, although in very cold areas they should be given some protection when they are young. Most of them are not very particular about the aspect of their position, and for this reason, they are especially valuable because they can be planted to cover a north wall. Some, such as *P. atalantioides*, will flourish in sunless spots and so give brightness with their blooms and berries to places, such as town gardens completely hemmed in by tall buildings, where no other plants would flourish. In addition pyracantha are quite indifferent to pollution and can thus be used in industrial areas.

They cause very little worry regarding soil, because they flourish in almost any soil, providing it is fertile. However, be sure that whatever its nature, the soil is well-drained. All pyracantha will grow very happily in clay, but you must take particular care here to see that water passes freely through it and there is no likelihood of it becoming waterlogged. As a very large number of other shrubs object to this condition you can drain the ground by putting a 45cm (18 in) deep trench across the site, and fill it with about 30cm (12 in) of rubble and a top layer of 15cm (6 in) of topsoil. Pyracantha will grow well in a chalky soil and equally in soil that is on the acid side without any signs of trouble.

All pyracantha resent being transplanted, so usually container-grown plants are sold by nurserymen; as we describe under When and how to plant, the seedlings or rooted cuttings are finally potted up before transferring them to their growing position outdoors.

Little attention is needed beyond watering during a period of drought, hoeing the surrounding soil to keep it free from weeds and mulching with garden compost, peat, manure or spent hops when the soil is moist in early summer (May). Being evergreens, they welcome being sprayed with cold water in the evening during dry weather.

When they are grown as wall plants, the sideshoots should be regularly tied in every year between late summer and mid autumn (July and September). To encourage side growths, any shoots growing forward that are not needed should be cut back to the stem from which they emerge between early and mid summer (May and June). When they are growing as specimens no pruning is necessary other than to keep them tidy and to size.

When and how to plant

Like other evergreen shrubs generally, pyracantha are best planted out between mid and late autumn (September and October) or during late spring and early summer (April and May) after the risk of the young plants being exposed to any severe winter weather and icy winds has passed. Although these periods are more usually recommended as being the safest, it seems that when they are container-grown (as they usually are), there is little reason why they should not be planted any time other than when the weather is likely to be severe. If this is done, however, it is important to see that they are kept well watered for a time after planting.

Since the majority of pyracantha have an ultimate spread of about 3m (10 ft), if several are planted in a group in a shrub border they need to be planted about 3m (10 ft) apart. When they are planted in a mixed bed of shrubs, the planting distance between a pyracantha and its neighbour is determined in the usual way by adding the ultimate spread of the former to that of its adjacent companion and dividing the sum by two. The ultimate spread of various shrubs is often given nowadays in nurserymen's catalogues or standard books on gardening.

Unless the previously-mentioned technique for making a pyracantha hedge is adopted, to get a good thick hedge quickly the planting distance should be 38–60cm (15–24 in).

As pyracantha are nearly always raised in containers, a hole for one that is intended as a free-standing bush should be dug so that it is about 10cm (4 in) greater in diameter than that of the rootball and of such a depth that the soil level in the pot is just at the surface of the soil in the bed when it is planted. Humus-making material, such as compost, manure or damp peat, should be mixed into the soil at the bottom of the hole. Tap the plant out of the pot and place it in the hole. Pack some of the excavated soil (not too tightly) round the rootball and firm it gently treading around the circumference of the hole. Finally level the surface of the soil, leaving it loose. Before planting, plunge the pot into water and keep it there until any bubbles cease to rise. At the time of planting insert a stake because pyracantha normally need some support in their early days.

When making a hedge, treat the plants similarly. When they are 20cm (8 in) tall, pinch out the growing tips to encourage basal growths. This should be done again later on.

If the pyracantha is intended to be a wall plant, it is best to plant it, leaning backwards slightly, about 30cm (12 in) in front of the wall and to train the young growths back to it in the first instance. This is because beds at the foot of a wall are so much under the eaves of the house that rain does not easily reach them and the soil keeps almost permanently dry. In this position it is important, prior to planting, to provide some wires spanning vine eyes driven into the wall or trellis, to which the young branches can be tied before they get disturbed.

Pyracantha can be raised from seed, but remember that only the species (not their cultivars) will be truly reproduced. Pick the ripe berries in late autumn (October) and squash them to obtain the seeds. Sow them in trays of J.I. seed compost or a soilless compost and put into a cold frame. When the seedlings are large enough to handle, prick them out into several seed trays. Ultimately they are transplanted into 8cm (3 in) pots and kept in the cold frame. The following late spring or early summer (April or May) plunge them into the soil or a specially-made bed of peat outdoors. In late autumn (October) you can make a start on planting out the young shrubs in their permanent growing quarters.

The alternative is to grow from cuttings that should be of hardwood and about 10–15cm (4–6 in) long. Take the cuttings in late autumn (October) and insert them in a bed of equal parts sand and peat in a cold frame. Pot them up in the following late spring or early summer (April or May) and plunge the pots into an outdoor bed of soil or peat. Finally, plant out the small plants in late autumn (October).

Pests and diseases
Stems and leaves are sometimes affected by aphides, particularly woolly aphides, that are detected by the presence of white, waxy tufts; spray with derris or malathion to control them. Scale insects are another menace. They make the plant sticky and sooty moulds develop. Spray with diazonin or malathion if the infestation is heavy.

As with other species belonging to the ROSACEAE family, pyracantha are likely to be attacked by fireblight, that blackens and shrivels the flowers and causes the leaves to wither and the branches to die back. If this happens there is nothing to do but dig up the infected plant and burn it.

A disease peculiar to pyracantha is pyracantha scab, indicated by an olive-brown or black coating on the leaves and berries. Spray with captan as soon as you see these symptoms.

Above right: two varieties intermingling will give even more colour interest

Some varieties to choose
The selection that follows lists excellent shrubs, that are easily available, to grow free-standing, or as wall plants, or for hedging. The figures given for ultimate height (first figure) and spread (second figure) relate to pyracantha growing as bushes. On a sheltered wall they normally reach greater height.

P. angustifolia	Grey-green leaves, with conspicuous clusters of orange-yellow berries that do not ripen until mid winter (December) and are sometimes retained until spring. 3×2.7m (10×9 ft). Will do best against a west wall.
P. atalantioides (*P. gibbsii*)	Considered to be the best red-berried wall plant. Good for sunless walls. Birds seldom eat the fruit. 3.6×3.6m (12×12 ft). Aurea has rich yellow fruits.
P. coccinea	Flowers in mid summer (June), followed by red berries. 3.6×3.6m (12×12 ft). Lalandei is possibly the most popular pyracantha. It has larger orange-red berries that smother the branches. 4.2×4.2m (14×14 ft).
P. crenulata	Orange-red berries. 2.7×3.9m (9×13 ft).
P. Orange Glow	Branches are inundated with long-lasting, bright orange-red berries. Good for hedging, as a bush, or on a north-facing wall. 2.4×3m (8×10 ft).
P. rogersiana	Freely produces reddish-orange berries. Makes an excellent hedge. 2.4×2.4m (8×8 ft). Flava is a very attractive bright yellow-berried version.
P. Shawnee	Comparatively recent introduction from America. Its masses of white flowers are succeeded by an abundance of yellow-to-orange berries as early as early autumn (August). Good for wall or border. It is claimed to be resistant to fireblight and scab. 3×3m (10×10 ft).
P. Watereri	Compact-growing shrub with masses of bright red berries. Good for a wall as a specimen, or as a hedge. 2.7×3.6m (9×12 ft).

RHODODENDRONS

Type	evergreen and deciduous flowering shrubs
Family	ERICACEAE
Flowering season	late winter to late summer (January–July)
Planting date	outdoors: mid to late spring (March–April) or autumn (September–October); from containers: anytime
Mature size/shape	prostrate to 12m (40 ft) spreading or bushy
Special use	Permanent ornamental foliage and flowering shrubs or small trees

Between them, the rhododendron and the rose have revolutionized British gardens, and it has all happened in the last hundred years or so. Rhododendrons were grown long before that but they were a rather dull lot and made no impact on ordinary gardeners. The first to arrive from Asia Minor in 1763 was *Rhododendron ponticum*, and it liked the British climate and soil so much that it soon escaped from gardens and began to naturalize itself. It is now the common rhododendron of many woodlands and some moorlands, a shrub much used as cover for game and also as a windbreak or hedge, but seldom nowadays as an ornamental garden shrub. Its purplish-mauve colour is too restricted, its flowers insufficiently impressive, to stand competition with the beauties that have since arrived. Nevertheless it is still a very common rootstock for other rhododendron cultivars. The name is derived from the Greek *rhodon* (a rose) and *dendron* (a tree).

The revolution began with the discovery in the mid-19th century of previously unknown rhododendrons in the Himalayas and in the mountain ranges and valleys of Burma, Assam and southern and south-western China. What started as a trickle became a flood and today botanists recognize 500–600 distinct species.

Not all the newcomers were beauties or even of much use to gardeners, but a great many were. What was really remarkable was the astonishing range of shapes, sizes and colour to be found among them. There were prostrate rhododendrons that crept along the ground and, at the other extreme, tree rhododendrons that could reach 10–12m (up to 40 ft); some with huge, and some with tiny, flowers in all manner of colours including scarlet, crimson, pink, salmon, apricot, yellow, purple and very nearly pure blue.

Because of the parts of the world from which they came, a good many of the new species were rather tender. Some needed greenhouse protection in winter, some grew well in places where the climate was exceptionally mild. But many were completely hardy everywhere and even the tender kinds provided the plant breeders with some magnificent material on which to work.

Looking back to the latter part of the 19th century it is possible to distinguish two distinct types of hybrid. One came from the nurserymen who kept their breeding programmes completely secret and crossed species and existing hybrids with the sole object of producing hardy, reliable, free-flowering shrubs. The other came from wealthy amateurs willing to record and publish the crosses they made and anxious to outvie one another in size of bloom, novelty of colour, richness of scent and everything else that made the new rhododendron so exciting.

The amateurs cared little if some of their seedlings were tender. The nurserymen, by contrast, concentrated on utility, and since, even in the hardiest rhododendron, the flowers and opening flower-buds can be completely spoiled by frost, they selected in the main varieties which flowered only in summer (mid May to mid June). So the amateurs produced hybrids of great beauty and variety with a flowering season from mid winter to late summer (January to July) and the nurserymen produced hardy hybrids which tended to look much alike in shape and size, had a concentrated flowering season, and differed chiefly in flower colours and quality.

The two races are still with us, the pedigree hybrids and the hardy hybrids, plus a great many species just as they grow in the wild. But we now know a great deal more about rhododendrons than we did, can select for gardens from all three groups with every expectation of success, and have developed means of growing rhododendrons even where it would have seemed impossible to do so a generation or so ago. The rhododendron has arrived as a shrub which does for the ordinary garden in spring and early summer what the rose can do so well for it from midsummer to autumn—fill it with colour and perfume and do it with a minimum of trouble or risk of failure.

In one respect rhododendrons are still at a disadvantage to roses. Most of them dislike

Right: magnificent view of hardy hybrid Mrs Furnival
Below: flower detail of hardy hybrid Gomer Waterer

alkaline soils so much that they can only be grown in chalk or limestone soils with special precautions or treatments. But those precautions are now fully understood and the treatments are available, and anyone can grow rhododendrons today.

Nearly all the shrubs that gardeners would regard as 'true' rhododendrons are evergreens, but botanists extend the genus to include what gardeners know as azaleas, some of which are evergreen and some deciduous. Most garden centres follow this horticultural practice and list azaleas separately, but a few adopt the botanical classification and put them under rhododendron, though with the garden varieties in a separate group under appropriate sub-headings. It is quite likely that botanists will one day also give the azaleas generic rank (they already fill a separate section or 'series' of the huge rhododendron genus) and there is so much to be said about them that we have already given them a section in their own right on page 30.

All rhododendrons prefer acid soils but they differ in their sensitiveness to it. For most, pH 5·0 to pH 6·0 is ideal, but many will grow well even up to pH 6·5 and some, including *Rhododendron ponticum* and some of the hardy hybrids, will get along quite nicely in neutral soils (pH 7·0) without special help. But usually, beyond pH 6·5, it will be necessary either to import acid soil and peat to make up beds for the rhododendrons, or to feed them two or three times a year with 'chelated' iron and manganese.

Chelates are complex chemical compounds which are now available in most garden shops, ready for mixing with water according to label instructions and applying to the soil. If special beds are prepared it is an advantage if they can be built up 30cm (12 in) or more above the level of the existing soil so that lime does not wash from this into the rhododendron bed. However, this means that another danger must be guarded against; raised beds can become very dry beds in summer. Rhododendrons can be watered, but if the mains water is 'hard' (alkaline), as it may well be in a chalk or limestone locality, this can introduce the very element you are trying to exclude. Rainwater is the ideal solution, and it is worthwhile putting a rain barrel where it can collect water from something like a shed or greenhouse roof.

All rhododendrons make masses of fibrous roots which bind the soil together into a tight ball. This makes them very easy to move even when they are quite big – a bonus for the gardener who can move them to other places if the original arrangement proves unsatisfactory, or can deliberately overplant at the outset to get a quick effect and then thin out later on.

If rhododendrons are to be moved from open ground, autumn (September–October) and mid to late spring (March–April) are the best planting seasons, but if they are obtained in containers rhododendrons can be planted at any time of the year provided they are properly looked after. But they should never be planted in exposed positions during wintry weather.

Bushes do not normally require pruning, but if they grow too large the branches can be cut back even to within a few inches of the soil level, although this will prevent flowering for at least one year. The best time for such hard pruning is in early summer (May) or immediately after flowering.

Rhododendrons, especially the species, usually set seed freely. This is almost dust-like and a pod can contain thousands of seeds, which is why the breeders were able to produce new varieties so quickly. But such tiny seeds are rather difficult to manage, seedlings take a number of years to reach flowering size, and those raised from hybrid plants are likely to differ greatly both from their parents and from one another. So in practice seed is not much used as a method of propagation except by specialists and breeders.

Nurserymen propagate mainly by grafting, usually onto seedlings of *Rhododendron ponticum*, and to a lesser degree by cutting and layering. Grafted plants have good roots and grow well, but if they produce suckers (shoots direct from the roots), these will be of the same character as the stock, not of the garden variety grafted on it. This accounts for many of the big bushes of *Rhododendron ponticum* to be seen in gardens. Their owners have failed to notice and remove the suckers which, because of their greater vigour, have gradually swamped and killed the garden variety. Ponticum suckers have narrower, darker green leaves than most of the hybrids, but the important point to watch for is any growth that is clearly of a different character from the rest of the bush. Trace such stems to their source and if this is at the roots or very low down on the main stem, more or less at soil level, they are almost certainly suckers and should be cut out with a sharp knife or secateurs.

By contrast rhododendrons raised from cuttings or layers are 'on their own roots' to use the gardener's phrase. The whole plant, stems and roots, is of the same kind, and suckers will bear just as beautiful flowers as stems from above ground and should be retained.

Most rhododendrons like to grow in dappled shade—the kind of shade provided by fairly thin woodland. If the cover trees are mixed deciduous

and evergreens, say some oaks and some pines, this is ideal. But these conditions are not essential and the hardy hybrids in particular will usually grow well even in full sun, provided the soil does not get too hot and dry in summer. One of the advantages of digging-in plenty of rotted leaves or peat before planting is that they both help to keep the soil cool and moist without making it too wet in winter; this should also be done each spring.

In addition to the 500–600 species there are now thousands of hybrid rhododendrons. Some nurserymen specialize in them and all garden centres offer quite a good selection. Here is a short selection of pedigree species and hybrids, together with some non-pedigree hardy hybrids which are still the toughest and easiest to grow (they are certainly the best where the air is smoke-polluted).

Bottom left and left: hardy hybrids Pink Pearl and Sappho

HARDY HYBRIDS

These average 3–4·5m (10–15 ft) in height and diameter when fully grown. or considerably more in moist, sheltered positions. Most of them flower in early to mid summer (May to June). The flowers are widely funnel-shaped, and measure 5–7·5cm (2–3 in) across.

Beauty of Littleworth	White-spotted crimsons.
Blue Peter	Violet-blue, the best of its colour.
Britannia	Scarlet with wavy-edged flowers. Slow growing and compact.
Christmas Cheer	Pink buds opening to blush-white flowers in mid spring (March).
Cynthia	Rose-red, very vigorous, hardy and reliable.
Doncaster	Crimson-scarlet, below average height.
Goldsworth Yellow	Apricot-pink buds opening to primrose-yellow flowers.
Gomer Waterer	White flushed mauve with yellow blotch.
Loder's White	Mauve-pink buds opening to pure white flowers in early summer (May).
Mrs Charles E. Pearson	Mauve-pink becoming nearly white.
Mrs Furnival	Rose-pink blotched with brown and crimson.
Mrs G. W. Leak	Similar to last in colour but a little earlier and a looser flower truss.
Pink Pearl	Rose buds opening to very large pink flowers. Rather lax habit.
Purple Splendour	Rich deep purple.
Sappho	Mauve buds opening to white flowers with almost black blotch.
Souvenir de Dr S. Endtz	Rose buds opening to pink flowers. Vigorous in growth.
Susan	Lavender-blue.

PEDIGREE HYBRIDS

These are best planted in thin woodland with dappled shade (sharp de-frosting caused by early morning sun may damage buds) and shelter from cold winds.

Angelo	Huge, sweetly-scented white flowers in mid summer (June). 3–4m (10–13 ft) when full grown.
Blue Diamond	Clusters of small lavender-blue flowers in late spring (April). 1m (3 ft).
Elizabeth	Large, deep red flowers in late spring (April). 1m (3 ft). Very hardy.
Hawk	Large pale yellow flowers in early summer (May). Up to 3m (10 ft). Crest is a particularly fine form.
Lady Chamberlain	Clusters of drooping, almost tubular orange-red flowers in early summer (May). Up to 2m (7 ft).
Loderi	Huge trusses of white- or pink-flushed, richly scented flowers in early summer (May). 3–4m (10–13 ft).
Naomi	Large pink- or mauve-tinted sweetly scented flowers in early summer (May). To 3m (10 ft).
Polar Bear	Large white flowers in late summer (July). 3–4m (10–13 ft).
Praecox	Magenta flowers in early spring (February–March). To 1·5m (5 ft).
Tally Ho	Brilliant red flowers appearing mid summer (June). About 2m (7 ft).
Temple Belle	Bell-shaped rose-pink flowers in early summer (May). 1m (3 ft).

SPECIES

As with the pedigree hybrids, species are best planted in light shelter such as thin woodland.

R. arboreum	Red, pink or white flowers from late winter to late spring (January to April). To 12m (40 ft).
R. augustinii	Blue or mauve flowers in late spring (April–May). 2 to 3m (6–10 ft). Electra is a fine blue form.
R. cinnabarinum	Cinnabar-red (vermilion) tubular flowers in early summer (May–June). To 3m (10 ft). The variety Blandfordiflorum has flowers yellow inside, and the variety Roylei purplish-red flowers.
R. discolor	Large pink flowers in mid summer (June–July). 3–4m (10–13 ft).
R. falconeri	Huge leaves and large cream flowers blotched with purple in late spring (April–May). 4–6m (13–20 ft).
R. fortunei	Scented lilac-pink flowers in early summer (May). 4–5m (13–17 ft).
R. leucaspis	Saucer-shaped creamy white flowers in early spring (February–March). About 50cm (20 in).
R. racemosum	Small pink flowers in mid to late spring (March–April). Up to 2m (7 ft). Forrest's Dwarf is a shorter form.
R. russatum	Small violet-blue flowers in late spring (April–May). Up to 1m (3 ft).
R. thomsonii	Blood-red flowers in late spring (April). 4–5m (13–17 ft).
R. wardii	Saucer-shaped yellow flowers in early summer (May). 3–4m (10–13 ft).
R. williamsianum	Bell-shaped pink flowers in late spring (April). Neat heart-shaped leaves. About 1m (3 ft).
R. yakushimanum	Rose-pink buds opening to white flowers in early summer (May). 1m (3 ft). There are numerous hybrids of this species, most of which retain its dwarf compact habit but extend its range to include all the rhododendron colours. These are very good garden plants.

Top: R. wardii, *an early summer-flowering species*
Centre: the pedigree hybrids Blue Diamond and Lady Chamberlain
Below: cluster of spring-flowering R. falconeri

SORBUS

Type	deciduous flowering and fruiting tree or shrub
Family	ROSACEAE
Flowering season	early or mid summer (May or June)
Planting date	late autumn to mid spring (October to March); from containers: anytime
Mature size/shape	60cm high × 45cm wide (2 × 1½ ft) to 7·5m high × 4m wide (22 × 12 ft); round-headed, conical, pyramidal, fastigiate

The genus sorbus is composed of 100 species of hardy, deciduous trees that were formerly included in the pyrus (pear) genus. The name comes from the Latin for the fruit of the service tree. Sorbus are easily grown on the whole and not particularly choosy about the soil or the position they are offered. Many of the species and hybrids are tolerant of shade and do not object to atmospheric pollution; this makes them very suitable for gardens in industrial areas. There are some members of the genus that are equally happy in coastal areas and exposed cold districts. They range in size from dwarf shrubs to larger trees. Unfortunately the most charming of the former, *Sorbus reducta*, is rare these days. It is an erect growing shrub with a height of between 30–60cm (1–2 ft) and has round, pinkish berries.

Sorbus trees reach heights of 6–9m (20–30 ft) and are largely sold as standards or as feathered trees. Numbers of them are very upright in their growth which enables them to be fitted into restricted areas but in many cases they are not really suitable for smaller gardens. However, in a built-up area, if there is space, *S. aucuparia* (mountain ash or rowan) is excellent for screening from sight any ugly or undesirable neighbouring object. Because of its mid-green, feathery leaves, with grey underneath, it provides a cheerful effect.

In order to facilitate the description of these species, it is necessary to consider briefly how their family is made up.

The sorbus genus is made up of three groups, and most of them belong to the first two.

Aria Members have simple leaves that are either toothed or lobed. In the main, they do well on chalky soil. The head of this group is the well-known *S. aria* (whitebeam).

Aucuparia The leading member of this category is the familiar *S. aucuparia*, or mountain ash. Plants in this group have pinnate leaves with numbers of leaflets. Quite a number of its members – species and cultivars – are short-lived on shallow chalk, preferring richer, deeper soils.

Micromeles The members of this much smaller class are different from those of the aucuparia in that the calyces of their fruits fall seasonally like deciduous leaves.

At this point it is appropriate to mention that there is a group of hybrids known as the 'Lombarts hybrid Sorbus'. This race has been raised by a famous Dutch nursery since the 1950s. It is made up of vigorous, elegant trees of upright habit, chiefly characterized by having larger and more unusually-coloured berries. They are not stocked by all nurserymen but they are worth searching out.

Regarding the habitat of these many species, a few such as *S. aria*, *S. aucuparia* and *S.*

Far left: Sorbus hybrida, *one of the whitebeams, forms a compact small tree*
Left: S. aucuparia *Xanthocarpa, a rowan or mountain ash*
Below S. a. Beissneri *is especially noted for the warm colouring of its bark*

bristoliensis are natives of the British Isles. So far, the latter has only been found growing wild in the Avon gorge near Bristol. The origins of the rest are widespread throughout the world – the mountains of Europe, Scandinavia, North America, Kashmir, Tibet, Manchuria, China, Japan and elsewhere. In addition, quite a number of the most attractive sorbus are hybrids or cultivars raised in gardens and nurseries.

With its autumn tints and coloured berries – that often ripen while the leaves are still green – sorbus can add a particularly beautiful touch to your garden. If you have the space you can grow some of the more slender, fastigiate species or cultivars as a specimen in the lawn or as an accent point in a shrubbery.

The small, upright, slender whitebeam species *S. minima* that does not grow to a greater height than 3m (10 ft) in ten years is a possibility in a smallish garden, as is the very upright, small tree *S. alnifolia submollis* (*zahlbruckneri*), a contrasting form to other whitebeams. It reaches a height of 2·5m (8 ft) or so in about the same time.

When a screen is required a mountain ash or whitebeam might fit the purpose most effectively.

Although the general tendency among the groups of trees is to grow upright branches, some are to be found with various shapes and habits that are valuable in creating a pleasing elevation in the garden. A few are rounded in outline, others are pyramidal, and columnar shapes are included among them. Also, a selection of habits such as horizontal branching, spreading limbs and arching branches all help to create an attractive design.

Cultivation and propagation

Sorbus will thrive in ordinary garden soil, provided it is well drained. If there is a fairly deep layer of topsoil they will grow satisfactorily on chalk. They prefer a sunny position but can grow quite well in partial or full shade. They are very accommodating as a whole and can withstand exposure to cold, high winds, salt-laden gales and atmospheric pollution.

As they are deciduous trees and shrubs, sorbus are best planted during suitable weather between late autumn and mid spring (October to March). One exception is when they are containerized – then they may be planted at any time. A second is when they are being planted at the seaside; it is better to postpone planting in this case until spring so as not to expose them to salt-laden gales just as they are starting to grow.

Bare-root trees are a problem in this respect because nurserymen are sometimes sold out so late in the season. So if you have an exposed garden it is advisable to buy good stock in the autumn and heel it under in a sheltered place until the worst weather has passed.

Fortunately, many sorbus are fairly slender, although they have some height, so the space allowed between them in a group or between neighbours is comparatively small. The best guide to spacing is to average the ultimate spread of the sorbus, and that of its neighbour.

Above: S. aria *Lutescens showing its silvery-white spring foliage. It produces bunches of deep red berries in the autumn*
Left and right: two forms of the rowan or mountain ash, S. hupehensis. *At right, the species and at left, the variety Pink Form*

When planting a bare-root sorbus tree, dig a hole large enough in diameter to allow its roots – after you have cut away all damaged and extralong ones – to be spread out in the bottom of it. It should be deep enough so that when planted the soil mark on the main stem, indicating the depth to which it was growing at the nursery, just shows above the soil surface in its new quarters. Mix a little garden compost or well-rotted manure with the broken-up soil at the bottom of the hole and, before filling it, insert a good stake between the roots so they do not get damaged, giving the tree support during its early years. As you replace the excavated soil, firm it well with your heel.

If the plant is pot-grown, remove the container and bury the rootball to a depth of the surrounding soil level without breaking it up and make sure that the soil round its edges is well firmed.

You can propagate species by planting seeds extracted from ripened berries in late autumn (October) right away in J.I. seed compost, using a cold frame. Transplant them a year later to a nursery bed and after three to five years plant them out in their permanent growing positions.

Hybrids and cultivars can be propagated by layering; rare kinds can be budded or grafted on to *S. aucuparia* stocks.

Disease

Apple canker produces severe cankers on the bark of sorbus and sometimes kills large shoots.

Fireblight, which blackens and shrivels the blooms and gradually kills the branches that carry brown and withered leaves, is likely to attack them, so cut it out and burn the infected wood.

Honey fungus may also attack sorbus and destroy it quickly.

Some varieties to choose

Sorbus adds an attractive feature to your garden if you can afford the space. They usually have white flowers appearing early to mid summer (May to June). The dimensions given are for the ultimate height and spread respectively.

Whitebeam

S. aria	Compact round-headed tree. Its leaves are greyish-white at first, then green above and densely white below, and finally golden-russet in autumn. Its berries are deep crimson in colour and it has a number of very attractive cultivars. 5·5 × 4m (18 × 13 ft).
S. a. Lutescens	Young leaves are a striking silvery-white in spring, becoming a greyish-green in summer. Its berries are a deep red and grow in large bunches on the more mature trees.
S. hybrida	Compact tree with green leaves and grey tomentose (dense covering of matted hairs) underneath. Its berries are globular and red and they grow in large clusters. 5·5 × 4m (18 × 13 ft).
S. h. Gibbsii (or *S. pinnatifida* Gibbsii)	An attractive cultivar that bears a good crop of dark red berries, too large for birds to tackle.
S. intermedia (Swedish whitebeam)	Round-headed tree that is very hardy and resistant to wind. It has large clusters of orange-scarlet fruits. 5·5 × 4m (18 × 13 ft).
S. minima	Small, slender tree with leaves that are green and have grey tomentose underneath, and speckled, scarlet berries. Suitable for a small garden. 3 × 2m (10 × 6 ft).

Mountain ash or rowan

S. aucuparia	Familiar tree with attractive greyish, downy winter buds that give pinnate leaves that turn orange and yellow in late autumn (October). It bears bright red berries. 6 × 3m (20 × 10 ft). It has several very fine varieties.
S. a. Aspleniifolia	Has fern-like leaves.
S. a. Beissneri	The young shoots are dark coral-red and the bark is a warm copper colour. It has bright red berries.
S. a. Edulis	Larger than usual sweet and edible berries.
S. a. Xanthocarpa	Berries are amber-yellow.
Lombart hybrids	These hybrids of *S. aucuparia* surpass all the other mountain ash varieties. They reach between 2·5–4·5m (8–15 ft) in height and from 2·5m (5–8 ft) in spread after being planted about ten years. The figures given for the individual plants in the following list are approximate heights.
Apricot Queen	Pale, orange-yellow berries. 4·5m (15 ft).
Carpet of Gold	Golden-yellow berries. 4·5m (15 ft).
Coral Beauty	Coral-red berries. 3·5m (11 ft).
Lombarts Golden Wonder	Large, golden-yellow berries. 4·5m (15 ft).
Old Pink	Large clusters of pink berries and pink-tinted leaves. 3m (10 ft).
Orange Favourite	Light, orange berries. 3·5m (11 ft).
Red Tip	Cream-white berries showing a red tip and red-tinted foliage. 2·5m (8 ft).
S. Embley	Small to medium-sized, erect-growing shrub whose former botanical name was *S. discolor*. It has sticky buds yielding leaves with up to 15 leaflets. Its leaves are longlasting and turn to a glowing red, giving a superb display in autumn. This beauty is enhanced by its glistening, orange-red berries. 6 × 2·5m (20 × 8 ft).

Left: bright yellow berries of S. Joseph Rock, an attractive small tree
Below left: S. sargentiana forms a small, pyramidal-shaped tree

S. hupehensis	Slow-growing tree with purplish-brown branches and slightly bluish leaves of up to 17 leaflets, and white berries. 5 × 3m (17 × 10 ft).
S. h. Pink Form	Has persistent, glistening pink berries.
S. Joseph Rock	Small tree with foliage that turns a superb crimson-purple colour in autumn. Its berries are yellow. 5·5 × 2·5m (18 × 8 ft).
S. prattii	Elegant large shrub or small tree with leaves composed of up to 30 leaflets. Its small, globose berries are pearly-white. 3 × 2·5m (10 × 8 ft).
S. sargentiana	Pyramidal tree with sticky, crimson winter buds, red leaf-stalks, producing clusters, 15cm (6 in) in diameter, of late-ripening, small, scarlet berries. 4·5 × 3m (15 × 10 ft).
S. scopulina	Slow-growing, columnar shrub or small tree with sealing-wax-red fruits. 3 × 2m (10 × 7 ft).
S. vilmorinii	Beautiful small tree or medium-sized shrub. Its fern-like leaves have up to 30 leaflets, and turn red to purple in autumn. Its berries are rose-red at first, then pink, and ultimately white, flushed rose. 3 × 2m (10 × 7 ft).

Micromeles

S. alnifolia submollis (or *zahlbruckneri*)	Very upright, slender, small tree. Its green leaves are deeply-veined, and turn golden-brown in autumn. Its berries are bright red and egg-shaped. 4·5 × 1·2m (15 × 4 ft).

SYRINGA

Type	hardy, deciduous flowering shrubs with fragrant flowers
Family	OLEACEAE
Common name	lilac
Planting date	late autumn–early winter (October–November); from containers any time
Flowering season	early–mid summer (May–June)
Mature size/shape	1·5–4·5m (5–15 ft) high and 1·5–4m (5–13 ft) spread; mainly rounded bushes, but a few are erect-growing

Syringa has been known for a long time. The Elizabethans called it the pipe tree because its wood was made into a musical instrument similar to that traditionally used by the god Pan known as pan-pipes or syrinx. The latter name has given rise to the genus name syringa.

Among the earliest species grown in gardens in England were *S. vulgaris*, brought from the mountains of eastern Europe during the 16th century, and *S. × persica,* that is said to have been cultivated in English gardens in 1640. In habitat the species is fairly widespread throughout the world. Like *S. vulgaris, S. josikaea* comes from eastern Europe; *S. microphylla, S. reflexa* and *S. sweginzowii* originated in China, while *S. amurensis* grows wild from Manchuria to Korea. Despite its name, *S. × persica* (Persian lilac) appears to have been brought from Afghanistan.

The genus syringa consists of 30 species of hardy deciduous shrubs and some small trees. Syringa – or lilacs – are much prized for their large, pyramidal panicles of flowers that are often very fragrant. They succeed the ornamental peaches, cherries and other spring-flowering shrubs and trees and continue flowering into mid summer (June). Syringa never form a true tree, although as bushes some species will grow as tall as 4·5m (15 ft) or sometimes even 6m (20 ft). This is because each growing shoot often ends in two hard buds of equal size that in spring sprout equally and vigorously, repeatedly producing forks. Syringa therefore rarely form a straight central stem and so remain long-lived bushes rather than trees.

Do not make the mistake of confusing the philadelphus (mock orange) with syringa. Although the philadelphus is often referred to as syringa this is quite erroneous since they do not even belong to the same plant family.

Although easy to grow, syringa often require a season or two to settle down, and are even then comparatively slow-growing. In many cases they are not true to colour until they have been in the garden for three years.

While some species grow fairly big after about 20 years, they never become unduly large. They are very suitable for small gardens because, in most cases, they are quite amenable to being cut back. In fact, you can rejuvenate overgrown bushes by pruning them back during the winter to about 75cm (2½ ft) above the ground. The larger-growing syringa, such as *S. × chinensis, S. josikaea, S. vulgaris* and *S. × prestoniae* (the Canadian hybrids) have heights and spreads up to 4·5m (15 ft) and 4m (13 ft) respectively. Among the several other species that are appreciably smaller are the rounded bush *S. × persica* with all-round dimensions of about 2m (6 ft), the beautiful, slender-branched, spreading shrub *S. microphylla* and the slow-growing, dense, compact, free-flowering bush *S. (palibiniana) velutina* – both with

Syringa vulgaris *Souvenir de Louis Spaeth is one of the best and most consistent single lilacs for the garden, having attractively-coloured, scented flowers and good, shrubby growth*

dimensions not exceeding 1·5m (5 ft); these can give the same effect in small gardens as the larger versions.

Although syringa are grown primarily for their large, colourful, scented blooms and their distinctive green leaves (that in the case of *S. vulgaris* are dark brown in autumn), there are at least two that have ornamental bark. One is the less common *S. reticulata* that can be readily trained to a short, stout tree with an attractive trunk. The other is *S. amurensis*, the older bark of which peels off to show dark chestnut brown. Also, one cultivar, *S. emodii* Aureovariegata has yellow variegated leaves.

Syringa thrive well in town gardens, particularly on industrial sites where their fragrant and prominent clusters of flowers enliven what might otherwise be a sombre environment.

Many of the choicest varieties grown at the present time are of garden origin. Particular mention must be made of the very lovely Canadian hybrids that were raised originally by Miss Isabella Preston of the Canadian government's Division of Horticulture in Ottawa in 1920.

Syringa make very handsome and colourful specimen shrubs. Alternatively, they are effective grown in shrub or mixed borders where, apart from their colourful flowers, their rather lighter, sometimes heart-shaped, green leaves make a much-appreciated contrast to darker foliage. The more dwarf species *S. microphylla* and *S. (palibiniana) velutina* are very good in a large rock garden.

The more bushy species and varieties are excellent for planting as informal hedges and also make good summer screens. Many varieties of *S. vulgaris* are particularly good for this purpose. In order to get the best out of them it is important to let the shrubs grow and flower freely. Some experts advocate allowing such a hedge to go its own way for one year and lightly pruning it the next, and so on.

Cultivation

In order to ensure maximum flower production, plant syringa in full sun. Although they will grow in partial shade they will not then be so floriferous. They thrive in any good fertile garden soil and can tolerate chalk.

Plant at any time in late autumn or early winter (October or November), provided the ground is not excessively wet. Those grown in containers can be planted at any time, but if it is in summer, take care to water well at the time of planting and also subsequently if the weather is dry.

Plant larger-growing syringa 3–4m (10–12 ft) apart if they are to be adjacent; allow a distance of about 1·5m (5 ft) with the smaller species. When planting them with other shrubs in a shrub border determine the planting distances in the usual way by adding the spread of the syringa to that of its neighbour and dividing by two. For a hedge plant the bushes about 2·5m (8 ft) apart, unless you are using a smaller type of syringa such as *S. microphylla*, when the planting distance should be

only about 60cm (2 ft).

Dig a hole wide enough to take the rootball comfortably and to allow the roots to spread out. Its depth should be such that the soil mark already on the main stem is level with the surface when it is planted. Fill the hole with soil and firm it well. As soon as growth becomes evident, cut back the shoots to a pair of buds so that a good bushy shape develops. Syringa need little attention once they are established. During the first season it is a good idea to pick off most of the flowers as they appear. In mid summer (June) they appreciate a dressing of sulphate of potash scattered around them and hoed in.

Remove all flowers as soon as they start to fade. After late autumn (October) and throughout the winter remove any crossing and weak shoots. Cut back all suckers as near as possible to the main stem or the root as soon as they appear.

Propagation

Syringa are propagated from 10cm (4 in) long heel cuttings or half-ripe shoots taken in late summer or early autumn (July or August). For the Canadian hybrids, take cuttings in early or mid summer (May or June). Insert them in potting compost either with mist propagation, or in a propagator at 16°C (61°F). Pot rooted cuttings into 10cm (4 in) pots and put in a cold frame. Transplant them to a nursery bed the following mid spring (March) and finally to their permanent home two or more years later.

Named varieties can be layered in spring and autumn. *S. vulgaris* varieties are sometimes budded or grafted on species seedling stock or privet; the advantage is that the latter does not sucker so much as the former, but it is better to grow them on their own roots because die-back and even death sometimes happen, especially with privet, owing to the basic incompatibility of stock and scion.

Pests and diseases

Leaves are sometimes tunnelled by lilac leaf miners. Also, shrubs are open to attack by willow scale insects. If the infestation of either of these is serious, spray with nicotine.

Flowers are sometimes killed by late frost, that also causes young shoots to die back. Such affected tissues are liable to become covered with a greyish-brown fungus due to grey mould (botrytis). Cut out any shoots affected with this. Honey fungus is also liable to attack and kill syringa. If this gains a really strong hold you will probably have to dig the tree out and burn it. Brown spots on leaves and blackened, withered shoots are due to lilac blight; treat by cutting affected branches back to healthy tissue. A spray of Bordeaux Mixture, repeated if necessary, can also help.

Silver leaf is another disease that might attack syringa and their varieties. It causes die-back of the branches that then carry leaves with a silvery tinge. Again, cut back to healthy tissue and paint the cut with a fungicidal paint. If the tree is badly affected dig it out and burn it.

Some varieties to choose

In the following selection the first figure given is the height of the shrub after about 20 years' growth and the second is the spread. Unless otherwise stated, the size of a variety is approximately the same as the species from which it derives.

S. × chinensis (Rouen lilac)
Broad, erect pyramidal panicles of fragrant purple flowers that appear in early summer (May); 3×2m ($10 \times 6\frac{1}{2}$ ft).

S. × hyacinthiflora
This is a variable hybrid, but the cultivars mentioned below are excellent. Flowers mainly in early summer (May), with single blooms; dimensions generally $2\cdot5 \times 1\cdot5$m (8×5 ft) after about ten years.

S. × h. Blue Hyacinth	tubular blue flowers with petals like hyacinths, that are mauve in the bud.
S. × h. Clarke's Giant	erect shrub with rosy-mauve to lilac-blue blooms in 30cm (12 in) long panicles.
S. × h. Esther Staley	carmine-red buds, opening to pure, bright pink.

S. × josiflexa Bellicent
An outstanding clone associated with the Canadian hybrids; has enormous panicles of fragrant, rose-coloured flowers; 4×2m ($13 \times 6\frac{1}{2}$ ft).

The Canadian hybrid cultivars are among the choicest syringas grown today.
S. × josiflexa Bellicent *(above) is a fine clone associated with them, and S. × prestoniae* Isabella *(top left) is a particularly vigorous and beautifully-coloured example*
Bottom left: S. vulgaris Maud Notcutt, *with large, erect-growing panicles is typical of the best single-flowered varieties available today*

S. microphylla (small-leaved or little-leaf lilac)
Has small leaves and erect panicles of fragrant lilac flowers during mid summer (June) and again in mid autumn (September); 1.5×1.5m (5×5 ft).

S.m. Superba	freely flowers from early summer to late autumn (May to October), with rose-pink blooms; 2m ($6\frac{1}{2}$ ft) high.

S. × persica (Persian lilac)
Bushy, rounded shrub producing 10cm (4 in) long, erect pyramidal panicles of fragrant lilac flowers in early summer (May); *S.×p.* Alba is a white version; 2.25×2.25m (7×7 ft).

S. × prestoniae (Canadian hybrids)
This is the species of a vigorous hardy race of cultivars flowering in early and mid summer (May and June); 4×2m ($13 \times 6\frac{1}{2}$ ft). Some of the most attractive varieties are listed below.

S.×p. Audrey	erect heads of deep pink.
S.×p. Elinor	semi-erect, slender, panicles of dark purple buds opening to pale lilac.
S.×p. Hiawatha	rich reddish-purple in bud, opening to pale pink.
S.×p. Isabella	30cm (12 in) long, slender, semi-erect panicles of mallow pink blooms; vigorous.
S.×p. Virgilia	compact shrub with 23cm (9 in) long, loose panicles of lilac flowers, deep lilac-magenta in bud.

S. sweginzowii
An open shrub of graceful habit that produces sweetly-scented, flesh-pink blooms in long, loose panicles in early and mid summer (May and June); 4×3m (13×10 ft).

S. (palibiniana) velutina (Korean lilac)
A modest-sized shrub of dense, compact habit with small, rounded, dark green leaves that are carried on slender, twiggy branches; bears numerous elegant panicles of lavender-pink blossoms in early and mid summer (May and June); 1.5×1.5m (5×5 ft).

S. vulgaris (common lilac)
An attractive shrub in itself, with heart-shaped leaves and erect, pyramidal panicles of lilac flowers; this species is the parent of the more popular syringa grown today; 3×2.5m (10×8 ft). These below flower in early summer (May).

SINGLE VARIETIES

S.v. Congo	large compact panicles of lilac-red flowers.
S.v. Marechal Foch	bright rose-carmine flowers in broad, open panicles.
S.v. Massena	late flowering with deep reddish-purple flowers.
S.v. Maud Notcutt	exceptionally large white flowers in 30cm (12 in) long, erect-growing panicles.
S.v. Primrose	very free-flowering, compact bush yielding small, dense panicles of primrose blooms.
S.v. Souvenir de Louis Spaeth	a very popular consistent lilac with wine-red blooms.
S.v. Vestale	a shrub of compact habit producing broad, crowded panicles of white flowers.

DOUBLE VARIETIES

S.v. Charles Joly	popular syringa with dark purplish, late-flowering blooms.
S.v. Katherine Havemeyer	broad, compact panicles of pure lavender.
S.v. Madame Antoine Buchner	loose, narrow panicles of rosy-mauve blooms.
S.v. Madame Lemoine	creamy-yellow buds opening to pure white.
S.v. Michel Buchner	large panicles of pale rose lilac.
S.v. Monique Lemoine	late flowering, pure white.
S.v. Mrs Edward Harding	popular, very free-flowering with claret-red, shaded pink late-blooming flowers.
S.v. Paul Thirion	late flowering, carmine buds opening to claret-rose, then turning lilac-pink.

In addition to the double blooms that make S. vulgaris Madame Antoine Buchner an attractive specimen shrub, its light green leaves can provide an effective contrast to darker-foliaged plants

VIBURNUM

Type	evergreen and deciduous fruiting shrubs
Family	CAPRIFOLIACEAE
Flowering season	mainly early–late summer (May–July), some bloom in winter and spring
Planting date	deciduous: late autumn–mid spring (October–March); evergreen: mid–late autumn (September–October), and mid spring–early summer (March–May)
Mature size/shape	bushy, round, spreading and erect; height 90cm–3·7m (3–12 ft), spread 1·5–4·5m (5–15 ft)

The genus viburnum contains some 200 species of evergreen and deciduous shrubs that are fairly widespread throughout the Northern Hemisphere. The famous plant explorer E. H. Wilson discovered a number of most attractive species in China, which he introduced into Western gardens during the early years of this century. *V. japonicum* hails from Japan and *V. dentatum* (arrow wood) was found growing wild in North America.

Several species have been discovered growing in Europe, in the Mediterranean region. These include the very lovely *V. tinus* (laurustinus) that flowers over a long period during winter, and has been cultivated in Britain since the late 16th century. Perhaps the most beautiful fruiting viburnum, however, is *V. opulus* (guelder rose or water elder), that grows freely in Europe, north and west Asia and Algeria, and in the moist hedgerows and edges of woodlands in the British Isles. *V. lantana* (wayfaring tree) is also a familiar hedgerow plant, particularly in the chalky downlands of Britain.

There are three distinct categories among viburnum species, all of which have a special beauty and value of their own. Some produce their flowers on bare wood in winter, while others flower in the spring and summer on fully-leaved stems. The third group follow their flowers in autumn with very decorative fruits ranging in colour from black to brilliant scarlet. A very large proportion of species fall into this category. Most viburnum have white flowers that are sometimes tinged pink in the bud, and carried in flat heads or rounded corymbs.

Fruiting viburnum make excellent small or medium-sized plants of varying shape for the shrub border. They are able to tolerate partial shade, and some species make good lawn specimens or ground cover. *V. tinus*, flowering from mid winter to early summer (December to May), makes a most attractive informal hedge, particularly for a shady position and in coastal areas. *V. japonicum* is useful grown as a wall plant.

Cultivation

Viburnum species must be grown in moist positions – dryness should be avoided at all costs. For this reason, they do not object to partial shade. They do best, however, in full sun, provided the soil is moist.

Usually, viburnum grown for their fruits should be planted in groups of two or three, so that pollination can take place without difficulty. All species grow well in any good, moist garden soil but do prepare the site by double digging and incorporating plenty of humus-making, moisture-retaining material such as well-rotted manure, garden compost, or peat, so that it is as rich as possible.

The deciduous species can be planted any time between late autumn and mid spring (October and March), provided the weather is favourable. Evergreens are best planted between mid and late autumn (September and October), and again from mid spring to early summer (March to May).

Above: V. sargentii *one of the most decorative of all viburnum, flowers in summer and is followed by long-lasting fruits*

If you are planting in groups, place the larger shrubs about 3m (10 ft) apart, and the more modest growers, like *V. davidii*, about 1·2m (4 ft) apart. Plant *V. tinus* shrubs for hedging about 60cm (2 ft) apart. Water the plants well before planting, and incorporate garden compost or rotted manure in the excavated soil before replacing it.

The deciduous shrubs, flowering in summer, need little regular pruning. Any that are overgrown can be thinned after flowering and any dead wood removed at the same time. Deciduous, winter-flowering viburnum are pruned in spring to remove flowered shoots and maintain the shape.

Evergreen species do not need regular pruning except to control size and remove old and dead wood. This should be done in early summer (May).

Leaf-curling aphides and whiteflies sometimes infest viburnum. The presence of whitefly is indicated by the undersides of the leaves being covered with black scales and fringed with white wax. *V. tinus* is particularly prone to attack from these pests. Both aphides and whiteflies can be controlled by sprays of a systemic insecticide.

Grey mould disease can be troublesome on viburnum and should be treated by cutting out and burning the infected wood, then painting the wound with protective paint. Sometimes pale or purple spots appear on the leaves, due to a fungus disease called leaf spot. If the disease is severe, spray with a fungicide such as captan or zineb. Occasionally, viburnum are attacked by honey fungus, which usually causes speedy death of the plant. The only treatment is to dig up the affected plant and burn it.

Propagation

Take heel cuttings about 8–10cm (3–4 in) long in mid or late summer (June or July). Insert them in a soilless compost in a propagating case with a bottom heat of 16°C (61°F). When they have rooted, pot in J.I. No 1 in 8cm (3 in) pots, and place in a cold frame for the winter. Alternatively, take softwood cuttings in early and mid autumn (August and September) and root them in a cold frame. In either case, transplant them to a nursery bed in late spring or early summer (April or May) and leave them for two or three years until planting them in their permanent home in winter.

Another method of propagating is to layer low-growing shoots in mid autumn (September). They will have rooted and can be ready for severing after a year. Species can be raised from seed, but it is a long process and it could take four to six years before flowers are produced.

Some varieties to choose

In the list given below, the dimensions for each shrub refer first to the height and secondly to the spread, both after about 20 years' growth.

V. betulifolium
One of the best fruiting, deciduous shrubs, this has an erect habit and long branches that are weighed down with bunches of redcurrant-like, persistent berries. Bears flat heads of small white flowers in mid summer (June). 2·4 × 1·5m (8 × 5 ft).

V. corylifolium
Medium-sized, deciduous shrub with white flowers that appear in early and mid summer (May and June) and are followed by good autumn colours in the foliage and long-lasting bright red fruits. 2·4 × 2·4m (8 × 8 ft).

V. davidii
Small, compact, evergreen shrub with deeply-veined dark green leaves. Small white flowers carried in terminal cymes appear in mid summer (June) and are followed by turquoise-blue, egg-shaped fruits. 90cm × 1·5m (3 × 5 ft).

V. henryi
Erect-growing, evergreen shrub with pyramidal panicles of white flowers produced in mid summer (June) and followed by bright red, then black, fruit. 1·8 × 1·2m (6 × 4 ft).

V. japonicum (*macrophylla*)
Handsome, evergreen shrub with leaves 15cm (6 in) long and 10cm (4 in) wide. Produces fragrant, white, rounded trusses of blooms in mid summer (June), and then red fruits. 2·5 × 3m (8 × 10 ft).

V. lantana (wayfaring tree)
Deciduous shrub with creamy white flowers opening in early summer (May) and followed by red, turning black, oblong fruits. Likes a chalky soil. 3 × 2·1m (10 × 7 ft).

V. opulus (guelder rose, water elder)
Large, vigorous, spreading deciduous shrub with leaves that colour richly in autumn. Produces white, lacecap hydrangea-like flowers in mid and late summer (June and July), and copious bunches of brilliant red fruits. 3·7 × 4.5m (12 × 15 ft).

V.o. Compactum	Smaller variety. 90 × 90cm (3 × 3 ft).
V.o. Fructuluteo	Pinkish, lemon-yellow fruits.
V.o. Notcutt's Variety	Larger fruits than the parent. Autumn tints.

V. rhytidophyllum
Fast-growing evergreen shrub that bears cymes of small, creamy white flowers during early summer (May). Its fruits are oval, and red, turning black. 3·7 × 3·4m (12 × 11 ft).

V. sargentii
Resembles *V. opulus* but has larger leaves, corky bark and purple instead of yellow anthers. Its fruits are long-lasting and bright, translucent red in colour. 3·7 × 4·5m (12 × 15 ft).

V.s. Flavum	Bears yellow berries.

V. tinus (laurustinus)
Winter-flowering evergreen with metallic blue, fruits, turning black. 1·8 × 2·1m (6 × 7 ft).

V.t. Gwenllian	Has small blue berries. 2·1 × 2·4m (7 × 8 ft).

Left: V. davidii, *at 90cm (3 ft) high, is an ideal shrub for a small border* Far left: *the fruits of deciduous* V. lantana *change colour dramatically as they age* Top left: *in addition to its bright berries,* V. opulus Compactum *has splendid autumn colour* Far left, above: *magnificent fruits of* V. opulus Nottcutt's Variety Far left, top: V. opulus *flowers in mid and late summer (June and July)*

YUCCA

Type	hardy and tender evergreen small trees and shrubs
Family	LILIACEAE
Planting dates	late spring–late autumn (April–October); from containers at any time
Flowering season	early summer–late autumn (May–October)
Mature size/shape	mainly rounded, foliage sometimes surmounting a short trunk; height 75cm–1·8m (2½–6 ft), spread 90cm–1·8m (3–6 ft)

There are 40 species in the yucca genus, consisting of evergreen, hardy and tender shrubs and small trees. Despite their sub-tropical appearance, a number are quite hardy in temperate districts. The name comes from the Carib word for cassava, though this is not related to the yucca plant.

These plants are natives of Central America, Mexico and the southern districts of the United States. The earliest to be introduced to cultivation in Britain, in about 1550, was *Yucca gloriosa*; this was followed by *Y. filamentosa* in 1675. The next to be cultivated in Britain was *Y. recurvifolia*, introduced in 1794, followed during the 19th century by *Y. glauca* (about 1811), *Y. flaccida* (1816), *Y. parviflora engelmannii* (1822) and *Y. whipplei* (1854).

Yucca produce very formal rosettes or clumps of narrow, usually rigid, bold leaves and tall racemes or panicles of drooping, bell-shaped, lily-like flowers. The inflorescence sometimes grows as much as 1·2–1·5m (4–5 ft) above the main body of the shrub or tree. This gives an effect of great stateliness and beauty, and an 'architectural' quality that is of great value in the garden. In California the shape has given rise to their popular name 'candles of the Lord'.

The real magnificence of yucca lies in their large, spiky, bold leaves. Some species, such as *Y. recurvifolia*, have extremely sharp spines at the ends that can very easily draw blood or damage an eye. It is therefore a wise precaution not to plant any of these in gardens where young children play. In any case, they should be positioned where they are unlikely to come into close contact with people. Some species have leaves of exceptional length and breadth: those of *Y. parviflora engelmannii*, for example, are 2–3cm (1 in) wide and 1·2m (4 ft) long, while those of *Y. recurvifolia* are up to 90cm (3 ft) in length. The leaves of *Y. gloriosa* (Adam's needle) are rather shorter, at

Above: Y. recurvifolia *can be impressive in a border. Its column of creamy-white flowers with spiky leaves at the base gives it a fountain-like appearance* *Right:* Y. gloriosa *has white flowers tinged with red*

between 30–60cm (12–24 in) long, but they can range from 8–10cm (3–4 in) in width.

The leaves of most of the species found in present-day gardens are greyish-green in colour, but notable exceptions with bright green foliage are *Y. brevifolia* (Joshua tree) and *Y. parviflora engelmannii*. *Y. gloriosa* Variegata has leaves that are striped and margined creamy-yellow, and *Y. recurvifolia* Variegata has foliage with a central band of pale green. In many species the leaves have white threads along their margins.

The flowering season of the yuccas varies from species to species. In general they fall into two groups – late summer to early autumn (July to August) and mid autumn (September) onwards. An exception is *Y. whipplei*, that produces blooms during early and mid summer (May and June).

exposed to salt-laden winds. They do well in full sun and are quite happy in poor soil, even tolerating shallow soil over chalk.

Plant yucca during late spring or late autumn (April or October), and container-grown plants at any time. Determine the space to be allowed between a yucca and its neighbouring shrub by adding together their ultimate spreads and dividing by two.

Although most of the yucca available from nurseries in Britain are hardy, it is wise to give them protection against frost in really severe weather. No pruning is necessary.

Yucca are not seriously affected by pests, but sometimes large brown spots with grey centres, due to leaf spot, appear on the foliage. If this infection is serious, spray with a fungicide such as captan or zineb.

To propagate yucca, cut off suckers with roots during mid or late spring (March or April) and plant them out at once in their permanent growing quarters.

Some varieties to choose

In the varieties listed below, the approximate dimensions given under each item are the height and spread after about 20 years' growth; they exclude the height of the flowering stalk. Assume, unless otherwise stated, that the size of any cultivar is approximately the same as its parent.

Y. brevifolia (Joshua tree)

Looks like a miniature tree with a small trunk. It has narrow, green, recurved leaves that are channelled on their upper surface and have small, tooth-like serrations along their margins. Its cream flowers often have a greenish tint and appear in early and mid autumn (August and September). $1·5 \times 1·5$m (5×5 ft). It needs careful protection from frost and is really suitable only for the most sheltered areas.

Y.b. jaegerana is a form that is rather shorter than the type and has smaller leaves and panicles.

Y. filamentosa

Stemless yucca that is useful for more forward positions in a shrub or mixed border. It produces dense clumps of leaves that are spreading or erect-growing and greyish-green in colour, with many curly white threads along their edges. Its 5–8cm (2–3 in) long, creamy-white flowers are carried in erect, smooth, conical panicles that grow up to $1·2$m (4 ft) tall, and appear in late summer and early autumn (July and August). Flowering begins when a plant is between two and three years old. 75cm $\times 1·2$m ($2\frac{1}{2} \times 4$ ft). *Y. f.* Variegata has leaves that are edged and striped with yellow.

Y. flaccida

Stemless species that forms clumps of long, lance-shaped, green or greyish leaves, characterized by sharply-pointed ends that bend downwards. They have curly, white, filament-like threads on their margins. Creamy-white flowers, carried in erect, downy panicles $1·2$m (4 ft) above the foliage, are

Usually the flowers are creamy-white or creamy-yellow, sometimes with a greenish hue, but an outstanding exception is *Y. parviflora engelmannii* that has aloe-like, tomato-red blooms. *Y. whipplei* has greenish-white flowers edged with purple. There is a legend that yucca flower only once every seven years, but this is not true; they will bloom nearly every year once they commence.

In size yucca range from 60–75cm (2–2$\frac{1}{2}$ ft) high with a spread of 90cm–1·2m (3–4 ft) for *Y. glauca*, to the $1·8$m (6 ft) height and spread of *Y. recurvifolia*. A particular exception is the rather spreading *Y. parviflora engelmannii* that can extend horizontally to about $1·8$m (6 ft), at a height of about $1·2$m (4 ft). All these dimensions are reached after about 20 years' growth.

Cultivation and propagation

Yucca are long-lived, and flourish in ordinary, well-drained garden soil. They will also thrive at the seaside, even in sand dunes that are fully

borne during late summer and early autumn (July and August). 1·5 × 1·5m (5 × 5 ft). The most commonly-seen variety is *Y. f.* Ivory.

Y. glauca

A low-growing plant with a short stem. It forms a rounded head of long, narrow, glaucous leaves that have a white edging with a few marginal white threads. Its 5–8cm (2–3 in) long, greenish-white flowers, appearing in late summer and early autumn (July and August), are carried in racemes that are 1·2m (4 ft) tall. 90 × 90cm (3 × 3 ft).

Y. gloriosa (Adam's needle)

The leaves of this species emerge in rosettes at the head of a slow-growing, woody trunk. They are recurving and about 45cm (18 in) long and up to 10cm (4 in) wide. The leaves are slightly glaucous and viciously spiked. The blooms, that first appear when the plant is five years old, are creamy-white and tinged red outside. They appear between early and late autumn (August and October). 1·5 × 1·5m (5 × 5 ft).

Y. parviflora engelmannii

This yucca is exceptional in having aloe-like, tomato-red flowers with gold inside; they are produced in long, slim panicles in late summer (July). Its thick, tough, bright green leaves are long and narrow. Again, this plant is susceptible to cold and needs a sheltered spot in order to survive. 1·2 × 1·8m (4 × 6 ft).

Y. recurvifolia

One of the most popular of the genus; it has greyish-green, long, narrow leaves that emerge at ground level when the plant is young, but appear later at the top of the slow-growing trunk. The outside leaves recurve, but the central ones remain erect. They have sharp spines on their ends. Panicles of creamy-white flowers grow on stalks up to 90cm (3 ft) high, and appear from early autumn (August) onwards. This species rarely blooms until the trunk is about 60cm (24 in) high. 1·8 × 1·8m (6 × 6 ft).
Y. r. Variegata is an attractive cultivar with leaves that have a pale green central band.

Y. whipplei

Stemless species that forms a round clump of greyish leaves. It has greenish-white, scented flowers, margined with purple, growing on a stem that sometimes reaches a height of 3·4m (11 ft). These blooms appear in early and mid summer (May and June). This species needs a warm, sunny position to survive. 1·5 × 1·5m (5 × 5 ft).

Top right: flowers of Y. flaccida *Ivory*
Top far right: Y. filamentosa *has a less formal appearance than some varieties of yucca*
Right: a fine specimen of Y. recurvifolia. *Its grey-green leaves top a thickish, fibrous trunk*

BIBLIOGRAPHY

Barber, Peter, and Phillips, C.E. Lucas. *The Trees Around Us* (Weidenfeld and Nicholson, London 1975)

Bonar, Ann. *Shrubs and Decorative Trees* (Ward Lock, London 1972)

Clayton, John. *Pruning Hardy Shrubs* (Royal Horticultural Society, London 1973)

Dawson, Oliver. *Shrubs and How to Use Them* (William Heinemann, London 1970)

Edlin, H.L. *Guide to Tree Planting and Cultivation* (Collins, London 1970)

Emberton, Sybil C. *Shrub Gardening for Flower Arrangement* (Faber, London 1973)

Gault, G.M. *Dictionary of Shrubs in Colour* (Michael Joseph, London 1976)

Gorer, Richard. *Quick-growing Shrubs* (William Heinemann, London 1976)

Gorer, Richard. *Trees and Phrubs* (David & Charles, Newton Abbot 1976)

Grounds, Roger. *Trees for Smaller Gardens* (Dent, London 1974)

Hammett, Keith R.W. *Plant Training, Pruning and Tree Surgery* (David & Charles, Newton Abbot 1974)

Haworth-Booth, M. *Flowering Shrub Garden* (Farrall Publications, London 1971)

Hillier, H.G. *Manual of Trees and Shrubs* (David & Charles, Newton Abbot 1974)

Hofman, Jaroslav. *A Concise Guide in Colour – Ornamental Shrubs* (Hamlyn, London 1978)

Johnson, Hugh. *International Book of Trees* (Mitchell Beazley, London 1973)

Lloyd, C. *Shrubs and Trees for Small Gardens* (Pan Books, London 1972)

Preston, G.H. *Climbing and Wall Plants* (Royal Horticultural Society, London 1973)

Seabrook, Peter. *Shrubs for Your Garden* (Floraprint, London 1973)

Smith, Geoffrey. *Shrubs and Small Trees for Your Garden* (Hamlyn, London 1973)

Wright, R.C.M. *Handbook of Plant Propagation* (Ward Lock, London 1973)

Wright, R.C.M. *Simple Plant Propagation* (Ward Lock, London 1975)

Shrubs and Decorative Evergreens (Ward Lock, London 1974)

Trees and Shrubs for Your Garden (Marshall Cavendish, London 1975)

INDEX